Joe

Joe
Rounding Third & HEADING FOR HOME

by Greg Hoard

Orange Frazer Press
Wilmington, Ohio

ISBN: 1-882203-37-2
Copyright 2004 by *Greg Hoard and Joe Nuxhall*
All rights belonging to Joe Nuxhall are assigned to the Fairfield Community Foundation
(the Joe Nuxhall Character Education Fund) and the Joe Nuxhall Foundation for the Young.

Ordering information: Additional copies of *Joe: Rounding Third and Heading for Home*
may be ordered directly from:

      Customer Service Department
      Orange Frazer Press, Inc.
      Box 214
      37$^1/_2$ West Main Street
      Wilmington, Ohio 45177

Telephone 1-800-852-9332 for price and shipping information
Web site: www.orangefrazer.com

Library of Congress Cataloging-in-Publication Data

Hoard, Greg, 1951-
   Joe: rounding third and heading for home / by Greg Hoard
     p. cm.
  Includes index.
   ISBN 1-882203-37-2
   1. Nuxhall, Joe. 2. Baseball players--United States--Biography. 3. Sportscasters--United
States--Biography. I. Title.

GV865.N89H63 2004
796.357'092--dc22
  [B]   2004050069

Jacket and interior design by Jeff Fulwiler

Printed in Canada

Dedication

To my wife, Cindy, who has always had more belief in me
than I've ever had in myself. Besides, she can take a little sun
and a mirror and make wonders.

Acknowledgements

Offering thanks after a project such as this is a little like trying to
count the blades of grass in the front yard. So many have been
generous with their time and memories, but there are those who have
been remarkable in nurturing this project.

First of all, Joe. God bless him. He was forever patient and
understanding, even when I asked him the same question over and
over. Not once did he say, "Are we there yet?"

There were times when I thought I was lashed to the helm of the
Hesperus, but Bob Nuxhall was always there to bail me out. Joe's
sons, Phil and Kim, pointed out side roads I would never have
discovered on my own.

Donzetta was always there. Joe says she is a saint. I will attest to
that. She offered humor and grace all along the way—as well as
perspective.

John Murdough and Jim Ferguson—who befriended me years ago,
when I first came to Cincinnati—propped me up on historical facts.
Without them, I would surely have crashed on the rocks.

The phone calls to "Fergie" in St. Petersburg, Florida always
began the same way: "Fergie, I am confused about something."

"You have never called me when you *weren't* confused," he said.

He was right.

I can't recall a time when he hasn't been right.

Marty Brennaman used to push my twin boys around in a double-
wide stroller during spring training. One night in Tampa, he was so
rowdy in this pursuit that he disturbed an entire college baseball
team. When they emerged from their rooms groggy and sleepy,
complaining about his rambunctious activity, he bowed his back and
told them all to go to hell.

Marty pushed me along in this endeavor and, once again in my
life, I offer him my thanks and gratitude.

Pat Casey, my boss in another life at Fox 19, gave me the time and the latitude to complete the project even when it wasn't easy or practical for him or my co-workers.

Thanks to Reuven Katz and Marcy Hawley, who made it possible and my family: Cindy, John, Joe, and Meg for their support in my frequent absence.

Meg wondered why I was in the basement all the time. The boys just wanted to know if I was ever going to help shoveling snow or mowing the grass again. Cindy's concern was her suspicion that I was so buried in the book that I was wearing the same clothes to work everyday.

Finally, special and immeasurable thanks to John Baskin, who whipped me back into shape and always served as my safety net.

"When you fall," he said, "I'll catch you."

I fell many times.

He never missed.

—*Greg Hoard, June, 2004*

Contents

Prologue/page 2

One **Different Times** page 14

Two **The Big Leagues** page 22

Three **War's Open Door** page 36

Four **Hayride, Train Ride** page 50

Five **Celebrity and Tragedy** page 68

Six **A Boy's Game** page 88

Seven **Heading South** page 110

Eight **Home Again** page 124

Nine **First Spring** page 136

Ten **Not Quite Paradise** page 152

Eleven **High Times** page 164

Twelve **A Minor Miracle** page 178

Thirteen **Back to the Bigs** page 194

Fourteen **Hanging With 'em** page 206

Fifteen **To the Booth** page 238

Sixteen **Life with Marty** page 252

Epilogue/page 272

Index/page 281

Foreword

February 1, 1974, that's the day I met Joe Nuxhall for the first time. It was my first day being employed by the Cincinnati Reds as their new radio play-by-play guy, succeeding Al Michaels.

I was just a name to Joe, but he was much more than that to me. I knew about Joe Nuxhall the player because I had his baseball cards. As I recall, that's the very first thing I said to him when we were introduced by Jim Winters, the Reds' director of broadcasting. Thus began a relationship that has lasted from then until now—a professional relationship, sure, but it has become much, much more than that. You can't sit next to a guy for that many baseball seasons and keep it strictly business.

During those early days, I followed him around learning the way things were done. He always and willingly satisfied my curiosity about the routine of a major league baseball announcer.

As time passed, I started to realize the high esteem that people held him in—and I'm not talking about just Greater Cincinnati, but everywhere I traveled: throughout the Midwest and the country, for that matter.

I've come to realize that a major part of his appeal to people is his total lack of ego. We are in a business that breeds egomaniacs and Joe Nuxhall is the rarest of the rare.

I've never seen him be anything but nice to his fans and their numbers are beyond comprehension. When people talk about legends in Greater Cincinnati, Joe Nuxhall is absolutely and unequivocally number one.

In all the years we have been together I have never heard one person, not one, say anything negative about him. Now, think about that, and then ask yourself if you know any one in the public eye you can say that about.

One of the things Joe excels in—and I'm certainly not talking about the game of golf—is his ability to tell a story and his amazing recall of events that occurred years and years ago. I wish I had that ability but I don't, and every time I think I have heard all the great stories of his baseball past, he surprises me with a new one.

Now, you, too, shortly will be privy to those great stories and I'm sure that some time during your reading of the book and my reading of the book, for that matter, I'll come upon a story that, yep, I've never heard before.

I could go on forever about Joe Nuxhall and the times we have had and all the laughter we have enjoyed. We have traveled the road together for thirty-one years now. I wish there were thirty-one more but, unfortunately, there won't be.

I'm sure that by the time you have finished this book you will have, if you don't already, a great feel and a great sense of what Joe Nuxhall is all about.

But take it from me, the "Old Lefthander" is special.

—Marty Brennaman

Joe

Two hours before game time on the final home stand of the inaugural season of Great American Ball Park, the Chicago Cubs are in Cincinnati to play the Reds, chasing a divisional title and the National League pennant.

Close to their goal, the Cubs are a cheerful lot. There is a lyric sense about them as they spring, light-footed, in and out of the batting cage.

Joe Nuxhall, ex-pitcher, is seated in the Reds' dugout, sneaking a smoke and considering the scene.

"It has been one hell of a year," he says, speaking very slowly. "Just one hell of a year."

His long sigh is an elaboration of this long and disappointing season, which began with such promise. A new era was on the wing, coinciding with the opening of this glittering ballpark wedged between the city's skyline and a southern turn in the Ohio River. This year, 2003, would be the year the Cincinnati Reds would reclaim its splendid history.

PITCHER TO PITCHER—JOE INTERVIEWS TOM SEAVER

IN 1978, WHEN HE WAS 16-14 AND FINALLY GOT HIS NO-HITTER, BLANKING

THE CARDINALS 4-0 ON JUNE 16.

IT IS

A youth movement would meld with veterans such as Barry Larkin and Ken Griffey, Jr., and the Reds would rise again, ripe with promise, much like the '70s, when The Big Red Machine affixed its trademark to the game.

But Larkin was aging and Griffey was often injured and the youth movement was on a slow and uncertain track. And four months later, even as promise still lingered in the mind, the ball club was stripped, reduced to a gaggle of wide-eyed Triple-A players and wounded, ineffectual veterans trudging their way toward season's end.

Hopelessly out of the race, ownership fired the management team and traded its most costly and promising ballplayers. A year that began with a merchant's song of anticipation was ending, in truth, with a dirge.

Great American Ball Park itself offered many tributes to the past—retired numbers graced the fences and statues lined the entrance—but in its first season, it produced nothing attached to that past. On the field, the Reds held, essentially, a major league tryout for the coming seasons.

For Nuxhall, who cast his lot with the Reds in 1944 as a 15-year-old pitcher, it was a picture of things gone wrong.

"I never thought," Joe says, "it would be ending like this. Who would have? Sometimes you got to wonder."

WHILE ALL THAT HE SEES RANKLES SOMETHING deep in his spirit, he is perfectly at ease in the dugout. He is perched on the edge of the bench, peering at the players on the field. He leans forward, his elbows resting on his knees. Even though his playing career ended nearly four decades ago, he is—at 75 years old—the pure portrait of a man awaiting a long-ago call to take the field.

Somewhere, the call echoes in his memory. Somehow, he wishes he could answer. Ability, always treacherous, dims but competition can burn as brightly at 75 as 17. And so it is with Joe.

Here, so close to the field, his concentration is unwavering. Nothing seems inviting or appealing enough to sway his eyes or thoughts from the field. It is a product of a hard-earned lesson from another time.

Cubs star Sammy Sosa is in the batting cage, delighting early-arriving fans with one crushing shot after another. The balls off Sosa's bat careen off seats deep beyond the outfield fences, bouncing off the concrete and plastic until the souvenir-hunters chase them down, cheering wildly, a forlorn exuberance in this hopeless season.

ALIVE AND PITCHING—ALL JOE EVER WANTED TO DO

WAS PITCH. BY THROWING BATTING PRACTICE, IT SEEMED LIKE HE MIGHT

REMAIN A PITCHER FOREVER.

"Gawd, he is strong," Joe says. "Anything middle of the plate and in, he is gonna take you bye-bye and now. You cannot give a guy like him anything he wants to see. Can not."

The fans love Sosa. The Cub slugger is one of the most popular players in the game.

"Good guy, too," Joe offers. "He makes time for the fans, as much as he can, you know. It irritates me 'cause a lot of guys don't do that anymore. It's all about them. But, it's the times and times change."

Joe turns his eyes to the seats, where more fans are beginning to arrive and mill about. He doesn't like what he sees. For the better part of sixty years, Joe has given the Reds organization the very best he had to offer, first as a player, then as a broadcaster, remaining loyal and true in every respect.

But this—this was hard to take.

Fully three-quarters of those in the stands are wearing Cubs hats, shirts, or jackets. It does not suit him, but he knows, like everyone else, that if it weren't for the Cub fans the park would be all but empty. These people have come from Indiana and Chicago.

They have come in motorcades, by SUV, by bus. They have come sensing a kill and a pennant. The Reds, once so proud, are weak and wounded prey.

Joe stubs out a spent cigarette on the dugout floor, his thoughts turning to better days. He played with Frank Robinson and Ted Kluszewski. Johnny Vander Meer had been his mentor. He had watched Bucky Walters pitch and seen Pete Rose, Johnny Bench, Tony Perez, and Joe Morgan put The Big Red Machine in motion.

"I remember when it was hard to get a seat for a game," Joe says. "Everywhere you looked there was red. The place was alive and if ya weren't behind the team, people would be on ya, all over ya.

"Look at this. This is like a home game for the Cubs. Has been all series," he says. "Hard to believe 'specially in this town."

JOE WAS CLOSING HIS FIFTY-NINTH YEAR with the organization, his final year as a full-time broadcaster. In the coming year, he would do half the season, retire from the broadcast booth, and serve the ball club in a different capacity. It is a contractual obligation, but not one that leaves him in peace. He is not ready to leave. He has not packed his bags. The ballpark is home and forever will be.

He tries to resign himself to the fact that soon he will not be behind

SILVER LINING

the microphone, telling the story of the Reds, something he has been doing since 1967.

"That's the plan," he says, his eyes never veering from the field, where one of the Cubs' newest acquisitions is taking swings in the cage.

"Randall Simon," he says. "Kid can hit. He's gonna help them in the playoffs. So is the other guy they got from the Pirates. What's his name? Ramirez? Aramis? Yeah, that's him."

"I figure sixty years is enough. Sixty years with one organization. That's long enough, don't you think?"

It is a rhetorical question.

For sixty years his life has been tied to the Cincinnati Reds in one way or another and for the better part of the last four decades his voice has been our connection to the Reds. "Joe *sounds* like baseball," said astute columnist Paul Daugherty. "He has been around it so long, its cadence is in his blood. In the summertime, we move to the easy rhythms of the game, on the porch, on the deck, in the yard, sitting staring at the night sky as Joe Nuxhall moves the games across the evening like a slow train to Memphis. This is Nuxhall's gift...."

HE WEARS A BALL CAP AND A LIGHT JACKET to ward off the premonitory chill that makes its way up from the river and slowly crawls over the walls of Great American Ball Park.

A steady stream of people stop by to greet him. Reds players. Cubs players. Coaches from both teams, some of whom he played against. Clubhouse boys. Security guards. Television announcers. Members of the grounds crew and the front office. Even the umpires.

They call him Joe.

They call him Nuxie.

They all want to know the same thing.

"How ya doin'?" they ask, a chorus.

He has a word and a smile for all. Most he knows by their first name.

This is not an unusual circumstance. It happens in every city, every stadium, every dugout or gathering where he might find himself. He is a man who prides himself on familiarity and acquaintance.

Sometimes, should his memory fail him, he turns to a friend.

"What the hell is that guy's name? Is it Billy? Bobby? Damn. I know he's on the TV crew. Yeah, *Billy!* What the hell is wrong with me?"

There is a very slight man on the field, wearing a Cubs jersey and cap, jeans and sneakers. He is in his 30's, perhaps. Hard to tell, really. His hair is blond, but with newly fashionable dark roots. One person after another approaches him for an autograph. Young players congregate around him, including Reds first baseman Sean Casey.

"Who the hell is that guy?" Joe asks. "The little guy. Who is that?"

Joe is told he is a rock singer and that he will throw out the first pitch that night.

Joe watches intently.

"Rock singer?" he says. "What's his name?"

"Eddie Vedder. Pearl Jam."

"Pearl what?"

"Pearl Jam. That's his band. Had some hits. 'Even Flow,' 'Yellow Ledbetter.'"

As Vedder breaks away from the group on the field and heads toward the dugout, Joe studies him closely.

"Pearl Jam?" Joe says. "Don't believe I ever heard of 'em."

Joe is a Sinatra man. Tony Bennett, Mel Torme.

Accompanied by a brace of marketing types, Vedder makes his way down the dugout steps.

MAN IN THE BOOTH—SAID A CINCINNATI SPORTSWRITER:

"AFTER 60 YEARS, ALL JOE SOUNDS LIKE IS SUMMERTIME. WHEN HE GOES,

WE'LL ALL BE A LITTLE COLDER."

"Hey," Joe says, reaching out to shake the rocker's hand. "Joe Nuxhall, nice to meet you."

Vedder stops and smiles. It is the smile of a delighted young boy. He tilts his cap back, looks at Joe, and says, "I know. Pleased to meet you. I have your baseball card."

"Is that right?" Joe says.

While he knows no stranger, he still is a little uncertain as to whom he has just met.

And why not?

It is the kind of curious confluence that might occur only within the bonds of baseball—Eddie Vedder, king of Grunge Rock, meets Hamilton Joe Nuxhall, The Old Lefthander. Vedder became famous with songs of rebellion and remorse. Nuxhall was a ballad of summer.

Lollapalooza, one might say, meets Percy Faith.

IT HAS ALREADY BEEN A FULL DAY: golf, a doctor's appointment, an interview and still he has a pre-game radio show to do before he makes his way to the booth for that night's game.

"Always something, always something going on," he says.

But he likes it that way. So when a producer from WLW radio tells him abruptly that he has two minutes to air, Joe starts to break away from his conversation.

It is not an easy thing for him to do. At the moment, he is talking with National League umpire Randy Marsh, who lives in Northern Kentucky and has known Joe since his boyhood, first as Reds pitcher and later as a friend. They are discussing Marsh's playoff schedule, when Joe gets another stern prompt.

"Ninety seconds, Joe!" the producer barks, more than a little impatient.

"I got ya," Joe says.

He shakes Marsh's hand, wishes him good luck, then stands on creaky knees, pausing for a moment as if he is making sure all things are in working order. Then he makes his way to the spot—just beyond the dugout—where the producer awaits.

He sits down, adjusts the headset, and offers a bright, "Hello, I'm here."

It is a short segment with Gary Burbank, WLW's afternoon-drive time personality. The discussion is light and breezy. And as Joe ambles through the prospects and leavings of this dreadful year, they laugh in

TWO PITCHERS PITCHING—JOE INTERVIEWS NORM CHARLTON, ANOTHER SOUTHPAW, AND ONE OF "THE NASTY BOYS," WHO TOOK THE REDS TO A WORLD SERIES SWEEP OVER OAKLAND IN 1990.

the face of another barren baseball season for the Reds. Joe likes Burbank. He appreciates his sense of humor.

"Ya just got to laugh," Joe says, even though he hates losing. "I mean, what else you gonna do?"

Writers, sportscasters, and members of the clubhouse crew stand around listening as Joe talks about nothing in particular.

Joe is being Joe, they say, and they love him for it. Few of them, however, notice his eyes. His eyes never leave the cage, where the Cubs continue to take batting practice.

Long ago, he learned the importance of studying the hitters. It was a hard-won lesson—June 10, 1944, the day his first big league manager handed him the ball and said, "Just do your very best."

He has never forgotten that advice, never forgotten that day.

The radio show completed, Joe returns to a spot on the Reds' bench. He resumes the position, elbows resting on knees, his eyes searching the field.

The Cubs bounce in and out of the cage, awaiting the next rotation.

"I like their chances," Joe says. "They sure got the pitching."

He seems a little tired although it will be a long while before he leaves the park and heads the van north on I-75, back to his home in Fairfield, where he has lived the past forty-six years. But there is no resentment in this man. While he is tired, he is not weary of the task. Surprisingly, he is completely immersed in this game, as meaningless as it is for his team.

One of the journalists on the field notices Joe's weariness. "Joe," he says, "you don't have to do it all. You can say no. You can take a break."

"What do you mean?" he asks.

"The interviews, the games. You don't have to do everything everyone asks you to do."

He chuckles at first. "No, no," he says. "Can't do that."

"Why? How come?"

"How come?"

He seems surprised at a question so transparently obvious.

"This," he said, looking out on the field and around the park. "*This!* All this. I had opportunities. I've had *this*. Baseball, my friend. *Baseball!* And, I always appreciated it. Appreciated the job. Still do. I guess I always will."

IT IS THE LAST WEEK OF HIS FIFTY-NINTH SEASON with the Reds, a little after six o'clock, about an hour before game time. It is time to head upstairs to the radio booth where he and Marty Brennaman will open the microphones and begin another Reds broadcast.

They may talk about Elvis. They may talk about tomatoes, or golf, or Marty's latest visit with his grandchildren in Chicago, or Joe's statue on Crosley Terrace, but it will all be wrapped around the night's game and the season and the thirty years they have spent together in the broadcast booth. And they will come across as friends, bound by far more than their proximity and longevity in the booth.

In some ways, they are an unlikely pair: Brennaman, the smooth, articulate Hall Of Fame broadcaster and Joe, the side-kick, his voice rich and rough and guided by a lifetime in the game.

Marty is wit and wisdom, no holds barred.

Joe is slow, measured, mixed—and, yes, sometimes confused. The score may not come as soon as we like. A name may be mispronounced. And that last fly ball, was it to right or left? Doesn't matter, really. Doesn't matter, because it's Joe.

"With certain people," said former Reds President Bob Howsam, who ushered Joe from the playing field to the broadcast booth, "you get a sense that they truly love the game and appreciate the people who make up the game. That's the way it is with Joe and it's been that way for a long time."

This night, like so many others, Joe will get a cup of coffee, fill out his scorebook, and take his position in the broadcast booth. It is a privileged position, high above home plate and, once more, he has the chance to see the game that became—and remains—his life.

Yes, he had opportunities and, at a very young age, younger than most, he grounded himself on the other side of that good fortune.

He planted his feet and his trust in what he viewed as a simple matter of affection, loyalty, and duty. Every day he would do what Bill McKechnie had asked him to do that day in 1944.

He would try to do his very best.

Over the years, it would result in a most uncommon union between Joe and all those who saw him play, listened to him on the radio, or just happened to run into him on a street corner.

His partner and friend, Marty Brennaman—a man who is not easily impressed—has seen it every day for over thirty years.

"I honest-to-God believe and I have said this many times," Brennaman says, "that Joe is the most beloved individual in this entire community. There is no question in my mind, none whatsoever. Joe is truly an icon and I thank the Lord that I have had the chance to work with him and be his friend."

Winter came early that year, the sky filled with gray clouds that swirled and twisted. The sun seemed interminably distant, without heat, occasionally shining through for a moment or two, then disappearing again. Even its light appeared pale and subdued.

It was just above freezing that day in early December, and the boys in the neighborhood had gathered to play basketball. They played when, where, and as often as they could. There were few conditions that stopped a game. They shoveled the snow aside, chipped ice off the court, anything to play.

If the older kids had the court, they improvised, found a rim in someone's backyard. By sixth grade, most had become accomplished dribblers on frozen, uneven ground.

Put the ball down on hard, cold ground, you never knew exactly how it would come back. It never came back true. Your hand had to find it, contain it, bring it back in control, and even then, even at forty degrees, the temperature took the touch from your fingers. The shot had

MIGHTY YOUNG JOE—ASSUMING HIS ACCUSTOMED PLACE—AT CENTER—JOSEPH

LEROY NUXHALL JOINS THE 6TH GRADE MADISON ELEMENTARY TEAM. IT WAS ALSO

HIS FIRST CHAMPIONSHIP.

to be more deliberate, more carefully aimed, released and not pushed toward the rim.

Was it down?

Yes, it was down!

And if you want to settle it, we will *settle* it!

That's the way they played, Joe, his brothers, and his friends: Gene, just two years younger than Joe; Bob, one year behind Gene; and little Don, six years younger than Joe and scuffling to keep up; and Jack and Bud Minnich.

It was an obstreperous group that found themselves outside that winter day, trying to elbow themselves into position under the makeshift basket, all battling against Joe, who was bigger and stronger and, consequently, better than the rest.

Joe loved basketball. He loved everything about it. Being bigger than most helped, and everything about the game seemed to come easily. The games had gone long and hard. The boys were engaged in their usual single-minded business of putting a beat-up leather ball through the netless hoop nailed to a telephone pole in the back yard of Joe's house on Vine Street.

They were children, innocently detached from everything outside tomorrow's homework, today's chores, and the goal to play hard. Of this important secular trinity, only the goal to play hard came to them naturally; homework and chores occurred largely under duress.

They were dimly aware of preserving their clothing, for school clothes and play clothes were the same clothes, and if they were torn playing ball, then punitive measures likely awaited. In this mid-century custom, the final arbiter was one's own mother, more implacable and unrelenting than any referee.

Sometimes they played barefoot, because they didn't want to harm their shoes. Shoes were not cheap, and there were a lot of feet in the Nuxhall house.

THE KIDS IN THE NEIGHBORHOOD were completely occupied by the moment. They didn't pay much attention to the papers. From time-to-time, they glanced at the sports pages, checked the box scores or read "the funnies."

Once in awhile, they listened to Fibber McGee and Molly on the radio, or Jack Benny. As for world affairs, well, world affairs were not exactly a part of their life. Their life—all that they knew—was Vine Street, Ford's Fields, and Madison Elementary School.

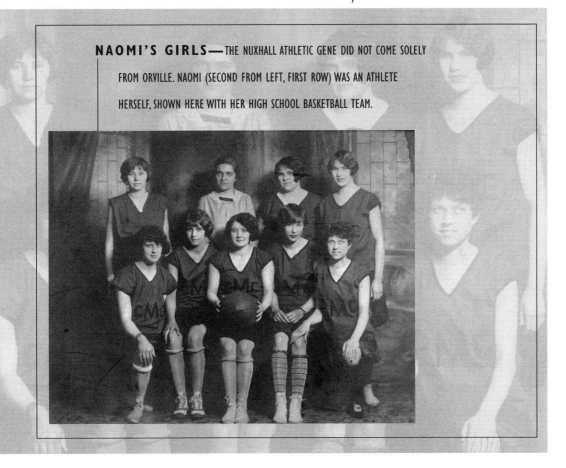

NAOMI'S GIRLS—THE NUXHALL ATHLETIC GENE DID NOT COME SOLELY FROM ORVILLE. NAOMI (SECOND FROM LEFT, FIRST ROW) WAS AN ATHLETE HERSELF, SHOWN HERE WITH HER HIGH SCHOOL BASKETBALL TEAM.

They played hard this particular Sunday—December 7, 1941—for they were trying to wring every moment out of the day before it was Monday morning again and time to go back to school.

"My boys didn't care much for school," says Naomi Nuxhall, her voice soft, thin, tremulous, like linen drapes in a summer wind. She turned 95 years old on Halloween, 2003. Understandably frail, her skin is almost translucent, her eyes as clear-blue and cool as an October morning.

Suddenly, Naomi is amused. She chuckles softly, bringing a long, thin hand to her mouth.

"School?" she says. "No, my boys liked sports. They did enough to pass and that was about it."

She is quiet for a moment, remembering things long since past.

"The boys were always playing games," she says. "They got that, you know, from their father."

She did remember that Sunday in December, the day the boys burst in from the yard, their clothes soiled, their shoes muddied, their cheeks flushed.

What was she to say when she, herself, didn't quite understand what had happened?

Their game had broken up late in the afternoon. The boys were tired and hungry. The temperature was beginning to drop as daylight drifted toward night, and the heat that had come from their physical exertions had already left.

Joe had not been in the house all day. When he and his brothers entered the back door, they walked into an unfamiliar stillness, except for the radio, which played louder than it normally did. His mother was in the kitchen.

Before Joe could ask if something was wrong, his mother told him that the Hawaiian Navy base called Pearl Harbor had been bombed by the Japanese.

It bothered Naomi that she could not convey the severity of what had taken place, but then again, should she? They were children. She understood that many Americans had been killed in the attack. She knew ships had been sunk and planes had been destroyed, even as they sat on the ground.

She could not envision the pain or the suffering or the shock of this event. And even if she could, how much should she tell her children?

She told them what she knew. They couldn't comprehend what had taken place and, in truth, neither could she.

"I had never heard of Pearl Harbor," Joe recalls. "I didn't know what to think. I just remember thinking that my parents seemed really sad and bothered by what had taken place."

"When you are a kid," says Bob Nuxhall, "things like that don't really soak in. You don't know what to make of it. Actually, I think, after Mom told us, we went back out and played some more basketball. We didn't know what else to do.

"That night, of course, we all sat around with Mom and Dad listening to the news on the radio. I remember that very well. Things so quiet. Just the radio."

It was a scene played out in millions of households throughout the country. The next day at Madison Elementary School, the Hamilton kids—like kids across the country—were called to assembly and told of what had taken place half-a-world away on an island in Hawaii.

Still and unusually orderly, they listened to President Roosevelt's

BE IT EVER SO HUMBLE—THE NUXHALL BOYS OCCUPY THE DINING ROOM TABLE ON VINE STREET.. JOE IS AT THE HEAD OF THE TABLE, SURROUNDED BY BROTHERS DON, GENE, AND BOB.

nationwide radio address. His voice was like no other, especially this day:

Yesterday, December 7th, 1941, a date which will live in infamy, the United States of America was suddenly and deliberately attacked by naval and air forces of the Empire of Japan.

The nation was going to war.

"People were scared and they were angry," Joe said. "I was what, 12, 13? All of a sudden you are hearing of places you had never heard of before. There was alot of uncertainty about what was going to happen. I just remember thinking that things weren't going to be the same, not like they had been. I remember talking with my folks about that."

At the time he remembered The Depression, the odd experience of standing in line with his parents for food and the sense of what?—yes, humiliation. This was bad, too, but different. Maybe worse.

On December 11th, the United States had declared war on Japan and Nazi Germany, and Joe kept hearing the names of distant places: Manila, The Philippines, Guam, Poland, Czechoslovakia.

HE STILL LIVED ON VINE STREET. He still went to Madison Elementary. His dad still walked to work each day at Baldwin-Lima Tool Works. His mom cooked and cleaned as she had done every day before the news had come from the President. His younger brothers played in the street and chased one another here and there.

All things appeared to be the same. But they weren't. The very community around him was changing, as one after another left for the war. Young men, boys, people he knew from around town, from the street and Ford's Fields.

"The Willis boys, Dick and Junior, they both signed up," Bob says. "Greg Grimes, him, too. That kind of brought it all home to us. They were a little older, but these were people we knew."

At The Soldiers and Sailors Monument in downtown Hamilton, the record is clear. During World War II, 13,539 men from Hamilton and Butler County served in the military, roughly one third of the entire male population of the county.

With so many men gone, women began to fill vacant positions at the plants and factories that fueled the economy of this southwestern Ohio community, and boys were welcomed in new places, places they had never been accepted before.

And life went on. Each day, the Nuxhall boys waited for their father to come home.

"We all had our favorite sports," Bob says, "but Dad loved baseball. Every day, if it wasn't too cold, he would come home and say, 'Who wants to throw?' And, we went out in the yard and he worked with us."

"You know, motion," Gene adds, "the proper way to throw a fast ball. Getting on top of the ball. Using your legs and hips. 'Course, he never let us try the curve ball. He was afraid it would hurt our arms."

"This is what he would do," Bob adds.

They are driven by the memory, the words coming fast, but each one careful not to spill over on the others' thoughts.

"If he didn't think we were throwing hard enough, he would yell. Remember?"

"Oh, I remember," Don says.

"'C'mon,'" Dad would yell. "'You can do better than that.' Then, he would take off his glove and catch us bare-handed. He thought that would make us try harder—and it did."

They are no longer young men, but the memories are ageless and in that moment, they are boys again, the brothers who walked in their older brother's shadow. And, always, any discussion of their father begins with a smile.

He was, after all, the man who rolled around with them in the house, never getting upset, never angered, when one window after another was broken by yet another thrown ball.

He was tough but understanding. *You will get better*, he said. *Try it this way*. As difficult as times were, a window could still be fixed; a spirit, a talent, *that* was something to be cherished and cultivated.

Sports were the Nuxhall family passion. It was certainly what Joe understood best. There were fewer worries and less confusion in sports. He wrapped himself in sweat and exertion.

When he couldn't physically play, he played the games in his mind, over and over.

What had he done right?

What had he done wrong?

His mother was right. He didn't like school. And he was too young for the army. So he would turn to sports. *That* would be his place.

And for longer than he could ever imagine.

Chapter two

Hamilton consisted of perhaps 50,000 people, yet its smalltown atmosphere mitigated its size. It was a factory town, strongly German-American, built around neighborhoods with German names like Lindenwald (which meant, literally, "linden forest"), none of the neighborhoods very far from the hulking industrial monoliths that employed most of the town.

The town's earliest incarnation was a military fort built in 1791, the vanguard for Arthur St. Clair's army, which was about to march north into its own massacre, a defeat that would stand famously as the worst military loss to Indian forces in American history. The fort, in due time, became the town center, its old and forgotten business seeming to have transferred onto various basketball courts and playing fields where Hamilton kids fought vengefully against all comers, as though informed historically, although most of them were not.

Its other famous monument was an odd tribute to another pioneer, Captain John Cleves Symmes, who, in the early 1800s proposed a theory that the earth was hollow—and inhabitable within. A famous historical expedition was mounted to find his imagined polar openings. The expedition was not

the BIG

CROSLEY FIELD, CIRCA 1939—ON HIS FIRST TRIPS TO THE FIELD,
WHAT HE REMEMBERED MOST WAS THE GRASS. HE HAD NEVER SEEN GRASS
SO GREEN.. HE WAS USED TO PASTURES AND FIELDS OF DIRT.

successful, of course, but it inspired a dedicated following in its time, becoming a monument to an unrelenting and unrealistic hope, something that factory workers and ball players sometimes needed in equal amounts.

Approaching the middle of the century, in the neighborhoods of Hamilton, the name "Nuxhall" was acquiring its own legendary status. Orville Nuxhall was a big, tireless, right-hander, 6-foot-1, over 240 pounds, so tough and competitive that it would have been unnatural for him *not* to have been called "Ox." He played in the Hamilton Sunday League, a pastoral-sounding appellation that belied its caliber of ball.

And now there was another Nuxhall, Ox's oldest son, Joe, whom many of them knew as "Sonny." Ox was inordinately proud of Joe, and he included the kid in the Sunday League games. If onlookers had ever been inclined to think of Joe's inclusion as mere nepotism, the kid's raw prowess soon instructed them otherwise. The story looped around town, from barbershops to drinking-holes. Ox had actually stuck Joe in right field in a game when he didn't have enough players, and word was, he was grooming the kid to be a pitcher.

And so the story spread.

The kid could play. He could field. He could throw. He was never overmatched playing with the men. Witnesses of Sonny's skills began to mount.

The skeptics had one question: Could he hit?

Fact was, no one knew. As confident as Ox seemed in Joe's ability, he would not let him bat. A lot of the pitchers could throw hard—himself included—but they didn't always have dependable control. Ox didn't want his son hit in the head by some 30-year-old factory worker, who might have had a couple of beers before the game.

The community seemed to agree with Orville and allowed him protective pride in his unusual offspring. The kid was tall, good-looking, mannerly; he would have made any parent proud. And so Sonny Nuxhall, only a few years removed from mother's milk, was given a privileged place in the men's game.

People in the neighborhood noticed things about Joe and his brothers, and it wasn't always their aptitude for sports. The Nuxhall boys, for instance, seemed to show up in the most unlikely places. Many found it curious that Joe, Bob, Gene, and Don—the whole Nuxhall brood— always had good seats when the circus came to town. The Nuxhalls

THE FAMILY OX—JOE'S FATHER, ORVILLE "OX" NUXHALL, WAS A LEGEND IN HIS OWN RIGHT. SOMETIMES THEY EVEN PLAYED IN THE SAME GAME, JOE RELIEVING THE OLD MAN, WHO WAS HEADED FOR THE WIN AND A BEER.

didn't have that kind of money. Everyone knew that.

In truth, they didn't. But the boys did have a curious nature and a knack for talking with anyone of any social status. Even at an early age, their abilities were unique and disarming. And Joe was the best.

The boys were intrigued by the circus, particularly the tough-talking, well-muscled men who handled the rigging and erected the tents. These men smoked cigarettes and spat tobacco juice. They hauled rope and pounded large wooden spikes in the ground with big, heavy hammers. They spoke with unknown accents and wiped their brows with large colorful bandannas.

They cursed and laughed and seemed to go wherever they wanted and do whatever they pleased. To the boys, these men were how they imagined pirates to be, except that they were landlocked, sailing across the flat and tideless Midwest in trucks, the tent poles merely another kind of mast.

They spoke continuously of distant places: Florida, Louisiana, Tennessee. They talked about places they would go: Toledo, Huntington, someplace called Chillicothe.

The boys loved listening to the roustabouts, passing the time of day. But they also learned something: Stick around, they were told, help us clean up after the show. And you'll get first-rate tickets to the show, every night, and free.

There was one catch. "We had to give them our belts before the show started," Joe says. "That way, they knew we would be there at the end of the show to help clean up. Why? Well, how the hell you gonna go home without your belt? Ya couldn't go home without your belt!"

Parents noticed if a boy came home without his belt. People noticed a lot of things back then. They noticed Joe working around Ford's Fields at night while the men played fast-pitch softball. There he was, night after night, pushing around an enormous cart filled with ice and soft drinks.

"Gawd, that thing was heavy," he says. "The drinks were a dime apiece, and for every one we sold we got two cents. That was pretty good in those days. Yeah, you were working, but you got to see the games. Trouble was, when the games were over, we had to go around and pick up all the empties. Crawling around under the bleachers. Seemed like it took forever."

The results of the games were dutifully reported in the *Hamilton Journal-News* each day by the man known in Hamilton as "The Commish," Hib Iske. Iske, who was connected everywhere, knew Joe and later he would make certain others knew him, too.

One summer, Joe stumbled upon a crew laying pipe not far from his house on Vine Street. Like the circus roustabouts, the crew's rowdy approach appealed to him.

Joe found the foreman, signed up, and went about the back-breaking work of digging ditches and laying pipe.

The foreman was happy to land such a big, strong, strapping, hard-working galoot. But it was a small town and word traveled quickly.

"Maybe two days on the job, I'm out there shoveling and working and the foreman walks up. 'Joe,' he says. 'How old are you?'

"Sixteen," I say.

"Tell me again," he says.

BOYZ N THE HOOD—THE NUXHALL BOYS WERE FOUND
ALL OVER HAMILTON, BUT THEY WERE FOUND MOST CONSPICUOUSLY
ON VARIOUS PLAYGROUNDS, BALL DIAMONDS, AND HARDWOOD COURTS.
JOE IS AT BOTTOM, LEFT.

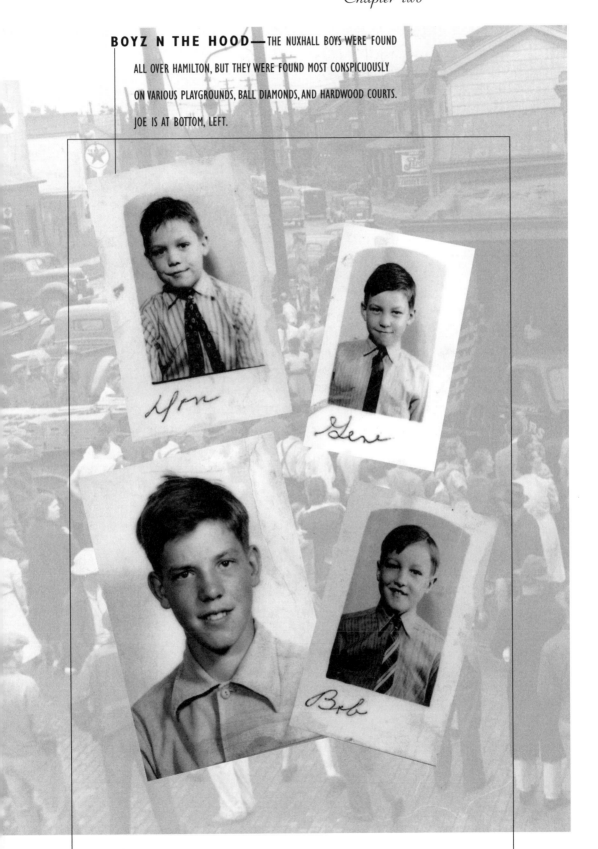

"Well, he is looking at me hard and all the other guys have stopped working and they are looking at me. I say, 'Uh, 13, sir.'

"He says, 'Check out, son. You're too young. Sorry to lose you. You're a good worker.'

"I hated to lose that job," Joe says. "It paid real well."

Joe loved his games, but he was not a typical sports fan. Occasionally, he would browse the papers, checking on the Cincinnati Reds. Once in a great while, he listened to a game on the radio.

"They had a segment I really liked," he recalls. "'Fans in the Stands' with Dick Bray—'*Brought to you by Rubel's Heidelberg Rye.*' He would just find someone in the stands and talk to them about the game. Maybe they would talk about McCormick or Lombardi. Maybe, the game before. I don't know why, but I really liked that. It seemed personal.

"You could tell Dick Bray really liked the game and the people. I liked the sounds around him that came through the microphone. The sounds in the background while they were talking."

Generally, the sound of the game drove Joe outside to find a game of his own. He was not one to sit and listen. To hell with listening; he wanted to get up a game.

He wasn't aware the Reds won the pennant in '39 and the Series in '40. At 10 and 11 years old, he was just too busy to notice.

Yet his success in Hamilton's Knothole League led him closer to big league baseball.

"Twice, maybe three times, the people who sponsored our team took us down to a game at Crosley," Joe remembers. "It was kind of a reward for a good season. We rode the bus and, gawd, what a place."

CROSLEY FIELD WHERE THE GATES OPENED, the turnstiles cranked. And, suddenly, one was met with the sounds and smells of baseball before ever coming close to the field.

Programs! Get your programs! Can't tell the players without a program.

The vendors' calls mixed with the crisp sounds of baseball: the bat against the ball, players loosening up for the game, but with a smart snap that you didn't see on any sandlot, anywhere.

"They threw so hard but so easily," Joe remembers. "I couldn't get over that. Just a snap and a throw and the mitt snapped and the guy on

THROWING PAINS—YOUNG JOE WAS NEVER MUCH OF A SPORTS
FAN. WHEN HE LISTENED TO GAMES ON THE RADIO, THE SOUND DROVE HIM
OUTSIDE, TO FIND HIS OWN GAME.

the other end kinda popped it outta his glove and whipped it right back. It was almost as if they could have done it in their sleep."

All this was mixed with the distant sounds of trains laboring into Union Terminal, which was maybe a mile from the ballpark.

Programs! Get your programs.

It was all the Crosley Field symphony, echoing through the tall passageways of the stadium, the cement corridors that also held the smells that signaled baseball: roasting peanuts, cigar smoke, beer, brats, sweat and perfume.

Peanuts!
Ice cold beer, here!
Programs...

From the seats, Crosley was a tapestry of plush green grass and red-brown soil with shining white lines stretching toward bases that looked like tight, white pillows.

It was a long way from the places where Joe had learned the game. There were times when he and his friends had used rocks and sticks for bases, and gunnysacks filled with sawdust.

Crosley had a look, her own character. Not too big, not too small, with graceful and distinguishing lines, that gentle terrace which climbed toward the scoreboard in left-center and challenged even the most graceful and adept outfielders. (It was here that The Great Bambino, Ruth, playing his next-to-last game and chasing a fly ball, tripped on the inclined terrace and fell on his head, storming off amid a cloud of curt Anglo-Saxon.)

The scoreboard stood high in left-center, obscuring the factories in the distance, as well as whatever it was you left behind before you came to the ballpark. Not only did it tell you what was happening in the game you were watching, it told you what was happening in places you had never seen or might never go: Ebbets Field, Sportsman's Park, Shibe, Yankee Stadium, Tiger Stadium, Wrigley, Fenway.

It was a window on the world, a slow, measured ticker tape of baseball, telling everything that was happening in the game that day.

In those early trips to the park, Joe noticed something about the players, even though he did not put names with their faces. He noticed how friendly most of them were, the way they made their way to the low brick wall that separated the field from the stands. He noticed that they talked and laughed, taking time with the fans.

Tucking their gloves under their arms, they signed scorecards, gloves, scraps of paper. They smiled. They seemed to know many fans by name.

Sou-ve-nirs! Get your souvenirs!

But of all the things he saw on those first trips to Crosley, one thing impressed him most: "The field. The greenest grass I have ever seen in my life," Joe says. "They were playing the Boston Bees, I think. I don't remember if they won or lost, but I will never forget the look of that field and the terrace out in the outfield. We were used to 'skin' infields, ya know, all dirt. We played in pastures. That place, that grass, it was like a carpet.

"It never crossed my mind that I would ever play there. How would I think that? I thought I would play basketball. As a kid, I always thought I would be a basketball player."

Joe had heard of Frank McCormick, Ernie Lombardi, and Paul Derringer, but only one Reds player really caught his interest, the pitcher Johnny Vander Meer. He identified with Vander Meer but not for the obvious reasons, not the back-to-back no-hitters in '38.

"I don't know that I even heard about the back-to-back no-hitters until years later," Joe says. "I just liked him, liked what I heard about him. I guess because he was a left-hander, and he just seemed like a good guy."

YEARS LATER, THEY WOULD BECOME FRIENDS and Joe was not disappointed in Vander Meer. "Everything I thought about him turned out to be right. If I ever had, what do you call it, a mentor, it was Johnny.

"He was a lot like McKechnie, straightforward. He talked to me a lot, talked to me about what it meant to be a big leaguer. He told me about little things. He talked to me about how everything you did—on the field, off the field—could, you know, have an impact on people. He meant an awful lot to me."

Joe never forgot the favor. As time passed, he would return it a thousand times over, telling this rookie and that one, over a beer or a cup of coffee, what it meant to be a big leaguer, what it took to be in the majors.

From Crosley to Riverfront to Great American Ballpark, as a player and a broadcaster, Joe was always there, sitting in the dugout or the clubhouse, smoking a cigarette, and talking quietly to one player or another.

He didn't tell them what to do. He tried to tell them what it all meant, how to react. He answered questions. He told them stories, parables from the past.

"I think it was '55, maybe '56, my best years," he says. "I had an awful night, got whacked around something terrible. I left the clubhouse and was going to my car. Like always, there were a lot of kids waiting outside for autographs.

"I always signed for everybody, but that night I didn't want any part of it. I told the kids, no. Just got in my car and left.

"There was this old guy who was always around the ballpark. I don't remember what he did, don't remember his name. The next night I pull in and get out of the car. He says, 'Joe, what you did last night, that's not you.'

"At first, I didn't know what he was talking about. Then, I realized. Just because it is going bad for you, you got no right to disappoint people. You are in the big leagues! Can life be so bad you can't make time for somebody? Since that day, I have never turned anyone down for an autograph. Sometimes, it's the small things, ya know what I mean?"

Ron Oester grew up in Cincinnati. When he was a small boy, he put the radio out on the lawn and listened to the game while he bounced a ball off the house or raced after high flies that he had launched into the air himself.

Aaron swings...It is deep...That ball is tagged. Oester is back. He jumps at the fence. Oh, my! What a catch! The crowd is going wild. Oester robs the Braves slugger of a homerun! Folks, Reds win again, 3-2. Talk about your great catches, we have just seen one. I'm tellin' ya, this Ron Oester, he is gonna be something!

"I imagined myself playing and Joe making the call," Oester says. "I think every kid does something like that, but for me, it was Joe making the call. Always Joe...."

Oester broke in with the Reds in 1978 and would eventually replace Hall of Famer Joe Morgan as the club's regular second baseman. It was not an easy act to follow, nor was it an easy entry into the game.

"I guess I first met Joe when I was with Indianapolis in Triple-A and they invited me to spring training," Oester says. "I don't know for sure, because it seems like I have known him forever. To me, he was a legend. When you first get to camp, it's kind of awkward, because you don't know that many people and you're worried about fitting in. But Joe would come along and talk. He made you feel comfortable.

"It wasn't just me," he says. "It was everyone. You meet him and you feel like he's been a friend all your life. You start talking with him and he's telling you stories and then, the next thing you know, he is telling you something about yourself as a ball player that you maybe never thought about before.

"He was like another coach," Oester says, "but it was different somehow."

Joe would pull a player aside to a corner of the clubhouse or the dugout and quietly offer an opinion or an observation, sometimes, even a stern word.

"He wasn't afraid to tell you what he thought," Oester says. "He would just lay it out. I remember one year, I was struggling. I wasn't driving in many runs. The year before I led the team in RBI's. It was '83, somewhere in there.

"He gets a hold of me after a game. He's got a Bud in his hand. He hands me one and says,'"O," you are being way too selective at the plate. Ya got to start making more contact. No contact, no chance.' And, he was right.

"Seemed like he was always right," Oester says. "He helped hundreds of guys and he still does. You hear him on the radio and he's Joe and you love him and that voice, but a lot of people don't know what he has done for so many guys who came through that clubhouse."

FOR DECADES, he was a person the players could count on. He was someone they could turn to for a story or a word of advice. He always had them laughing. He always had them thinking.

"I played with Joe back in the '60s," says Tommy Helms, Rookie of The Year in 1966. "By that time, he had been in the game over twenty years. I was in my 20's, and it seemed like he knew everything and everybody. Even back then the guy was a walking history book.

"Damn guy had something on everyone. Every guy in the league. What he could hit. What he couldn't. Tendencies, you know. It was like

THREE OF A KIND—IN THE SPRING OF 1955, THESE PITCHERS CAME TO CAMP WITH A 31-18 RECORD FROM 1954. THAT'S JACKIE COLLUM (7-3) AT LEFT, JOE (12-5), AND ART FOWLER (12-10).

he had some big ol' mental catalogue. I always thought if he hadn't gone into broadcasting, he would have made one helluva manager. He had it all. He could deal with players. Knew the game inside out. And the fans loved him."

Helms is quiet for a moment, running the idea of Joe as manager around in his mind.

"Makes perfect sense," he says. "Wonder why no one ever thought of that?"

he great Cincinnati baseball scribe, Lee Allen, said that the ball yard fan was by nature isolationist, his sport excluding all else but his interest in the game. "This type of fan," Allen said, "even considers global war as a personal affront designed to ruin his enjoyment of baseball."

Ruin in the war years was a relative term but suffice it to say that the face of baseball was certainly altered. The Reds cut back on their travel accommodations, and in 1942 the players traveled in two Pullman cars rather than three, introducing the privations of the upper bunk to those who had previously slept downstairs. (The *Enquirer*'s baseball writer remarked that the boys weren't complaining, however; an upper berth still compared quite favorably to a foxhole.)

On the eve of Opening Day, 1943, fans were warned that ferrying one's self to Crosley Field by taxi would violate rationing regulations, and the club itself asked fans to give back foul balls. The ushers collected them, and they were sent to the servicemen.

"SONNY"
1941

THE HAMILTON KID—HERE, JOE IS 13 AND PLAYING
IN THE HAMILTON SUNDAY LEAGUE; SOMETIMES HE FOUND HIMSELF
PLAYING ON THE SAME TEAM AS HIS FATHER, ORVILLE.

Lee Allen pronounced even the ball a war victim. Its core, made of balata instead of rubber, came from the juices of tropical trees, and Allen said it was "dead as the hopes of a cellar team." Nearly half of the first thirty games of the 1943 season ended in shutouts, prompting the Reds' Frank McCormick to compare the balata balls to hitting concrete.

By the Opening Day of 1943, the war had taken an incredible toll. Gripped by the patriotic fervor that swelled throughout the country, millions had entered the armed services, among them, some of baseball's greatest.

Ted Williams, the last man to hit .400 in a season, was a pilot in the Marine Corps. Joe DiMaggio, who hit in fifty-six straight games in the summer of 1941, was in the Army. (That was also the summer when Cincinnati kids, in a high school summer history class, took a poll of the greatest Americans of all time and named the Yankee Clipper Number 1, followed by George Washington, who occupied a distant second.)

Two days after Pearl Harbor, Cleveland's Bob Feller, the most dominant pitcher in baseball, winner of 76 games from 1939 through 1941, enlisted in the Navy. Of his voluntary four years in the service, Feller once said, "I just thought there were more important things than being a ballplayer."

Detroit slugger Hank Greenberg was drafted and later reenlisted. Yankee power-hitter Hank Bauer was twice wounded, and Braves pitcher Warren Spahn won the Bronze Star for bravery while leading a unit in the Battle of The Bulge.

From 1941 through 1945, there were sixteen teams in major league baseball, each team composed of twenty-five men. Of the 400 men on those rosters during the war years, 340 were drafted or enlisted. Another 3,000 would leave the minor leagues.

When the '41 season opened, there were forty-one different leagues operating in minor league baseball. By 1944, there were only ten.

On Opening Day in 1942, a record was established. Of the 400 men who took the field that day, a hundred of them had never played in a major league game.

"We were losing the very best the game had to offer," said former Reds President Bob Howsam, who served as a test pilot during the war. "But the game went on and it endured because it had to. President Roosevelt wanted it to continue. He wanted baseball to be there for the people."

Clyde King pitched ten years in the majors, from 1944 to 1953. He was an 18-year-old right-handed pitcher from Goldsboro, North Carolina, who—admittedly—slipped into the game during its leanest years.

"There is no question that the quality of play was down during the war years," King says. "Hell, so many of our great players were gone. But our game was still entertaining and I think, I swear, we did our part. It wasn't a complete circus during the war. Some of us were good enough to stick around after the war was over."

Baseball may not have been a complete circus, but it was crowded with castoffs and veterans who were persuaded into coming back for one last round. "A strange collection of flotsam washed up on the major league shore," Lee Allen described them.

Jimmie Foxx, the great home run hitter who played in the shadows of Babe Ruth and Lou Gehrig, came back in his late 30's. Paul Waner returned in his early 40's. Babe Herman came back at 42, eight years after he had retired.

The Washington Senators had Bert Shephard, a war veteran who pitched on an artificial leg. Hod Lisenbee was a rookie in 1927 with the Senators. At age 46, he pitched for the Reds.

Phil Weintraub, a rookie in '33 with the Giants, had bounced back and forth from the minors to the majors for twelve years. In 1944, he won a spot with the Giants and on April 30th, against the rival Dodgers at the Polo Grounds, he doubled twice, tripled, and hit a home run. By day's end, the 36-year-old left-handed hitter out of Chicago had 11 runs batted in, one short of the record held by Hall of Famer Jim Bottomley.

Weintraub never played after the '45 season and those 11 runs batted in on April 30, 1944, represented just over five percent of his career total. In seven years, Weintraub drove in a total of 207 runs. Beyond that one-game performance, Weintraub was known for two other things: He was a marvelous dresser and an accomplished accordion player.

THE ST. LOUIS CARDINALS, for all their glory, were so talent-desperate that they placed an advertisement in *The Sporting News.*

If you are a free agent, and have previous professional experience, we may be able to place you on one of our clubs. We have positions open on our AA, B, and D classification clubs. If you believe you can qualify for one of these good baseball jobs, tell us about yourself.

The Cards asked for personal information and concluded: *Write Today.*

The advertisement marked a precipitous fall for a World Championship team that once prided itself on a minor league system of more than thirty teams developed by Branch Rickey.

But after a battle with club owner Sam Breadon, Rickey had moved to Brooklyn and his trusted and loyal scouts quickly followed.

When it came to finding ballplayers, Breadon was no match for Rickey, but then, few were. While Rickey had taken the best of the St. Louis scouting team with him to Brooklyn, then increased the staff four times over, Breadon's plea to the masses was a bust; only some half-dozen replies were considered worthy of the most meager scrutiny.

Sometimes, extreme methods were used to find players. The Salem Senators, based in Oregon and part of the Western International League, heard about a pitcher who was having success in their area—he was the top pitcher for the state penitentiary.

Undeterred, club officials approached the warden with a proposal. On the days he was scheduled to pitch, the convict could be ushered to the park by prison guards and returned to the lock-up after the game.

The request went as far as the governor's desk, where it was denied. It was noted that while the man in question was of considerable skill, the governor must decline since the pitcher's offense was shooting a policeman.

The pitcher's reputation, after all, would precede him, bringing a subtle pressure to the game. What might happen upon the occasion of a third strike? Would the umpire—the policeman of the game, one might say—suddenly find *himself* in the line of fire?

THESE WERE TIMES when players like Denny Galehouse and Chet Laabs left their factory jobs on Friday, jumped a train, and joined the St. Louis Browns wherever they were playing, and Pete Gray, a one-armed outfielder, gained a starting position in the major leagues. Losing his right arm at age six after falling off a truck, he learned to throw and hit with his left hand. A shoemaker made him a special glove with little padding and loose fingers but he preferred to field bare-handed, actually being quicker on ground balls than many of his glove-wearing compatriots. He debuted against Detroit in April of 1945 and went one-for-three. In all, he played 77 games and batted .218, a testament to both the war years and an indomitable spirit.

Throughout the war years, the hardest working men in the game—those most challenged—were the scouts. "We not only had to find ballplayers for the major league teams, we had to find players for our minor league affiliates," said Rex Bowen, then working for Branch Rickey and the Brooklyn Dodgers.

"In those days it was different. Some teams had between fifteen and twenty-five minor league teams. Mr. Rickey called me into his office and handed me a fistful of train tickets.

"He said, 'I want you to go across the country holding tryout camps and find me the best ballplayers available.' You have to understand. When Mr. Rickey asked you to do something, you did it with fervor.

"So, we started out. From Holyoke, Massachusetts, to San Mateo, California. We held twenty-seven different tryout camps. Mostly we saw young high school boys and older men and most of 'em weren't up to scotch."

One such stop, in Indianapolis, led to the signing of first baseman Gil Hodges and pitcher Carl Erskine, but they, too, would be called to service.

"That was 1943," Bowen recalls. "The following year, we did the same thing through the southern states. Those trips were the foundation of our success in the '50s. That, of course, and the addition of Jackie (Robinson) from the Negro League.

"Everybody else in the game was out there working, too. But Mr. Rickey was insistent on building the kind of system we had back in St. Louis. Still, everybody had the same goal, trying to find players, players who could run and throw and had some power. Sometimes you just felt, well, like you were spinning your wheels."

THE PLAYERS WHO WERE MOST REALISTIC knew they weren't ready for the big leagues. "Hell, we were all young. A lot of guys weren't really developed yet," says Clyde King, "but this was opportunity. This was a chance to play in the big leagues."

The scouts found themselves bird-dogging all over the country, from one town, one county, to the next, watching industrial league games, Sunday leagues, continually searching for players worthy enough—given the conditions—to wear a major league uniform.

Scouts guarded their secrets well. Unlike today, information on a player or a prospect was never shared. The very best, such as "Wid" Matthews, another in Rickey's employ, relied on a network of "sub" scouts or commission scouts, who themselves leaned heavily on high school coaches and people who, as Bowen put it, "knew the game, just didn't think they knew it. People who had an eye for real talent."

Rickey's scouting staff corresponded with hundreds of high school coaches around the country and on a regular basis.

The Reds' scouting staff was not as deep as the Dodgers', and while limited in number, it, too, was continually beating the bushes. In Cincinnati, the need was clear. The Reds, so rich in pitching just years before, were in dire need of arms.

Pat Patterson, Bill McCorry, and Eddie Reis worked for the Reds. In the summer of '43, Reese told Patterson and McCorry about a right-handed pitcher from nearby Hamilton, Ohio. Reis's lead was Hib Iske, who ran the recreational leagues in Hamilton. Reis told Patterson and McCorry this was a player worth their time. They could find the guy playing in the Hamilton Sunday League.

The description was simple: Big guy. Probably in his mid-30's. Throws hard. The name, they were told, was Nuxhall, Orville Nuxhall. Nicknamed "Ox."

The three scouts made the trip to Hamilton to see Nuxhall play and he was as described: a big, strong, right-hander. They liked his competitive nature. He had a toughness about him that appealed to the scouts. They didn't know how successful he would be, but they did know he would not back down. They watched him throw, watched him run a little bit, and tried to gauge his interest in playing ball for a living.

They were undeterred by his age—he was 34—and his weight—he was pushing 250 pounds—and they offered him $150 a month and an assignment to Ogden, Utah, in the Pioneer League, Class C Ball. Orville Nuxhall thought it over but not for long, and he declined the offer.

He worked as a millwright and a stationary engineer. He had a wife and five kids to feed: four boys and a baby girl. It just didn't seem to make sense. Orville was known throughout the area not only for his physical stature and ability in baseball but also for being a practical and sometimes stubborn sort.

Patterson and McCorry didn't give up easily, but sensing Nuxhall's stance was firm, they began to relent. Reis, meanwhile, was looking around the field at the other players. One in particular caught his interest, a tall player tossing with others in right field. Reis pointed him out.

The scouts liked his motion and his size. They asked Nuxhall about him.

Nuxhall seemed a little surprised by the question. He smiled and told the scouts it was his oldest son, Joe. "Sonny," folks called him.

How old is he? they asked.

Nuxhall said his son was 14, just finishing eighth grade at Wilson Junior High School.

Fourteen? Awfully young, even for the times.

But the kid's size was impressive and his movements belied his youth. Here, they thought, might just be a find.

Joe threw for the scouts, never giving the activity much thought at all. He was there to play and this just seemed a passing circumstance.

PATTERSON, McCORRY AND REIS left Hamilton impressed. The kid could throw, no doubt about that. He was raw and rough, but they could work that out and he would surely be an easy sign. What 14-year-old boy would turn down a big-league contract? Still, maybe he was too young. Maybe McKechnie and Warren Giles, the Reds' general manager, would frown on signing a kid so young.

But was 14 *that* young? Cleveland had signed Feller at 17 out of Van Meter, Iowa. In his first two big league starts, he struck out thirty-two batters, then went home to finish high school.

What about Dizzy Dean? Dean was an 18-year-old cotton picker. Rickey's scouts found him playing sandlot ball in Texas. Brash and zany, he was the perfect embodiment of his nickname. He won 120 games his first five seasons. "Son," he liked to ask new batters, "what pitch would you like to miss?"

Waite Hoyt signed at 16. So did Mel Ott.

The scouts talked it over on their way back to Cincinnati. There was only one thing to do: File their report, make their recommendation, and wait to see what the bosses had to say.

The Reds' brain trust reacted quickly. Giles, the general manager, and his assistant, Gabe Paul, called the scouts to the Reds' main office in the Union Central Building on Vine Street in downtown Cincinnati. Manager Bill McKechnie attended the meeting, as well.

McKechnie, the scouts figured, might be the hardest sell of all. Though he liked to build his teams around pitching and defense, he also liked veterans.

Giles, Paul, and McKechnie were impressed with the report on Nuxhall. Patterson's word carried a lot of weight. He was one of the most respected scouts in the game.

But, understandably, they wanted to see for themselves, especially McKechnie. Like everybody else in the league, they were chasing St. Louis and not catching up. Their numbers were dwindling quickly.

With the war's end nowhere in sight, harder times appeared to be ahead. No prospect so enthusiastically recommended could be dismissed. Besides, Reis said, Hib Iske, his contact in Hamilton, had told him he had already sent a letter to Brooklyn about Nuxhall. This lent urgency to the situation. No one wanted to lose a local prospect to the Dodgers. How would *that* look?

What should they do?

Reis had a quick answer. Iske had a number of boys in Hamilton he believed were prospects. Tell him all the boys would be brought in for a workout, but the first player they wanted to see was young Nuxhall.

The arrangements were made. Joe would work out for McKechnie and his staff on a day when the Reds didn't have a game. His father was working that day, as was his grandfather, but Bud Dubois, Joe's junior high school basketball coach, agreed to drive Joe to the city for the audition.

Dubois was just as intrigued as Joe, maybe more so. He could only wonder where this might lead.

They arrived at Crosley, entered through the players' entrance, and were taken to the clubhouse, where they were greeted by McKechnie's coaches.

Joe changed into a uniform, laced up his spikes, grabbed his glove, and made his way to the field, where he met McKechnie for the first time.

DuBois went to the box seats along third base at Crosley, propped his two-tone, wing-tipped shoes on the rail and watched as Joe began to throw. He had brought along a camera and took a picture from his seat. He wanted to preserve the moment.

There was Joe, throwing from the mound. McKechnie, Estel Crabtree, and Hans Lobert took up a position behind the mound.

McKechnie leaned on a bat and watched Joe.

McKechnie didn't like kids, especially kid pitchers. He preferred veteran players, men who had been through the games, brought some thought to the clubhouse.

He favored players who recognized situations before they occurred and, consequently, knew the possibilities, and reacted naturally in each breach the game presented.

REUNION—WHEN JOE MADE THE REDS' ROSTER, HE AND THE DEACON RELIVED HIS FIRST MOMENTS WITH THE TEAM. AT RIGHT IS BILL MEKECHNIE JR., AND PAUL FLORENCE IS AT LEFT.

If, then. . .

If, then. . .

Think before the act is required. Be so in tune with the game that the required act is a matter of rote.

His standards were high, seldom met by kids. Kids didn't think. Kids acted and reacted with no experience to draw upon. Kids gave you extremes. He wanted polished, cool performance.

But he would not prejudice his observation of the kid.

After all, there was a war on.

And the government seemed to have all the pitchers.

God knows, major league baseball didn't have them.

McKECHNIE MADE SURE THE WORKOUT was leisurely at first, allowing Joe to get used to the surroundings. He wanted him to be at ease. Only then would he see what he had to offer.

First, they watched him loosen up, looking at his motion. They asked him to throw off the mound. He took a few ground balls and ran a little. Then came the litmus test. In those days, the extra players—the guys who were not starters—always came to the park on off-days to hit and take infield.

McKechnie instructed them to grab a bat and jump in against the kid. Joe threw and worked up a thoroughbred sweat.

He gave up some line drives, and he sneaked by a fastball or two. Perhaps it was his youth that shielded him from any anxiety that would ordinarily stem from such an experience. Perhaps it was the fact that he had never thought about being a big league player.

Whatever beneficent spirit guided him that day, Joe threw well.

"Just throwing one strike after another," he says. "First ten pitches, eight for strikes. Throwin' strikes left and right. I was probably somewhere between 85 and 90 miles per hour. Who knows? They didn't have the radar gun yet. I was just out there lettin' my natural stuff come through."

When the workout was over, McKechnie thanked Joe for coming and wished him luck.

Nothing else was said.

DuBois and Joe drove back to Hamilton, wondering what would take place.

McKechnie, meanwhile, made his way to Giles' office on the grandstand level at Crosley, where he made his case. He strongly suggested the Reds offer Nuxhall a contract.

Giles was impressed.

This was McKechnie, groomed under John McGraw and Frank Chance, a man devoted to veteran players, but also one gifted in spotting young talent, and he was endorsing a 14-year-old pitcher.

Giles listened as McKechnie assessed the young left-hander's ability. But his mind was already made up. McKechnie's opinion was enough. He had developed players like Pie Traynor, Kiki Cuyler, Paul Waner, Chick Hafey, Wally Berger, Vince DiMaggio, Frank McCormick, Johnny Vander Meer.

No one else thought *they* were ready.

McKechnie did, and they were.

THERE WERE THINGS THAT WERE INEXPLICABLE about McKechnie.

Why *did* he keep that beat-up old chair in his office that went back to the '20s and his days with the Pirates, the leather split, ticking falling out on the floor?

But the man had genius. Especially, it seemed, when it came to pitchers.

Vander Meer was 3-5 as a rookie in '37. The next year, under McKechnie, he was 15-10 and threw back-to-back no-hitters.

In June of 1938, the Reds purchased Bucky Walters from the Phillies. Walters had won 29 games in the previous two-plus seasons. In his first three seasons under McKechnie, he won 50 games. The story was similar with Paul Derringer, the Kentucky firebrand who won 45 games in 1939 and 1940. His 2-1 win over Detroit clinched the 1940 World Series title for the Reds.

Long before McKechnie finished talking, Giles' mind was made up.

They would offer the kid a contract.

Giles arranged a meeting with Orville Nuxhall and made a generous offer for Joe—$175 a month to play for Ogden in the Pioneer League in Utah.

As Giles spoke, Orville Nuxhall wrestled with his thoughts. He didn't want his boy to work in a factory, forced to work back-to-back shifts. He wanted his son to have an education and wear clean clothes. The boy was also on the brink of a dream that had once been *his*. But he was just 14. He wanted all his kids to have a chance to enjoy their youth.

Orville was torn by the alternatives. The money was good. The opportunity was great. But the time was not right. Joe was too young.

At first, Giles was stunned. He sat back and listened as Orville offered the reasoning behind his decision.

Finally, Orville said, there was one last matter—Joe's desire to help his junior high school basketball team win a third straight city title.

Joe, he told Giles, wants that very badly.

"Thank you," Orville said, "but not now."

It was one of the hardest things he had ever done.

"THAT WAS A LOT OF MONEY IN THOSE DAYS, $175 a month, maybe as much as Dad was making, but my parents didn't like it," Joe says. "They thought I was too young. They knew how important education was and, truthfully, I really didn't want to do it. They knew that. We had won two straight championships in basketball at Wilson and I wanted to go back and try to win a third."

Giles was immediately impressed with the Nuxhalls, their son, and their priorities.

He was vice president of the Reds, World Champions in 1940, the oldest professional franchise in the game. He was a candidate for league president, possibly commissioner, and he had not anticipated this kind of honesty or innocence. He had not foreseen junior high school basketball as an obstacle to a career in professional baseball.

Warren Giles admired the Nuxhalls and he believed this kid could play. He had come to believe he might be another Bob Feller, another Dizzy Dean or Waite Hoyt.

He told Orville Nuxhall he understood.

But while Giles was a man who respected education, civility, honor, and devotion, he was also one who didn't give up easily.

Several weeks passed. As Labor Day approached, the Reds were in second place, floundering far behind the first-place Cardinals. Giles was busily going through his notes. His thoughts kept coming back to Nuxhall. He called Gabe Paul into his office. Paul was not only his trusted assistant manager, he was also his friend.

The idea, he told Paul, had just come to him. Maybe it was too late, maybe not.

Paul listened as Giles explained.

Labor Day Weekend was coming up. They had a series with St. Louis. Ask Joe to make the road trip. That way he could see what big league baseball was all about. They would roll out the carpet. That would surely convince him to sign.

As Giles energetically described his plan, Paul was doubtful. But he had learned that his boss was right more often than he was wrong.

Paul hastily left the office. It was Wednesday. He had a little over twenty-four hours to work everything out.

"Mr. Giles was a good man," says Bobby Mattick, a Reds farmhand who would coach for the club and eventually become one of its best scouts. "But in those days the heads of ball clubs, they were kings. They expected you to do what they asked and *now*. No questions asked, no excuses. And, by God, they usually got what they wanted.

"Warren Giles? I'm tellin' ya, best stand up straight when you talked with that man, no kiddin' about that. Cross him and it was trouble."

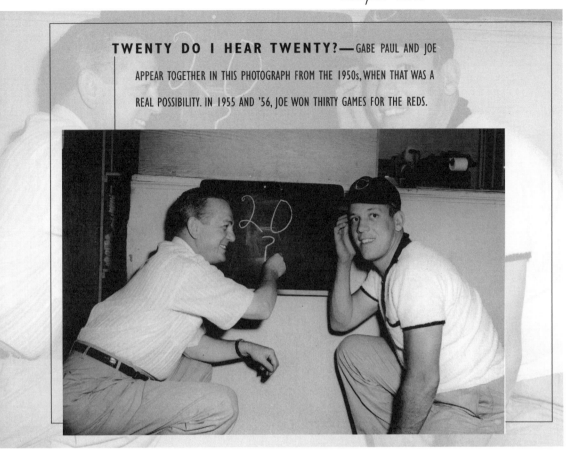

TWENTY DO I HEAR TWENTY?—GABE PAUL AND JOE APPEAR TOGETHER IN THIS PHOTOGRAPH FROM THE 1950s, WHEN THAT WAS A REAL POSSIBILITY. IN 1955 AND '56, JOE WON THIRTY GAMES FOR THE REDS.

To that point in his career, Paul had risen quickly in baseball, moving up the ladder from the lowest rungs to his position of trust under Giles. He prided himself on being Giles' good right hand, and he took great pleasure in the success they had achieved together.

In all the years he had worked with Giles, he had learned that sometimes the smallest task could lead to the largest results. But he wasn't sure he could pull this off in twenty-four hours, all this scrambling around for a 15-year-old pitcher.

Paul pulled the files and started working the phone.

Chapter four

he Reds' plan for the 15-year-old Nuxhall was filled with peril. It was good that Gabe Paul trusted his powers of persuasion, for he would need them.

First, he had to convince the Nuxhalls that it would be fine for their son to go on a three-day road trip with a bunch of major league ball players. What about school? And how would Joe react? The little journey was, after all, nothing short of a recruiting trip.

Giles thought the trip would sway the boy's opinion and lead him closer to signing a contract, and Paul knew very well that Giles was right far more than he was wrong.

So he would use every bit of his considerable charm to convince the Nuxhalls what a wonderful opportunity this was for their boy.

The contract was on the table. A $500 bonus and $175 a month.

When Paul finally got an answer at the Nuxhall home, he explained to Orville and Naomi that the ball club would like Joe to go with them on the weekend trip to St. Louis, just to see what big league baseball was all about.

HAYRIDE,

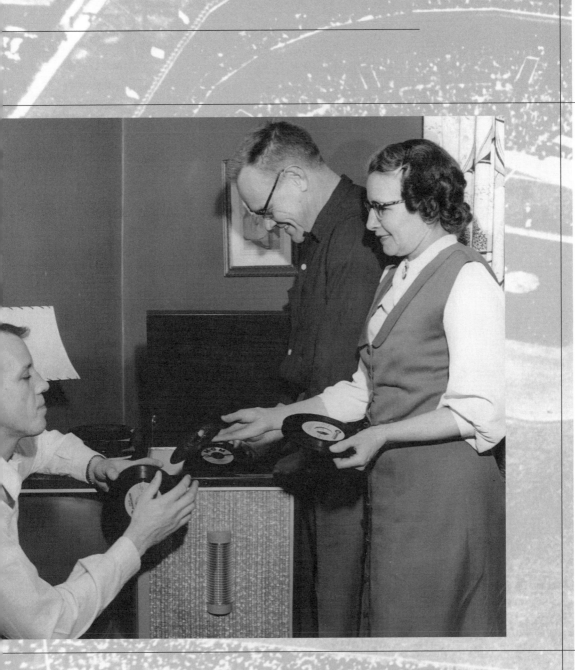

FAMILY MATTERS—JOE WITH HIS PARENTS, ORVILLE AND NAOMI. WHEN HE WAS ON THE ROAD IN THE EARLY YEARS, JOE WAS ALWAYS TRYING TO GET BACK HOME.

RAIN RIDE

Orville and Naomi had many questions. A thing like that would be very expensive. They were honored and impressed, but they didn't have the kind of money to pay for such a trip.

Paul assured them all expenses would be paid. Joe would have a room at the team hotel. He would be taken care of in every way.

Naomi worried about his meals. What would he eat and where?

Paul said he understood their concern, but Joe's meals would be paid for by the team and would be taken at the hotel. Joe, like all the rest of the players, would have a room at the Coronado Hotel.

Orville and Naomi began to soften. Finally, they agreed, with the provision that someone kept an eye on their boy. Paul assured them that would be done. Of course, Paul added, they should be aware that manager Bill McKechnie was a devoutly religious man and would not allow Joe to get involved in anything untoward.

When, they asked, would Joe have to leave?

Tonight, Paul said. Joe would need to be at Union Terminal in Cincinnati by 11 o'clock.

There was a problem, they said.

Joe wasn't expected home until much later in the evening.

Paul, always confident in his abilities, anticipated an unpleasant conversation with Giles.

"I WAS OUT ON A HAYRIDE," JOE SAYS. "Me and a bunch of my buddies, Eddie Greisinger, Andy Lambros, a bunch of us. Just out having fun. The last weekend before school started. We were out in the country, out by Camp Campbell Guard, a summer camp.

"It was getting on toward dark, when here comes Mom and Dad in the car. I'm not sure how they tracked us down. I think they called one of the other parents to find out where we were exactly. I'm wondering what in the world is going on.

"He says, 'Come on, you got to go. The Reds want you to go with them to St. Louis.' It was like a dream or something.

"St. Louis? With the ball club? Hell, I was just on a hayride. Now, St. Louis. We hurried on home. I packed my little bag. One of those old cloth jobs we used to have. You know, like an old gym-bag with the leather loops for handles.

"Didn't take long 'cause I didn't have much: a shirt, socks, pants. I think I had a jacket. And here we go. Still picking off pieces of hay on the drive. You been on a hayride? The hay sticks to everything."

IMPORTANT NOTICE

The attention of both Club and Player is specifically directed to the following excerpt from Major League Rule 3(a):

"No Club shall make a contract different from the uniform contract or a contract containing a non-reserve clause, except with the written approval of the Advisory Council. All contracts shall be in duplicate and the Player shall retain a counterpart original. The making of any agreement between a Club and Player not embodied in the contract shall subject both parties to discipline by the Commissioner; and no such agreement, whether written or verbal, shall be recognized or enforced by the Commissioner."

National League of Professional Baseball Clubs
UNIFORM PLAYER'S CONTRACT

Parties   The_____CINCINNATI BASEBALL CLUB COMPANY_____

herein called the Club, and_____JOSEPH NUXHALL_____

of__1224 E. Vine St., Hamilton, Ohio_____

Recital   The Club is a member of the National League of Professional Baseball Clubs. As such, and jointly with the other members of the League, it is a party to the National League Constitution and to agreements and rules with the American League of Professional Baseball Clubs and its constituent clubs, and with the National Association of Professional Baseball Leagues. The purpose of these agreements and rules is to insure to the public wholesome and high-class professional baseball by defining the relations between Club and Player, between club and club, between league and league, and by vesting in a designated Commissioner broad powers of control and discipline, and of decision in case of disputes.

Agreement   In view of the facts above recited the parties agree as follows:

Employment   1.   The Club hereby employs the Player to render skilled service as a baseball player in connection with all games of the Club during the year____194 5____including the Club's training season, the Club's exhibition games, the Club's playing season, and the World Series (or any other official series in which the Club may participate and in any receipts of which the player may be entitled to share); and the Player covenants that he will perform with diligence and fidelity the service stated and such duties as may be required of him in such employment.

Salary   2.   For the service aforesaid the Club will pay the Player an aggregate salary of $__175.00__ (One Hundred & Seventy-Five Dollars) per month_____, as follows:

In semi-monthly installments after the commencement of the playing season covered by this contract, unless the Player is "abroad" with the Club for the purpose of playing games, in which event the amount then due shall be paid on the first week-day after the return "home" of the Club, the terms "home" and "abroad" meaning respectively *at* and *away from* the city in which the Club has its baseball field.

If a monthly salary is stipulated above, it shall begin with the commencement of the Club's playing season (or such subsequent date as the Player's services may commence) and end with the termination of the Club's scheduled playing season, and shall be payable in semi-monthly installments as above provided.

If the player is in the service of the Club for part of the playing season only, he shall receive such proportion of the salary above mentioned, as the number of days of his actual employment in the Club's playing season bears to the number of days in said season.

Loyalty   3.   (a)   The Player will faithfully serve the Club or any other Club to which, in conformity with the agreements above recited, this contract may be assigned, and pledges himself to the American public to conform to high standards of personal conduct, of fair play and good sportsmanship.

(b)   The Player represents that he does not, directly or indirectly, own stock or have any financial interest in the ownership or earnings of any Major League club, except as hereinafter expressly set forth, and covenants that he will not hereafter, while connected with any Major Lague club, acquire or hold any such stock or interest except in accordance with Major League Rule 20 (e).

Service   4.   (a)   The player agrees that, while under contract or reservation, he will not play baseball (except post-season games as hereinafter stated) otherwise than for the Club or a Club assignee hereof; that he will not engage in professional boxing or wrestling; and that, except with the written consent of the Club or its assignee, he will not engage in any game or exhibition of football, basketball, hockey or other athletic sport.

Post-season Games   (b)   The Player agrees that, while under contract or reservation, he will not play in any post-season baseball games except in conformity with the Major League Rules; and that he will not play in any such baseball game more than ten days after the close of the Major League championship season any year covered by this contract, until the following training season, or in which more than two other players of the Club participate, or with or against an ineligible player or team.

Assignment   5.   (a)   In case of assignment of this contract to another Club, the Player shall promptly report to the assignee club within 72 hours from the date he receives written notice from the Club of such assignment, if not more than 1600 miles by most-direct available railroad route, plus an additional 24 hours for each additional 800 miles; accrued salary shall be payable when he so reports; and each successive assignee shall become liable to the Player for his salary during his term of service with such assignee, and the Club shall not be liable therefor. If the player fails to report as above specified, he shall not be entitled to salary after the date he receives written notice of assignment. If the assignee is a member either of the National or American League the salary shall be as above (paragraph 2) specified. If the assignment, either outright or optional, is made to

He laughs then. It is a soft laugh, the same laugh that often comes to him when he looks through the yellowed pages of the scrapbooks his mother and aunt began keeping in the early '40s, the chronicles of his rise through knothole ball, junior high school, major league baseball, high school, the minors, and back to the big league. The stories pasted to the decaying pages are sometimes exaggerated, sometimes not completely tied to fact; sometimes they are colored by others attempting to take a presence in Joe's rise to notoriety and success.

He begrudges no one in that regard, however. It is like the story he so often tells: "The day I first pitched in the big leagues, there might have been 3,000 people left in the stands," he says. "In the time that's past, I have probably met 30,000 people who said they were there."

And there is the laugh again, the soft laugh of a man who finds his own past difficult to comprehend.

Often, as he looks through the scrapbooks or ransacks his memory for details of things like the hayride and hasty trip to Union Terminal, the laugh comes, rich and raspy, always followed by the same words: "Beats the hell outta me."

Joe would end up spending much of his life in train stations, bus stations, and airports, packing and unpacking, heading to one city after another, one game after another. This one, on that September night in 1943, was maybe the most difficult of his life.

"Oh, I worried about him something terrible," his mother, Naomi remembers. "I knew the ball team would take care of him, at least I hoped they would, but here is my boy going off and on such short notice, for the first time on his own. I don't believe I slept much 'til he got home. I just kept thinking to myself, 'McKechnie, the manager, is a good man. He will take care of Joe.' Still it was hard to sleep."

Joe remembers his father pulling into the Union Terminal drive. "I was looking around. I had never seen anything like it," he says. "Even at that hour of the night, there were people everywhere, all heading somewhere.

"Dad says to me, 'You're supposed to go to Gate 15. All the players will be there. Mr. Paul will be there with your ticket.'"

Orville Nuxhall pointed the way, and Joe turned and walked toward the gate. Any trepidation he may have felt was dispelled by the wonder of all he was seeing. His father had told him to hurry, that his train would leave at 11:20, but what a place this was! A thirteen-story half-dome, as if it were the sun setting at the end of the boulevard. Inside, the concourse rotunda soared magnificently upward, and each of the brilliant murals of Cincinnati's working life seemed as big as an infield. Union Terminal was a major north-south transfer point for troops, and on some days as many as 20,000 passengers passed through.

There was zebrawood paneling, and enough marble to have paved all the streets in downtown Hamilton. Never had Joe seen so many people moving about in one place.

Now arriving from Philadelphia...
Now departing for Atlanta...

The announcements came quickly, in a confusion to the ear, yet suggesting that these distant places were not so distant after all.

Joe hurried down the caverns of the terminal, milling his way through the crowd to Gate15. The trains huffed great gasps of air, their whistles blowing long, loud, almost deafening.

St. Louis! All aboard!

As he approached the gate, he was met with another sight, a line of well-dressed men, bags in tow, each receiving a ticket from a man who seemed to be fully in charge. It was Gabe Paul, who turned, smiled, and handed Joe his ticket.

Each Pullman car had twelve upper-berths and twelve lowers. There were two bedroom compartments, one of which went to the manager of the team and the other, generally, to the traveling secretary. The team occupied two Pullman cars, separated from other travelers.

Veteran players—McCormick, Frey, Vander Meer, Walters— received privileged status, lower berths in the middle of the car away from the screeching sound of the wheels.

"I got an upper at the end of the car right above the wheels," Joe remembers. "Damned hard to sleep. Swaying back and forth, all that racket, and just, you know, the unknown, the mystery of it all."

Like his mother back in Hamilton, Joe didn't sleep much that night. It was not only the feel and the sound of the train that disturbed him, but the sounds of the players making their way back from the club car, some of them clumsily.

The berths were not designed for someone over six feet tall and once a comfortable spot was found, someone bumped into the side of

ROAD WARRIOR—JOE GETS OFF THE TRAIN AT WINTON PLACE AFTER RETURNING FROM A ROAD TRIP TO NEW YORK IN THE 1950s.

the railing. Or someone laughed, and someone else said, "Where the hell am I? What's my berth?"

They groaned. They sighed. They shushed one another, warning, "Don't wake The Deac." Then there was more muffled laughter.

"What made it worse, it was a 'Milk Run,'" Joe says. "It seemed like we stopped every twenty minutes. Just as you are starting to get comfortable, you are slowing down to a stop and there is all this racket. And just as you are about to drop off again, here you go chuggin' off, lurching ahead, the train jerkin'. Maybe they were used to it. I wasn't used to it."

Nonetheless, when the train pulled into Union Station in St. Louis about 7:30 the following morning, Joe found that he was far more prepared to greet the day than most of the players. They were, as a lot, slow moving and thick of speech.

McKechnie, however, was not and neither was Paul. McKechnie moved about energetically, clearly in command of his time and space. He smiled, seeing one or another of his boys who had overstayed his time in the club car. They were allowed their little diversions. Baseball was a hard life, and McKechnie understood why some in the game might seek a drink or two.

HE WAS AN UNUSUAL SORT IN BASEBALL, a church-going man who sang in the choir and was said to be baseball's only thirty-third degree Mason. He was pious and paternal, known throughout baseball as The Deacon. McKechnie was also a teetotaler, but he did not impose temperance on his players unless it was absolutely necessary to improve performance on the field. He had learned over the years that even his most direct intervention was not always successful.

While managing Pittsburgh, McKechnie was confronted with two players who loved nightlife and all its seductions: eventual Hall of Fame shortstop Rabbit Maranville and the productive pitcher, Moses Yellowhorse, an American Indian.

Confronted with a series of antics, McKechnie decided that the only way to keep Maranville and Yellowhorse in line was to room with them, which he eventually did. But even that didn't curtail their extravagant nocturnal activities.

Lee Allen tells the story:

"All went well until one night McKechnie, in a deep sleep, dreamed that he was hanging over a precipice, while vultures pecked away at him. He awoke to find out that Yellowhorse was braced against the frame of the window on the top floor of the hotel, holding the midget Maranville at arm's length out the window. And the Rabbit was busily catching pigeons as they landed on the roof, handing them to Yellowhorse, who added them to the aviary that the room had become."

McKechnie didn't have those kinds of problems with his Cincinnati club. Yet he always kept an eye on who was moving slow, who was late, and who was a no-show for breakfast.

Limited in ability as a player himself, he valued preparation, conditioning, and discipline. He liked players who placed a value on their own talent. He had a particular spot in his heart for those who had less ability than others, but worked to hone their skill to its highest level.

As always, McKechnie studied his players as they made their way from the Pullmans. He was 5-foot-10 inches in height, but his bearing and posture made him seem much larger.

"There was a dignity about McKechnie," says John Murdough, who began his career with the Reds in the ticket office in 1941 and rose to business manager after a stint in the service. "He never used a swear word, but he could dress you down in a minute. It didn't matter who you were.

"He had those eyes, just freeze you in your tracks," added Murdough. "He didn't even have to raise his voice. But the words, because you knew he was right, would just level you."

The players, some more sheepishly than others, passed under McKechnie's steady gaze. At his side was Paul, the benefactor. Paul made sure the players' rooms were ready, that transportation awaited.

Paul was well turned out that morning, in another fine suit, his tie neatly crimped, his freshly shaven face lit by the beacon of a broad smile. He greeted the players by name as they made their way from the station to the street and the cabs that would take them to the team hotel, the Coronado on Grand Avenue. He was especially bright with Joe.

"He gave me a five-dollar bill," Joe says. "He told me it was spending money. In those days, five dollars would go a long way."

Joe wondered how he would spend that much money. He wondered, too, if he would ever stop finding remnants of the hayride from the night before. All through the night, all morning, ticking had just seemed to mysteriously materialize—from a sock, on his shirt, in his hair.

Thankfully, no one seemed to notice the fallout from Joe's hectic travels of the previous night. In fact, other than Paul and McKechnie, few seemed to pay him much attention at all. McCormick, who stood 6-foot-4, measured Joe up and commented on his size for being such a young man. Vander Meer had offered a gracious welcome, but most just nodded or dropped a quick word of greeting.

To Joe, the ballplayers didn't seem all that open to conversation and he found himself unusually reluctant to speak up. There was something about the players, though. Somehow they seemed different from the people back home.

IT WAS HARD TO SAY EXACTLY WHAT set them apart. Some were rough like the people around the circus. Others were smooth and quiet like teachers he had known. Joe found himself content to listen, catching parts of conversation here and there.

They talked about their last game, their last series. After beating the Cubs on Tuesday, 3-2, Jimmie Wilson's fifth-place ball club had come back to beat the Reds 12-9 Wednesday and 3-1 the following day.

Everyone agreed they should not be losing to the Cubs. Of course, someone said, it was always good to see Ival Goodman again and Derringer, good old Oom Paul. What was Giles thinking, trading those guys to Chicago? Goodman had spent eight good years with the Reds. Derringer was with the Reds for nine years, and four times he won over twenty games.

Most did acknowledge that Derringer had dropped off in '41 and '42. What did he win, a total of twenty-two games? And he wasn't doing so hot with the Cubs.

Joe listened as they talked on about their last meeting with the first-place Cardinals, the defending World Champions.

Hell, they could be handled.

The Reds had taken two of three from the Cards just a week ago at Crosley, but you had to admit, they were an impressive bunch. Musial hitting around .350 again, not an easy out in the crowd. Mort Cooper on his way to twenty wins. Yep, they were getting it right in St. Louis.

Joe soaked it all in.

The players talked about Musial most. How to pitch him. How it did no earthly good to throw at him. He was too quick. His eyes were too good. He said he always knew what the pitch was because he could see the rotation of the ball. Could you believe *that*?

He had this peculiar batting stance in which he compressed himself into a coiled figure armed with a bat and, as one of the writers said, "appeared to be peering at the pitcher around a corner." Musial could have hit .300 with a fountain pen, said another.

And even if you hit him, now everybody else is ticked off and here they come and before you know it, you got a three-run inning on your hands, maybe worse, and then Musial is back and damned mad and rips one into the alley.

Musial, ironically, had much in common with Nuxhall. Although Musial was an old man of 24, he had once been a pitcher himself, a blue collar southpaw like Joe, with a reputation for wildness and inconsistency. Signed at 17, he won eighteen games as a pitcher at Daytona Beach in 1940, playing the outfield when not pitching. Hurt his shoulder making a diving catch. Goes to Class C Ball, then the International League, and hits .426 in a September call-up by the Cardinals.

And here he is, two years later, flat wearing out the league. Shouldn't be that easy.

No. Hell, no!

If Union Terminal back in Cincinnati had seemed enormous to Joe, Union Station in St. Louis seemed even larger, more hectic. Someone said it was the busiest train terminal in the entire United States. Joe didn't doubt it. Besides, he was too busy wondering what was next.

Train rides were far better than hayrides, he was beginning to think, and they had not yet reached the grandeur of The Coronado Hotel.

Outside the terminal, Gabe Paul directed the players toward a line of cabs and Joe noticed a certain pecking order. McCormick was the first to board, followed by Frey, Vander Meer, and the other front-line players. Joe was in the back of the pack with Paul and McKechnie bringing up the rear.

The cab ride wasn't long and St. Louis out the window didn't look that much different from Cincinnati, just another big river city. The cabs traveled from the station up Grand Avenue to the hotel.

"It was an incredible place," Joe says. "Inside—and I'm telling you this was an impressive place—we were all given a key. Somebody told me all I had to do was sign for my meals and take care of the tip."

Joe didn't quit understand.

"I had never tipped anybody in my life. Hell, I was 15. Never had any money to tip, never had any reason to tip."

Looking back, he would later understand that he disappointed a lot of waiters and bellmen on his three-day stay at The Coronado.

The ball club had determined it would be best to give Joe a single room at the hotel, an honor usually reserved for the top stars on the club. In this case, however, it was a matter of prudence. They thought it best not to toss the young boy in with a veteran player, who might be wandering about St. Louis when he wasn't at the ballpark.

Joe was fascinated by his room: twin beds, perfectly laundered sheets, a view of the city, and something called "room service."

"Let's say I took full advantage of room service," Joe says. "As I recall, I had breakfast and lunch in the room and I didn't hold back, eggs, bacon, club sandwiches, just signing away."

He had eaten all he wanted, investigated every corner of the room, and there were still hours before he was to report to the ballpark.

What to do next?

Joe decided he would take a walk.

He was not looking for landmarks or libraries. He was just aimlessly walking along when he landed upon something very familiar.

"Batting cages," Joe says. "I think it was something like ten or fifteen balls for a quarter. That five dollars Gabe Paul gave me, spent it all right there. Every bit of it that first afternoon. My hands were a mess, blisters all over."

That was the extent of Joe's tour of St. Louis. The rest of the trip he, like many players to this day, limited his travels to roundtrips from the hotel to the ballpark.

His exploration of St. Louis complete, his pockets empty, his hands nearly bleeding and game time approaching, Joe headed back up Grand to the team hotel.

"I ran into Chuck Aleno in the lobby. He was a third baseman, played some outfield. He and Tony DePhillips, a back-up catcher, I think that was his only year with the club, they asked me if I wanted to go have something to eat with them.

"They had this fancy restaurant there at The Coronado. They ordered steaks. So I ordered steak. I tell ya what, if nothing else, I got my three-squares on that trip. Count on that. I had never eaten like that in my life.

"One night steak, the next liver and onions with cole slaw and baked potato. I tied it on, brother. Back home, with the kids and all, having pork chops was a big deal. Most of the time it was macaroni and cheese,

YOUNG AND INNOCENT—WHEN JOE PITCHED IN THE

MAJORS FOR THE FIRST TIME, THE NAME "MUSIAL" BARELY REGISTERED.

HE HAD HEARD THE TALK, BUT IT DIDN'T MEAN MUCH TO HIM. NOT THEN.

soup beans and cornbread. And you better come when Mom called 'cause if you didn't, it was gone. I mean *gone*!"

Joe picked out four postcards to commemorate his trip to St. Louis. One was of the skyline, another depicted Forest Park, and two extolled the virtues and décor of the restaurant at the Coronado.

SPORTSMAN'S PARK WAS A BIG, BROAD, spacious ballpark at the intersection of Dodier Street and North Spring Avenue and it served as the home for both the Cardinals and the Browns. It seated 34,000 people, seeming to stretch out forever toward right- and left-center field. It was 426 feet to the deepest point of the park just left of dead center and 422 feet just right of dead center.

"Pitcher friendly, you might say," Joe recalls, "except for right, which was real short."

Left-handed hitters were lured by a porch that stood just 309$^1/_2$ feet from home plate. It was a park that shaped the makeup of the Cardinals, a line-drive hitting bunch, who fielded well and relied on solid pitching.

Larry McMannus, the Reds' equipment manager, gave Joe a uniform, number 39. It fit well and felt good, except for the fact that it was wool flannel and St. Louis in September was like a blast furnace, sucking the life out of any breeze even before it could bestir itself.

The Reds were a well-conditioned ball club. McKechnie insisted on that, but in these conditions the fittest of all succumbed to a flop-sweat. Joe, throwing on the side for Coach Hans Lobert, found himself swimming in sweat and the smell of wet wool.

Fans were beginning to enter the park when Lobert, impressed with Joe's mechanics, instructed him to head to the outfield to shag balls during batting practice. Clyde Shoun was with him.

Shoun—nicknamed "Hardrock"—was a slender left-handed pitcher from Mountain City, Tennessee, who was having a good year for the Reds, on his way to winning fourteen games.

"For some reason, the fans were letting him have it pretty good," Joe says, "razzing him about one thing and another, how the Cardinals were gonna beat us, how he was nothing, and the Reds didn't have a chance.

"He didn't turn around for the longest time, just letting it go by and, then, I guess he had enough. He turned around and just let loose. He is saying things I had never heard before. Let's just say the language was way off-color. I didn't know you could talk to people like that.

"I had never heard anything like it, not working around the circus, not around the parks back home, and certainly not when I was playing in the Sunday League. He was blazing at those folks.

"Funny thing, didn't slow 'em down one bit. They just kept bringing it right back at him. Me, I just started to move away a little bit, quiet like. I didn't want 'em to start in on me."

For three days, Joe lived the big league life. He did everything the rest of the players did except play, though he wished he could. That night he watched Vander Meer lose, 5-4, to the Cards. On Saturday night, Joe Beggs lost a 2-1 game and in Sunday's doubleheader, Shoun, much to the delight of his friends in the bleachers, lost a 1-0 decision in the first game.

Only Bucky Walters' efforts in the final game prevented a series sweep. Walters shut out the Cards, 4-0.

Each day, Joe became more convinced that Musial was the best hitter he had ever seen and each day he came closer to the conclusion that he could, in fact, play at the big league level. Maybe this was the thing to do. The money was very good, $500 to sign and $175 a month. On the train ride home, he decided he would talk it over with his parents.

Maybe, he thought, he could make enough money in baseball that he could buy his folks a farm. They had always talked about wanting a farm.

They had once lived near Oxford, Ohio, and Orville loved to hunt and to take long walks in the country. Joe thought that maybe he could help his father get back to the country.

Once back in Cincinnati, Gabe Paul thanked Joe for making the trip and said he hoped he had enjoyed himself. Paul told Joe the Reds would stay in touch.

"By the way," Paul asked, "Did the five dollars get you through the trip?"

Joe told him about the batting cages.

"Well," Paul said, smiling, "I'm glad you spent it on something productive."

Paul didn't know then how things would work out with Nuxhall, but he did know there was something about the young man he liked. There was in his demeanor a complete lack of pretense or self-absorption.

The Reds went on to Chicago, and Joe went home to Hamilton and the consideration of his future.

"We talked about it for several days, Mom, Dad and me," Joe recalls.

"Having a chance to be a professional ballplayer was not something that happened to just anybody."

Joe's parents urged him not to rush to a decision. They recognized his enthusiasm and excitement after the St. Louis trip and wondered if his ideas would change as time passed. Orville restrained his own excitement.

"You see," says Naomi, "that was something Orville always wanted for himself. But, of course, he couldn't do it. He had five children and a household to keep."

Orville's dream may have been lost, but he kept it alive for his sons. Working second and third shifts—sometimes back-to-back—supported his family but not his private ambition.

Orville, Naomi and Joe decided to wait. If the Reds had an offer now, they would probably have one later. They agreed that Joe should have his youth. School was starting soon, which meant basketball was right around the corner and Joe wanted to return to Coach Bud Dubois' team at Wilson for what could be a third championship season.

A week or two had passed when Giles phoned, assuring the Nuxhalls that the Reds' offer still stood. Orville thanked him for all the things he had done for Joe, but they were not ready to sign.

But they did come to an agreement. "We agreed that once that basketball season was over," Joe says, "and if I could finish that freshman year and not have to go to spring training, 'cause that would cut into the school year, if they would agree to those conditions, I would sign."

After another consultation with Paul and McKechnie, Giles accepted every stipulation. That fall, Orville Nuxhall and Warren Giles arrived at a gentlemen's agreement. Joe would sign before the next season began.

ON A COLD WINTER NIGHT some sixty years later, battling health problems and facing what would probably be his final year in the broadcast booth, Joe offered a long sigh. Recently diagnosed with lymphoma and enduring a battery of chemotherapy treatments, the Old Left-hander looked back on the boy he had been more than a half century before.

"Ya know," he said, "I don't think I knew what it all meant. I'm sure I didn't. Being a professional ballplayer was something, something to be proud of. But at the time, I didn't know how hard it would be or what I would be giving up...."

Chapter five

ord of Joe's trip with the Reds had spread throughout Hamilton. Orville was filled with pride, and he and Naomi were met with questions wherever they went.

Had Joe signed a professional contract?

Was he about to sign a major league contract?

It was just a matter of time, right?

Were they excited?

Were they worried about their boy being away from home for the first time?

Many reveled in his achievement, assuring the Nuxhalls that they had, of course, seen all this coming from the very first time they had witnessed Joe out playing with the men on Sundays. The well-wishers, the curious, as well as the envious, all spoke of wealth and success as if both were preordained. There was not even a passing thought as to the notion that Joe might not make it in the pro ranks. Naomi and Orville thought about that possibility a lot.

"The questions went on and on," says Naomi. "Everyone was interested in what Joe was going to do."

CELEBRITY

THE HAMILTON BOYS CLUB—JOE HOLDS COURT IN THE NUXHALL LIVING ROOM. BY THIS TIME, GENE (AT RIGHT) IS AT OHIO UNIVERSITY. DON AND BOB (FROM LEFT) ARE STILL IN HIGH SCHOOL.

nd TRAGEDY

It is a rainy, cold afternoon in December. She is seated in a soft recliner in her apartment, which she shares with her sister, Dorothy. The apartment is less than three miles from Joe's home, and the entire family stays close.

Joe's oldest son, Phil, is there, too, and particularly attentive to his grandmother and great-aunt, both of whom have suffered hearing problems from birth. He gives them long, gentle hugs, often prompting his grandmother in discussion, and she and Dorothy seem to have a special connection with him.

"Grandma," Phil says, speaking loudly, as if he were addressing a crowded room, "what was it like when Dad came back from St. Louis the first time?"

She studies his lips and there is a pause before she speaks.

"Everybody seemed to be talking about it. There was a little piece in the paper, I believe. 'Course it was nothing like what would come later."

She and Dorothy call it *Joe's First Adventure*. Dorothy, at 89, is six years younger than Naomi. They wear broaches at their collars and are dressed for company: slacks and pressed blouses. Their hair is freshly done, their makeup is in place. The apartment is neat and clean, filled with decorative dishes and doilies on the tables.

Despite their years, they are an energetic pair. Not that long ago, they say, maybe ten years ago, they took a train trip to Alaska. It was part of the adventuresome Naomi's desire to see every state in the union.

"Beautiful country," she says, "but, oh, how I do hate trains. Too noisy. Too much motion."

Naomi is the heart of the family, a little bit of a woman in stature, who raised four sons, buried a daughter, as well as three husbands. She is clearly the matriarch, clearly thankful for her time on this earth, and equally thankful for her sister's presence.

Still, it is obvious that she views her little sister as somewhat excitable. While Naomi is quiet and deliberate, giving thought to every word and every response, Dorothy is ebullient and excitable. Naomi's hands float in conversation. Dorothy's are given to quick starts and stops.

From time to time, Naomi gives Dorothy a motherly, cautioning glance, as if she wished her sister would calm down just slightly. Dorothy doesn't seem to notice.

"We all worried a little when Joe made that first trip, the trip to St. Louis," Dorothy says. "He was so young. He hadn't even started high school. Papa Joe was concerned."

"Yes, we worried," Naomi interjects, slowly. "But I trusted he was in good hands. I liked the manager. What was his name? McKechnie. Yes, that's right! He seemed like a good man. Besides, Joe was always self-sufficient for his age, more responsible and grown-up than most. Now, when he was younger, he had the wanderlust.

"He was always running off somewhere. I remember once when he was maybe just four years old, he asked me if he could go down the street to play with another little boy. I told him he could. I got busy doing things around the house. A few hours later I started wondering about him. I looked around outside and didn't see him. About that time, the phone rang."

The phone call was from her father, Joe Gailey, "Papa Joe," who lived on the other side of Hamilton on South C Street. "He says, 'Guess who I've got here? Joe! He walked all the way over here to see me.' It had to be three or four miles. He'd crossed two railroad tracks and the river just to see his grampa. I do believe that was the longest walk he ever took in his life."

Joe doesn't remember the walk. He does remember the story and the motivation.

"Grampa," he says, "always took care of me, always had candy for me. I'm sure that's why I set out."

NAOMI AND DOROTHY LAUGH, remembering the plucky little boy whom they once found at the very top of a telephone pole, his legs wrapped around the pole, his pockets filled with an endless supply of rocks. Naomi's thin, expressive hands rise before her face, then come to rest in her lap. It is the ancient expression of mothers, at once exasperated and delighted with the exploits of their children.

"Sometimes I wonder how he ever made it," she says. "He had climbed up there and he was throwing those rocks at first one thing and then another. I guess he just wanted to throw at something. He was always throwing at something.

"But other than that kind of thing Joe was never any trouble. He was a good boy. All the boys were good. Of course, I'm sure they did things they never told me about. Or, if they did, it was years later and too late to do anything about it. To this day, I don't know how he got up that pole and I couldn't tell you how he got down, because I couldn't watch."

Naomi never saw Joe walk the Black Street Bridge, the exploit for which he was most famed in the neighborhood. The bridge crossed the Great Miami, perhaps seventy feet above the water. On a dare, Joe walked across the top of it. His brother, Gene, told Naomi, and she scolded him. The next time someone dared him, Joe was back on top of the bridge, balancing himself and grinning, all the way across. She was glad she never saw that. The telephone pole was bad enough.

"That trip to St. Louis was the beginning of his celebrity, if that's what you would call it," Naomi said. "He had already gained some recognition for knothole baseball and his basketball in grade school and junior high school. But this was bigger than all that.

"You know," she says, her eyes still and pure at 95. "He has handled so much and so well. I am proud of my Joe. I'm proud that he was able to do what he wanted to do."

She is quiet for a moment, sitting still in her chair, her thoughts traveling quickly through the past.

"I never thought that anything like this would ever happen to me or anyone in my family," she says. "It is somewhat astonishing."

JOE CAME HOME FROM ST. LOUIS to a hero's status, to promise and celebrity.

"But he never let that affect him," Naomi says. "He was never influenced by anything of that kind. One thing I told him seemed to make an impression. I always told him, 'Treat others the way you would want to be treated.' He has done that. He does that today."

Back home, Joe returned to the world of Hamilton and Wilson Junior High. Room service, train rides, steaks, all were just a memory. Other kids, even his brothers, wanted to know what it had been like. He didn't know what to say.

How do you explain a world so different? How do you explain just signing your name in payment for a meal, or crisp, clean sheets on the bed every night? How would he explain sitting in the dugout with McCormick and Vander Meer, and being treated like just another member of the team? He couldn't explain.

Joe said the trip was fun and that the Reds had been very good to him. He left it at that. Saying anything more, he felt, would be something close to boasting.

He was ready to get back to the routine of school and the new ground of ninth grade. He did not relish academics, but there was something about the order of school that he liked. Each day was measured, prede-

MEASURING UP—WHEN JOE SIGNED WITH THE REDS, THE PHOTOGRAPHERS CAME CALLING, BRINGING ALONG THE INVENTIVE NEWSPAPER IMAGERY OF THE PERIOD. JOE IS FLANKED BY BOB, AT LEFT, AND DON.

termined, and topped off by his favorite class, which was gym.

With no freshman football at Wilson Junior High, Joe tackled the unknowns of algebra. He sampled Spanish and struggled with English.

"And," he says, "I'm sure everyone who has ever listened to me over the years would guess that by now."

After school, he delivered papers, the *Hamilton Journal-News*. His route consisted of 112 homes and shops downtown, and Joe walked the route daily. The carefully hurled papers broke cleanly, landing on doorsteps and against entryways with immaculate control.

Thirty-seven batters, if he chose to think in baseball terms, down in order, and if every pitch had been a strike, each day of his route would have been the equivalent of a 12-inning game.

No one was happier to see Joe back in his schoolboy routine than Louis "Bud" Dubois, Joe's health teacher and junior high school basketball coach. Dubois, a product of Ohio University, had taken a special interest in Joe and, admittedly, had a personal interest in his return to school.

Towering above most his age, Joe had helped Dubois' Wilson teams to back-to-back junior high school championships in '42 and '43. DuBois' own star had risen in the community, and the success of Wilson's basketball team had made headlines in the local press.

Without Joe, Dubois would have had just one more collection of undersized ninth graders with little hope of defending the school's back-to-back titles. In addition to his height, Joe was a player who made those around him better, always challenging his teammates. With his sense of time, space, and separation, Joe had an uncanny sense of how the game should be played. His primary flaw was his temper.

At one point, DuBois was sure he would lose Joe. The thought pained him as a coach and troubled him as a teacher. Joe had talked with him after the Reds had made their initial contract offer. Dubois told Joe he thought he was too young to sign a pro contract. He feared Joe would be buried in the minor leagues, and he told him that during these war years, baseball teams were groping for players.

"It was his influence and my parents' that led me to turn the first offer down," Joe says. "I always felt like Mr. DuBois was someone I could count on. I trusted what he said."

DuBois valued Joe's trust. When Orville asked him to drive Joe to the workout with the Reds because he was working another double shift, DuBois quickly obliged. He watched closely that day and sensed the

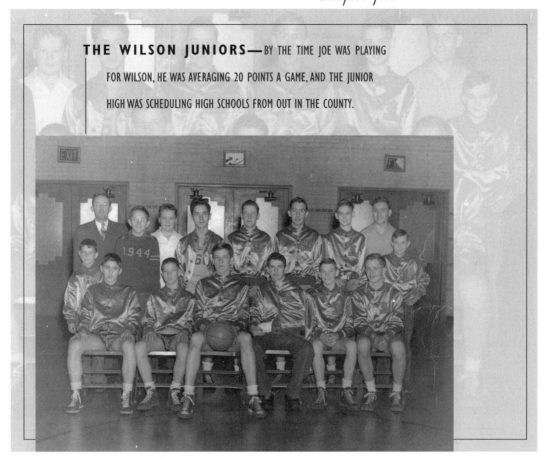

THE WILSON JUNIORS—BY THE TIME JOE WAS PLAYING FOR WILSON, HE WAS AVERAGING 20 POINTS A GAME, AND THE JUNIOR HIGH WAS SCHEDULING HIGH SCHOOLS FROM OUT IN THE COUNTY.

Reds' interest was far more than a passing fancy. He talked with McKechnie and the coaches. He knew that while baseball was plucking players from everywhere to fill its ranks, Joe was viewed as a bona fide major league talent.

Their eagerness to land such a prospect at such a young age was obvious. And, Dubois guessed, there were probably other motives, including the draw at the gate created by such a story. *Local Youth Makes Good!* Bud could already see the headlines.

Dubois was troubled by the entire situation. He knew of Orville's excitement with his son so close to being a professional ballplayer. He had talked with Orville many times. From the booming voice on the basketball court, he always knew exactly where Orville was sitting. Orville's was the loudest voice anywhere, drowning out anything that dared compete. DuBois knew Orville wanted a pro career for his son and wanted it badly.

But DuBois wasn't sure how Joe truly felt. Joe used phrases like "the honor" of such an opportunity and "the privilege."

What did he *really* want? DuBois certainly wasn't sure if this was the right thing for a boy in the ninth grade. But should he interfere at all? It wasn't as though he himself were a completely disinterested spectator. Certainly he would have liked to have kept Joe at center on his basketball team another year.

Joe remembered DuBois as a great coach and teacher. "Lots of times toward the end of practice, it would start getting dark in the gym and he wouldn't turn on the lights," Joe says. "It would get darker and darker and then he would tell us to practice our free throws.

"Well, it was hard seeing and we always complained. He laughed at us and then he would say, 'Okay, let's have a competition. Best out of ten free throws and whoever gets the most, I will beat them blindfolded.'

"He beat us every time. Somebody would hit six or seven, maybe eight. No matter what it took, he beat us and did it with a towel or bandana tied around his eyes."

The lesson was about timing, rhythm, and knowing where one stood. Bud DuBois seemed to have all those things in balance. Barely 15, those qualities were not yet aligned in Joe's world.

EACH FALL, THE BOYS FROM WILSON turned out for basketball tryouts, and the best of the lot were named to the Wilson Junior High School varsity squad. Normally, the varsity consisted mostly of ninth graders, but Joe not only made the team as a seventh grader, he became a star, which wasn't a surprise.

Standing head and shoulders above most, Joe had been a successful player at Madison Elementary School, where he led his team to the grade school championship in 1941, a title earned despite some rather unorthodox rules often imposed by his coach, N.B. LaMonda, who was also principal at Madison.

LaMonda, a stern and disciplined man, had a keen sense of fair play. In addition to Joe, who was already taller than LaMonda, the Madison squad included a quick bunch of raw-boned ball handlers: Dickie Apgar, Joe Wriggle, Earl Jones, and Earl Piegert.

"I remember once we were playing Taylor and they couldn't even get the ball," Joe says. "Mr. LaMonda called timeout and he told me I was not allowed to go under their basket to rebound. I couldn't go past half court. I could rebound under our basket, but not under theirs.

He wanted them to have a chance in the game. As it turned out, we still beat them pretty badly."

"We loved to watch him play but I used to get so mad and so did his father," his mother says. "In grade school and junior high, even in high school, they would grab him and hold him and the officials wouldn't even call a foul. There were times I couldn't watch. It was awful what the officials let the other teams get away with. The other players would hang all over him. Still, Madison managed to win most of the time."

By the time he was playing for DuBois and Wilson Junior High, Joe was averaging nearly 20 points a game, leading his team in scoring and rebounding.

With Joe under the basket, Dutch Hamm and Don Barger at forward, and Don Tullis at guard, Wilson honed its skills by scheduling county high school teams: Oxford Stewart, Union, Ross, and Hamilton Catholic, playing better than .500 ball against high school juniors and seniors.

During the '42 championship season, Joe led the Wilson Knights to a 9-2 record and scored 176 points. The second leading scorer on the team was Hamm, with 69 points.

Bill Moeller was a young sports writer with the *Journal-News*, who at the conclusion of the 1942 season dubbed Joe a superstar. "'Sonny' features the pivot shot and is especially adept with either hand," wrote Moeller.

DuBois' team caught the city's interest, and so did Joe. Basketball fans were fascinated by the young man who dominated opponents, scoring points at an unheard of rate: 21 of his team's 40 points in a loss to Wayne High, 26 of 38 in a win over Reily, 20 of 44 against Middletown McKinley.

Moeller was captivated by Joe's play and eventually promised his readers that Nuxhall would become the most successful athlete "to ever emerge from these parts."

After Wilson repeated as champion in 1942, Joe's success in basketball was no longer a novelty. It was expected.

In the early weeks of the '43-'44 season, Moeller included two paragraphs on Wilson's win over Amanda. "Joe 'Sonny' Nuxhall picked up where he left off last season and scored 23 points as Wilson Junior High defeated Amanda, 29-17, Thursday night at the Wilson Gym. Tom Hamm, the other veteran on the squad, counted the other six points."

Week after week, the headlines continued, in bigger and bolder type,

Moeller yielding more space to Bud DuBois' Knights.

Each year, the Miami Valley Championship seemed to come down to a meeting between Hamilton's two junior high schools, Roosevelt and Wilson. Hamilton was, and remains, a city that recognizes and cherishes its own, honoring achievements of every kind—especially those earned on the playing fields. By mid-January, 1944, the attention given the game between Roosevelt and Wilson sent a wide ripple through the community.

"As I remember, they moved that game to Hamilton High because so many people wanted to see it," Joe says.

Both teams entered the gym undefeated and played the game before 1,800 fans, said to be one of the largest crowds ever to see a basketball game at Hamilton High.

"To that point in my life, I can't remember playing before a louder crowd," Joe says. "The noise never stopped. It seemed like they were even yelling during timeouts."

That night, Wilson prevailed, beating Roosevelt, 29-23. But Roosevelt was getting better at finding ways to deal with Joe. He had been held to 13 points, seven below his average.

The papers duly noted that the two teams would meet again in February, in what would probably amount to the championship game of the Miami Valley League.

ANOTHER STORY WAS UNFOLDING in the Nuxhall home. Often, and well into the evening, Joe and his father talked about what awaited him. The Nuxhalls had given their word: When the basketball season was over, Joe would sign a contract and begin his professional career with the Reds. Over and over, Orville asked the question. "Is this what you want to do?"

Joe didn't hesitate. He told his father he had no doubts. After the trip to St. Louis, and seeing the games against the Cardinals, he was sure he could be successful.

Orville wondered if his son understood the ramifications. He would never be able to play amateur sports again. Joe said that he understood. Orville told him it would mean no more basketball, no baseball, no football at the scholastic level.

Joe was steadfast. Still, Ox was left to question. Was this the best for his son? Had his own enthusiasm influenced his son too much?

Naomi struggles with the question for a moment, then decides.

"I have always thought," she says, "that Joe got the idea from his father that he had better do this and he better do it well. I don't know that he felt pressured or threatened," she adds, "just a father's influence."

At that time, there was a bit of a rift in the family. "Papa Joe" Gailey was not enamored with the idea of a career in professional baseball for his grandson. He argued against it. Like many of his generation, he regarded baseball as one step above the circus, a traveling show that offered little long-term security.

"Papa was a huge baseball fan," says Dorothy, "but he just didn't think it was a good life for Joe, or any of the other boys. He wanted them to get a good education and find a good job."

Papa Joe had spent his youth keeping the power plant alive at Beckett Paper Company. He was a small, proud man who wanted more for his children and grandchildren. Naomi, his oldest daughter, was the first family member to get a high school education, Hamilton High, Class of 1926.

Papa Joe envisioned college for his eldest grandson, a white collar job, a life away from dirt and boiler rooms and double shifts. Joe Gailey liked to dress up and wear ties and he did so at every opportunity. Even in his advanced years, Gailey cut a figure, wearing his felt fedora at just the right angle.

Papa Joe wanted more for his namesake than the traveling show of baseball, but—in the end—he was certain the athletic deities had already chosen his grandson and oh how he loved to watch him play.

So many times on Sunday he climbed the stairs at Beckett to the tower that overlooked Ford's Fields. From there he looked down and watched Joe pitch. He even bought a telescope to get a better view.

While the debate over Joe's future continued, Naomi's attention was turned to a more important matter. Her baby girl, Evelyn, just two years old, had shown a susceptibility to congestion, and she was frequently ill.

While she did her best to nurture her boys, her mind and heart turned to Evelyn. In the deep winter months, there were frequent visits to the doctor. The baby's colds became more virulent. All that winter, Evelyn improved, then faltered.

Soon, everything—the bills, basketball, Joe's future, Papa Joe's concerns—seemed secondary. She was consumed with Evelyn's health.

The only girl and the baby in the family, Evelyn was the treasure of the Nuxhall household. All the boys—Joe, Gene, Bob and Don—loved to play with her. Always so rough and tumble, the boys lost their edge in

Evelyn's presence. The same boys who scraped and wrestled about the backyard were careful and caring with Evelyn.

The man everyone knew as Ox, tough and hulking, became a gentle bear around his daughter.

"Big, hard, tough guy," says Don Nuxhall, Joe's youngest brother. "That's the picture everyone had of Dad. Kind of no-nonsense. Just looking at him, you might think he was one of these people who got in fights all the time. But he was nothing like that at all.

"He spent as much time with us kids as he possibly could. He played ball with us. He taught us. He coached us. He took us fishing and swimming and showed us how to ice skate. He taught us how to play hockey. He always made time for us."

The boys worshiped their father and cherished their time with him. "I loved to hear him sing," Bob says. "He would have a couple of beers and then he sang all the old barroom songs: 'Roll Out the Barrel,' 'Sweet Adeline,' 'Down by the Old Mill Stream.'

"He had that big baritone voice. Sometimes, when Evelyn wasn't doing real well, he sang to her very quietly."

Naomi and her sons remember how Ox wrapped his great arms around the little girl with soft blonde hair, and looked into her green eyes.

"We loved her very much," Bob says. "She was our baby sister."

Like Joe and Naomi, Bob cannot defeat the catch in his voice when his thoughts turn to Evelyn.

"You know," he says, clearing his throat, "there is only one picture of the entire family. I still have it. All four boys, Joe standing taller than Dad, Mom holding Evelyn. I look at it all the time.

"We were very fortunate to have one another. Mom kept things together and Dad, well, he had a gentle side and if we ever had a problem, he was always there to talk us through it." Bob pauses for a moment, then laughs. "When it came to getting a whippin', we always wanted Dad to do it. 'Cause as big and strong as he was, you knew you would get one big swat and he would say, 'That's it.'

"But, Mom, sweetheart that she is, would say, 'Get me a switch. Get me the belt.' And you knew you were gonna get several licks. Although we never got one that we didn't deserve."

WHILE JOE AND THE WILSON KNIGHTS ascended toward a third straight championship and Joe's reputation continued to grow, Evelyn's health

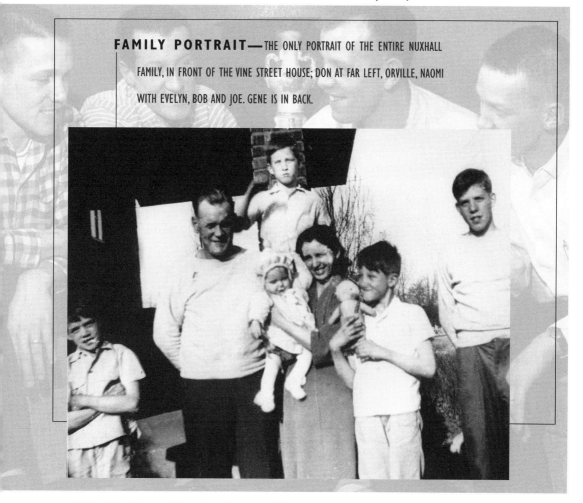

FAMILY PORTRAIT—THE ONLY PORTRAIT OF THE ENTIRE NUXHALL FAMILY, IN FRONT OF THE VINE STREET HOUSE; DON AT FAR LEFT, ORVILLE, NAOMI WITH EVELYN, BOB AND JOE. GENE IS IN BACK.

shifted back and forth. She would improve from time-to-time, but the cough wouldn't go away and everyone in the Nuxhall family, forever optimistic, felt the little girl with the ready smile would get better.

It was just a cold, just the flu.

They would nurture her back to health.

"Honestly," Naomi says, "I don't remember much about those days except how sick she was."

Naomi cloaked herself in prayer and hope, holding her daughter as closely as she could, as if her very embrace had some healing effect. But Evelyn's cough lingered and worsened.

"It didn't seem right or fair," Bob recalls. "God was giving Joe so much, so many wonderful things and we were so happy. At the same time, something so horrible and awful was happening to us as a family."

On Thursday night, February 13, 1944, Joe scored 20 points before another roaring crowd in Wilson's 44-23 win over McKinley. That victory clinched Wilson's third straight Miami Valley Championship.

The next day, Bill McCorry and Reds Public Relations Director Lee Allen were in Hamilton discussing Joe's contract with Orville. Orville listened intently as McCorry and Allen assured him the Reds would give Joe every opportunity to make the big league club. Orville signed the contract and McCorry and Allen returned to Cincinnati.

Five days later, Joe was in the Reds' executive offices in downtown Cincinnati. Papa Joe Gailey had driven him to the meeting. Papa Joe was there to honor the Nuxhalls' promise and make sure the Reds would honor theirs: Joe would be permitted to finish school, no spring training, no immediate assignment to the minor leagues.

Warren Giles and Gabe Paul assured Joe's grandfather they would abide by their word. They complimented Mr. Gailey and the Nuxhalls on their integrity. Matters in baseball, they said, weren't always handled in such good faith.

The contract was signed—a $500 signing bonus and $175 a month for the 1944 season. The Reds had included a clause, heretofore unknown. Joe would receive $300 of the bonus on execution of the contract and the remaining $200 if he remained on the big league roster for the first sixty days of the season.

On the drive back to Hamilton, Joe noticed that his grandfather seemed annoyed by something.

"Oh, he was annoyed all right," says Dorothy. "Papa Joe was sure Joe could have gotten more money out of the Reds, if they had pushed it. He was certain they wanted him badly enough that they would have paid more."

But without representation or professional counsel, the contract was signed, and Joe's life changed immediately. The phone rang all the time. At first it was Bill Moeller from the local paper and the Nuxhalls were glad to hear from him. Then a barrage followed: Cincinnati, Dayton, Columbus, Dick Bray, who did "Fans In The Stands," Joe's favorite part of the Reds radio broadcasts, called.

Their modest home on Vine Street popped with flash bulbs.

There was Joe combing his hair. Joe doing his homework. Joe standing in the yard with his father. Joe holding up his hands, described as large beyond belief. Joe with a spade, digging in the garden, standing beside his mother.

PALS—AT A TIME THAT SHOULD HAVE BEEN JOE'S HAPPIEST, THINGS WERE GROWING STEADILY WORSE FOR HIS BABY SISTER, EVELYN.

Naomi wore a print dress and a smile, which disguised her anxiety from the eye of the camera.

"I wish," she says, "I could tell you all the emotions I had in those days, but I can't. I didn't want anything to diminish what Joe had achieved, but it was such a difficult time."

Joe's story found its way across the country, from New York to San Francisco. Everywhere baseball was played, the account of the Reds' new 15-year-old pitcher was carried—even in Italy, where an English newspaper reported: "The Cincinnati Reds are getting ready to break Waite Hoyt's and Mel Ott's record of being the youngest athletes to play major league ball. Both started at 16. The Reds have signed 15-year-old Joe Nuxhall...He will report when school closes in June."

Each day's press seemed to carry a story, a photograph, or a cartoon about Joe. One drawing depicted McKechnie spiriting Joe from the cradle. Friends and acquaintances wrote letters of congratulations or phoned the Nuxhalls to offer good wishes and kind thoughts.

No request for an interview was denied; no phone call went unanswered. Editors loved the story and wanted more, and reporters were glad to give them more. Jack Armstrong wasn't fiction anymore. His name was Nuxhall and he came from Hamilton, Ohio.

On February 23, 1944, Warren Giles sent a letter to Joe regarding his recent signing. "Dear Joe," Giles wrote, "I want to tell you that I think you have handled yourself in a fine manner through the whole negotiation. You have proved to be an honorable boy by wanting to retain your amateur standing through your basketball season.

"We all believe you have a chance to become a good pitcher and I want you to know that we will give you every opportunity and see that you get in good hands for development."

Giles, who had grown up in the small town of Tiskilwa, Illinois, population 700 or so, was already developing a certain affection for Joe.

"My father always liked Joe," says Bill Giles, chairman of the Philadelphia Phillies. "I think he saw something in him that he admired, that small-town, down-home nature. Dad talked about him a lot, the fact that he was so appreciative and humble and that he worked very hard at the game and that he never gave up. Joe was cut from an old cloth and a different time."

On Wednesday night, March 1, twelve days after Joe signed his contract, Evelyn was extremely ill. Her cold and cough had progressed into pneumonia. Nothing the doctors tried seemed to help.

"I will never forget that night, walking into the house," Joe says. "Mom was holding her in her arms and rocking her. Evelyn was having real trouble breathing.

"We were all scared. She was so young, so small. She got worse and worse and my dad called for an ambulance.

"They took her to Fort Hamilton Hospital in the middle of the night. She never came out."

Evelyn Nuxhall died at 2:30 in the morning, Thursday, March 2, 1944.

"We were all sick with grief," says Bob Nuxhall. "I don't think any of us ever really got over it. We were being given so much and so much was taken away."

The calls and letters of congratulations were replaced by condo-

GENERAL OFFICES
307 VINE STREET

REDS

CROSLEY FIELD
FINDLAY AT WESTERN AVENUE

Founded 1869 — The First Professional Base Ball Club in America

THE CINCINNATI BASEBALL CLUB CO.

NATIONAL LEAGUE

Cincinnati

Zone 2

February 23, 1944

Mr. Joe Nuxhall
1224 Vine St.
Hamilton, Ohio

Dear Joe:

Here is a copy of the contract you signed, but which I forgot to sign when Bill McCorry took it up to you.

I want to tell you that I think you have handled yourself in a fine manner through the whole negotiation. You have proved yourself to be an honorable boy by wanting to retain your amateur standing through your basketball season.

We all believe you have a chance to become a good pitcher and I want you to know that we will give you every opportunity and see that you get in good hands for development.

Any time you or your father want to come down to a ball game, just let us know and we will be glad to take care of you and in case you want to bring a friend or two, we will take care of them too.

Sincerely yours,

WCG/FL
enc.

Warren C. Giles
Vice-Pres. & Gen'l. Mgr.

lences. Where there had been so much laughter and excitement, there were tears and silence.

The next day, Joe received a telegram from Warren Giles.

Terribly sorry, Joe, to learn of the grief in your family. You have my deep sympathy and please express the sympathy of our organiza-tion to your mother and father. If anything we can do please call us.

Warren C. Giles
Vice President, Cincinnati Baseball Club

"I was pretty much, I don't know, numb to everything then," Joe says. "But I do remember that Mr. Giles came to the funeral home. That meant a lot to me and to the family. He was always very good to me and to the family."

When Joe speaks of his sister, his speech is very slow, very soft, com-pletely measured. "I don't know how we got through it," he says. "I really don't. But it is like so many things. You have to go on. There is nothing else you can do.

"I always wonder, if we would have had the medicines and the doc-tors and all the things they can do now. I always think about that."

There is another long pause.

"She would have been 62 this year," he says. "Still young by today's standards. I wonder what she might have done in her life."

Evelyn was buried on Saturday, March 4, 1944, at Greenwood Cem-etery in Hamilton.

Two hundred miles away, in Bloomington, Indiana, the Reds gathered for spring training. All the talk was about the 15-year-old left-handed pitcher Giles had signed to the club. Waite Hoyt, the Hall of Fame pitcher and inimitable radio broadcaster, was drawn to the story.

Hoyt, who signed at 16, felt a certain kinship with this young man he had yet to meet. Hoyt had heard about him: talented, big, strong, and quaintly naive. Hoyt dashed off a note requesting an interview that would be aired on his radio show.

His request was declined. Hoyt was informed the Nuxhall family was still in mourning over the loss of Evelyn.

On March 18th, Hoyt sat down at his typewriter at the team head-quarters in the Hotel Graham in Bloomington, Indiana, and wrote a second letter. He was embarrassed and saddened and not quite sure what to say. He wanted to express his sorrow, as well as an encouragement he felt was due and needed.

Dear Joe,

I realized after I sent the letter, about the unfortunate loss of your sister, and I understand your position perfectly.

Regarding a future radio date, I will not be back in Cincinnati until around April 1st. I'll get in touch with you around that time.

I've been working out with the Reds—and I guess I am getting too old. Can't take it any more. I might add though, you've got a lot of boosters up here. They're expecting fine things from you.

In the meanwhile, best of luck—and I'll look forward to seeing you in the early part of April.

Sincerely,
Waite C. Hoyt

Joe and his family had suffered a great loss, but at the same time his family was expanding, growing larger than he could ever imagine.

Grief is a long darkness but, like the night, it recedes, giving way to new light. Joe would forever hold Evelyn's memory in his heart. He would also go on, although he would no longer take anything for granted.

Too much could be lost too quickly.

Chapter six

John Elwell, busy in his office at Wilson Junior High, was somewhat surprised when he was told that a student had requested a personal meeting. The principal's office was not the most popular place at school, and he did not receive many requests from students.

The request, he was told, was from Joe Nuxhall. Elwell paused over the possibilities. He had seen the stories in the papers and the repeated proposition that Joe, given his contract with the Reds, might choose to quit school. Knowing Joe's parents and his grandfather, he never gave that idea much credibility, but maybe he was wrong.

For one of the few times in his tenure as principal, Elwell entered a meeting with a student as the most anxious party involved. Elwell was an imposing figure and, by the nature of the times, an advocate and

THE REDS GO IN FOR CRADLE SNATCHING, SIGNING UP JOE NUXHALL, 15 YEAR-OLD HAMILTON, O. BOY

A B O Y '

FATHER-SON BATTERY, 1944— WHEN JOE WAS

OFFERED HIS FIRST CONTRACT, IT WAS A MOMENT FOR ORVILLE, AS WELL.

PERHAPS HE COULD HAVE BEEN A MAJOR LEAGUE PITCHER, TOO.

GAME

practitioner of corporal punishment. A trip to see Mr. Elwell often meant "the hose."

"He didn't hesitate to beat your butt," Joe remembered. "He had this hose and he would rap you with it."

So no one intentionally asked to see Mr. Elwell. Yet Joe had to. There wasn't any way around it. He gathered himself, thought about what he had to say, and—shy to the point of speechlessness—stopped by the office after school.

Elwell welcomed him and asked what was on his mind.

"Any trouble?" he asked.

"No," Joe said. "No, sir, not at all."

"Well, then," Elwell asked, "why do you need to see me?"

Joe struggled to find his voice.

It was just that he had signed this contract with the Reds, he said, and Opening Day was coming up and, well, he was wondering if maybe he could skip school to be with the team when the season opened and would that be all right? The Reds, well, they were kind of expecting him and he would sure like to be there, it being the first day of the season and all, and, boy, he hoped it would be okay.

Elwell did his very best to hide his amusement. That was all it was, a boy trying to honor his commitments. He did not smile. If he felt laughter welling up inside himself he gave no hint of it. Here was a boy impeccable in attendance—though not the best of students—asking permission to cut school.

The principal said nothing for a moment, then he looked at Joe. "I think that would be okay," he said, "as long as you don't make it a habit.

"And," he added, sternly, "don't think about missing your final exams."

"No, sir!" Joe said, scrambling from the office.

Elwell may have sat for a moment contemplating the possibilities opening to the boy sitting nervously in front of him. He may have even considered skipping school himself, just to watch him. Whatever he may have thought, he would have had to have been unconscious not to understand the wonder of this child from Hamilton making an appearance in a major league uniform when he was not yet 16 years old.

And in that, he would not be alone.

The baseball writers fanned the embers of that notion every day in the Ohio press, how the Hamilton manchild would spring fullgrown from the brow of junior high school and into the pros. The idea caught on across the nation. Throughout the spring, hyperbole about the gangly novice who couldn't attend spring training because he had to attend grade-school filled the sports pages.

McKechnie, known for his development of pitchers, had also contributed to the journalistic fervor. Before camp began in 1944, a reporter from the Associated Press in Pittsburgh asked The Deacon about the young left-hander. What were his chances of sticking with the club?

"His father was a semi-pro player and he's been coaching the kid ever since he was 9 years old," McKechnie said. "Last year the young southpaw pitched two no-hitters and two one-hitters...That was against 18 and 19-year-old players.

"I plan to keep him all summer if he continues to show promise. Whether he gets into any games or not, he'll get every opportunity to be a big leaguer."

On Tuesday, April 18th, the 1944 season began. The Reds played the Chicago Cubs. That morning—instead of going to school—Joe boarded the bus in Hamilton and rode to Brighton's Corner in Cincinnati. From there, he walked to Crosley Field and entered the park through the players' entrance.

The same morning, Si Burick, the sports editor at the *Dayton Daily News*, drove to the ballpark, all the while thinking of this kid signed in the winter and not yet 16 years old. Regardless of what the Reds did— and they weren't expected to do much that season—Nuxhall, he decided, was the story.

Though Nuxhall had not been in Bloomington for spring training, he was the subject of much discussion during training camp. Could he possibly stick with the big league club? everyone wondered. And if so, for how long?

Burick was not stuck on that aspect of the story. Regardless of what McKechnie or Warren Giles said, experience and reason told him Nuxhall was a short-timer, at best headed to the minors and probably in short order.

What intrigued Burick was the human element of Nuxhall's signing. What if this "Boy Wonder" was *his* son? Whether success or failure lay ahead, it was a fascinating tale that reached beyond the usual scope of the sports pages.

Burick was a rabbi's son, tall, dapper and quick-witted. He was given to puns in conversation, his favorite being wordplay on a popular automobile commercial: "Wouldn't you really rather have a Burick?"

He was gifted as a reporter and columnist, having gone to work for the *Daily News* when he was only a few months older than Joe. He had been working so long and so well that he was named to the writers' wing of baseball's Hall of Fame in 1982.

By 1944, Burick was covering his fifteenth consecutive Reds' opener. He was well known in the game, well respected and not easily misled. Ever proper and precise on the page, he enjoyed insider status in baseball, sharing in the jokes, as well as matters that seldom left the clubhouse. It was a position earned over time and gained through the trust of the players, managers, and front-office executives he had come to know over the years, not just in Cincinnati, but throughout the country.

Burick had written about everyone in baseball from the formidable Ruth to the elegant DiMaggio and when Secretariat won horse racing's Triple Crown, Burick would write these notable lines: "Secretariat is everything I am not. He is young, he is beautiful, and his sex life is all ahead of him."

On this day, however, he would write about the kid.

He located Joe about an hour before game time, sitting in the dugout and twirling his glove in his hand. Notebook in hand, Burick approached the youngster.

"This must be quite an experience for a boy of your age," Burick said.

"Yep, it is," Joe replied, offering no elaboration.

Soon, Joe left the dugout and began to throw with the other players.

Burick found him tall, husky, gawky. "He was a little on the open-mouthed side," Burick wrote, "but after watching him a while, I decided the expression was natural with him. The kid definitely was not awed...

"He is no figure of grace walking. Maybe he never will be. He's big all over and a little knock-kneed...He threw the ball soft-like to begin with and gradually picked up steam. The kid left-hander can throw all right. He is naturally fast."

But Burick was not convinced this was a storybook tale, and he shared that with his readers. Yes, excitement surrounded this boy and his talent, but there were reservations, and Burick recounted Nuxhall's casual approach to the pre-game regimen:

THE BIG PITCH—JOE WAS RELAXED BEFORE HIS FIRST GAME IN MAJOR LEAGUE BALL. "IN THE JAMS," HIS TEAMMATE, WALKER, SAID, "GIVE THE HITTER YOUR BEST PITCH." AND SO HE DID.

"That's amazing, isn't it," I said to Estel Crabtree, the Reds' coach-outfielder.

"You'd think he's been doing this sort of thing all of his life," said Crabby.

"Maybe he is just a typical left-hander," suggested Bill McKechnie.

It was not exactly a compliment. Burick lingered in the dugout watching Nuxhall's every move and his interaction with the older players. When young Joe returned to the dugout, Burick sat down near Gee Walker, a 36-year-old outfielder on the club.

"Hasn't got a worry and there isn't a trace of excitement in him," Gee whispered.

"No imagination, I guess."

Then Walker launched into a discussion with Nuxhall:

"Lemme give you a tip, kid," Walker said. "And remember it now and for all time. In the jams, no matter what anybody else wants you to throw, you give the hitter what you consider your best pitch. Your best one, understand...No matter what you know or don't know about the batter you are facing , that's the best thing for you to do...Give him your best."

"Thanks, Gee," the youngster said, leaning back then and staring out towards the field, apparently oblivious to what should have been the most exciting scene he had ever known in his young life.

Burick ended his column there, offering no conclusions, no predictions. He was not yet sold on the young Nuxhall and neither were the Reds.

THAT DAY, APRIL 18TH, 1944, the Reds lost to the Cubs, 3-0. Joe didn't make it into the game, and he wouldn't for some time. He seemed to be a part of the team, yet he wasn't. Each day, McKechnie and the coaches would watch him throw or watch him pitch batting practice.

But he never got the call. "It was kind of odd, just being there and not really knowing what was going to happen," Joe said. "I remember being frustrated and feeling like I could help. I remember trying to be patient and trying to pick up what I could from the other pitchers and players.

"I never asked what was going to happen or if I was going to get in," he said. "I figured they knew what they were doing and some decision would eventually be made."

As the season wore on, Joe's story began to fade. The Reds were within striking distance of first place in the National League and playing better than most expected. When Joe's lack of playing time came up, McKechnie said he was waiting for the right time and the right place. In his science of pitching and pitchers, McKechnie knew the danger of a shattering first experience.

The Reds had been involved in an inordinate number of close games, he said. And he wasn't about to put a talented but untried pitcher in that situation.

The problem was Joe's continuing wildness during batting practice and his sessions with the coaches.

Crabtree told writers he loved Nuxhall's spirit and talked about his experience calling balls and strikes during simulated games. When Joe

THE YOUNG LION—THIS IS THE OFFICIAL PHOTO

OF JOE IN 1944, HIS FIRST TIME IN BIG RED WOOLIES. JOE BEGAN

BY THROWING HEAT, AND, UNFORTUNATELY, STAN MUSIAL RETURNED IT.

didn't get a call he thought he deserved, he glared at the coach and spit and stomped and retook the mound, throwing each pitch with more determination and more mustard. The difficulty was, that in this case, more mustard did not mean more strikes.

The day Joe finally got his chance, the Reds were forty-four games into the season, four games above .500 ball, tied with the Pirates for second place, and three-and-a-half games behind the league-leading Cardinals. With the Reds hopelessly out of the game, McKechnie decided the time was right.

By the second inning, the game was slipping away. Bill Lohrman had pitched a scoreless first inning for Cincinnati, but in the second the Cardinals began stringing together base hits. Four runs had scored on the right-handed Lohrman when McKechnie pulled him, calling on Ed Heusser to stop the St. Louis rally.

Heusser would win thirteen games that season for the Reds, but this was not one of his better days. The Wild Elk of the Wasatch didn't record an out. The first-place Cardinals sprayed Crosley Field with singles, the runs continued to mount, and the fans began to groan their disappointment.

Now McKechnie's patience was growing thin. It would almost have been better if the Cardinals had been hitting the ball out of the park or off the fences, but led by Stan Musial's example, Marty Marion, Whitey Kurowski, Walker Cooper, and the rest of the St. Louis line-up produced what seemed like an endless stream of line drive singles. They could have been bowmen shooting arrows around the field: left-center, right-center, up the middle, down the line at third.

McKechnie was just four years beyond a World Championship, when the 1940 Reds won a hundred games and beat Detroit in the World Series, its first championship since the club's tainted 1919 Series win over the Chicago "Black Sox." Foreshadowing the more boisterous celebrations of the late 20th century, ecstatic Cincinnati fans turned over a streetcar.

In that not-so-distant time, Paul Derringer and Bucky Walters pitched in five of the seven Series games and won four of them. Some credited McKechnie's reputation as pitching strategist, although the players were convinced they won because of The Deacon's old tie, which he wore every day, even sleeping in it. "It may have helped the team," said one writer, "but it didn't do much for Deacon Bill; by season's end his gravy looked like someone had spilled tie on it."

FAST BALLS, SNOW BALLS—IN LATE SPRING,
BEFORE HIS MAJOR LEAGUE DEBUT, JOE WENT OUTSIDE FOR THE
PHOTOGRAPHERS AND HAMMED IT UP ON HIS VINE STREET LAWN.

And so the old strategist watched the numbers climb on the scoreboard. He recognized in the Cardinals' dugout the ease and comfort that comes with a large lead and an accomplished team.

In 1940, he had Frank McCormick, Lonnie Frey, and Bill Werber in his infield; Ernie Lombardi behind the plate; Harry Craft and Ival Goodman in the outfield. First baseman McCormick, who reported to the Reds in 1938 with a piece of straw luggage bound together by rope, was the National League MVP, having driven in 127 runs.

His pitching was as good as any in baseball. Two twenty-game winners: Bucky Walters and Paul Derringer. Three more who won twelve games or more: Junior Thompson, Milkman Jim Turner, and Joe Beggs.

In 1925, The Deacon led the Pirates to a World Championship with Pie Traynor, Kiki Cuyler, Max Carey, and five pitchers with fifteen wins or more. He had ten players on that team that hit close to .300. Cuyler led the club with a .357 batting average, and that was only good enough for fourth in the league.

In '28, he won the pennant managing the Cardinals. Sunny Jim Bottomley was on that team. So was Frankie Frisch, Chick Hafey, and Rabbit Maranville. Grover Cleveland Alexander was the third best pitcher on the staff. He was 41 years old and won sixteen games. Imagine that, Alexander your third best pitcher. Of whom Grantland Rice once said, "He could pitch into a tin can." Two years later, having overcome the handicaps of epilepsy, deafness, and double vision, Alexander retired with 373 wins.

Of those halcyon days, only McCormick and Walters were left. The bounce and vigor The Deacon saw in the Cardinal dugout had departed with all the others. Now what did he have?

Woody Williams, Gee Walker, Max Marshall, Dain Clay, Joe Just, Tony Criscola, Eddie Miller.

Eddie Miller, who that day, while playing shortstop, threw the ball to an unoccupied base in the second inning. No runner, no fielder. Just threw it into empty space. McKechnie watched as the Cardinals ran, nearly danced, around the bases. What on earth was Miller thinking?

Every day, McKechnie realized how far he was away from 1940. Just four years had passed and he was in a different world. He didn't have position players. He didn't have pitching. He had Walters, Heusser, and Clyde Shoun. And the rookies: Jim Konstanty, a 27-year-old right-hander; Arnold Carter, a left-hander; and, of course, the kid, Joe Nuxhall,

MOTHER MCKECHNIE—IT WAS NOT THE DEACON'S FAVORITE

ROLE, LOOKING AFTER A BROOD OF BABY-FACED RECRUITS. BUT THE WAR LEFT

HIM NO GOOD ALTERNATIVE.

who had been signed that winter and had not been in a game yet.

A cartoon appeared in the *Cincinnati Enquirer*: Matron with youngster in tow accosts The Deacon, saying, "Sonny may need his slippers in Boston—I hear it's very cold and damp there in May—and here's his cough syrup just in case!" Another shows McKechnie as a bespectacled, slightly perplexed mother hen, surrounded by baby chicks, including the fledgling Nuxhall, pecking his way out of an egg.

McKechnie liked the kid. The Deacon liked his manners, his devotion to the game, and his talent.

"He is not just a wartime find," McKechnie said to an Associated Press reporter from Pittsburgh. "This kid can be something in the big leagues."

So while these were not pleasant times for McKechnie, he was a patient man, taught to be so by both baseball and the Bible. His earthly devotionals must center once again on strategy. It was only June, and his boys were not yet out of the race. They were only out of the game.

With Heusser struggling, McKechnie and his coaches Hans Lobert, Estel Crabtree, and Jimmy Wilson decided they would make a move to save the pitching staff, if not the game.

They decided on Buck Fausett. Fausett had been called up from the minors to fill out the roster. Warren Giles, like every general manager in the big leagues, was using every means available to keep his team stocked with players.

Fausett was a third baseman by trade. This day, he would pitch. Called "Leaky"—what else?—by the other players, Fausett didn't balk at the assignment. After all, he was finally in the majors, a rookie at the age of 36. Sure, he would pitch. He would have sold peanuts if McKechnie had asked him.

Leaky would throw six and two-thirds innings, surrender six runs on ten hits and six walks, and further cement his unfortunate sobriquet into club legend. He would strike out two, who were subjected to unbridled ridicule upon returning to the Cardinal dugout. By that time, it was St. Louis 13, Cincinnati 0.

McKechnie decided, mercifully, that Fausett had taken enough.

The Cardinals, meanwhile, clapped hands, encouraged one another, and tallied their hits and runs.

It was now the eighth inning. Time to try the youngest pitcher on the staff, in fact, the youngest pitcher ever to take the mound in a major league game.

McKechnie turned to Lobert and Crabtree.

"Tell the kid to warm up," he said.

The coaches didn't respond.

"Go ahead! Get him up. He's not here to sit the bench. He's here to pitch. Let's get him in there."

When the coaches didn't respond, McKechnie barked.

"Joe, warm up!"

When he saw no movement from the other end of the dugout, he yelled again.

Louder.

Again.

And louder still.

"Joe! Nuxhall! Warm up!"

IT WAS JUNE 10TH, 1944. Joe Nuxhall was still 15 years old, and just days ago had finished the ninth grade at Wilson Junior High School in Hamilton, Ohio.

At 6-foot-3 and 195 pounds, Joe was reasonably graceful. He had shown that in Butler County where he had first gained notice on the sandlots and basketball courts.

That said, he was not Gene Kelly, and baseball spikes and the concrete floors of a dugout had never been a judicious match.

"He must have called to me three times," Joe said. "I wasn't paying attention. I never thought they would put me in the game. I figured I would just sit there until they decided where they were going to send me. Tell ya the truth, I was shocked."

He scrambled to his feet, grabbed his glove, did a small skate on his spikes and then hurried up the steps of the dugout. On the last step, he stumbled and fell face down on the field, and there was laughter in both dugouts.

He heard the laughter, but it was nothing to him, a meaningless soundtrack. His focus was entirely on the ball in his glove.

As he began to warm up in the bullpen, the Cardinal dugout was drawn back to the game. Leading 13-0, they had long since lost concentration on anything other than who was up next. Dinner plans had long overtaken the score as the chief topic of discussion. Then they saw the kid.

The kid was throwing hard.

The fans began to notice Nuxhall and the crowd of 3,500 at Crosley took a renewed interest. Many of those in the park, like the players, knew about the kid.

Dan Litwhiler was a starting outfielder for the Cardinals. "Everybody was curious," Litwhiler said. "We had all heard about him and read about him in *The Sporting News* and the papers. Fifteen years old. Signed to a major league contract and they put him right on the roster.

"He was a big story. We watched him warm up real close. He was a little wild at first, but then he seemed to settle down and get loose. It was just like the papers had said. We could tell. He might be a kid, but he could certainly throw hard."

AT FIRST, IT HAD SEEMED LIKE any other game to Joe, not that much different from the Sunday League back in Hamilton.

McKechnie gave him the ball with a simple instruction that he adopted and used on countless occasions over the past seven decades.

"Just throw strikes," The Deacon said. "Do the very best you can."

Joe retired the first man he faced—George Fallon—on a ground ball to short. Pitcher Mort Cooper followed and drew a walk. Augie Bergamo, the center fielder, followed and popped out in the infield on a full count pitch. Joe was on the verge of beginning his career with a scoreless, hitless inning.

The next hitter, Deb Garms, walked.

Two out, two on base.

Stan Musial was up next, the National League's batting champion.

He stood at the plate and regarded Nuxhall with the tranquility of a man holding a cup of beer twenty feet behind the screen. It was the demeanor that had already unnerved veteran pitchers in the league.

"Here I was all over the place, in the dirt, off the screen," Joe remembered, "and he just stood there looking at me like I was threading needles."

So Nuxhall threw Musial a fastball.

It was all that he had, and Musial responded by scorching it into right field, scoring another run.

"He hit an absolute rocket," Joe said. "He blistered it."

The Cardinal batters were waiting on Nuxhall, taking his first pitch. The first pitch to the outfielder Litwhiler was over his head and into the screen. He decided he would take the next one, too. That one went into the screen, as well. Litwhiler took a walk.

"Four pitches," he said. "Didn't take the bat off my shoulder. Kinda went downhill for Joe after that. We got several more runs off him, but we could see why the Reds signed him at such a young age. An arm like that doesn't come along very often."

"All of a sudden, I couldn't throw a strike," Joe said. "Couldn't come close. Damnedest thing. I guess I finally realized where I was and what I was doing. Dumb as I am, helluva time to get smart. But, you know, three weeks before that I was pitching to junior high school guys in Hamilton. My nerves just started getting to me."

He walked four straight hitters and threw two wild pitches along the way. Five runs scored against Nuxhall and at 18-0, two outs in the inning, McKechnie called time out and made his way from the Reds' dugout to the mound.

"Well, son," The Deacon said, not unkindly, "I think you've had enough."

Joe gave The Deacon the ball and walked back to the dugout. McKechnie called on Jake Eisenhart to get the last out.

"I remember when McKechnie took him out, Nuxhall walked off the field with his head high," said Litwhiler. "We knew he had good spirit and we knew the Reds weren't gonna give up on him, not with an arm like that. Kid almost got out of the inning. He was real close. We figured we would hear from him again."

The Reds' radio announcer was Waite Hoyt, who began his major league career at age 16 with the Yankees. A reporter asked Hoyt what he thought of Nuxhall's debut.

Hoyt said that Nuxhall was jittery and telegraphed his pitches. "His pitching wasn't slugged," Hoyt said. "He was just wild."

Paul B. Mason was a reporter for the Associated Press. After the game, Mason asked Nuxhall if Musial's single had unnerved him.

"Guess then is when I was *really* nervous," Joe said. "Things just weren't going right. I walked the next three men I faced…I don't know who they were. You see, sir," he added, quickly, almost apologetically. "I don't know all their names yet."

He was young. He was gifted, yet humble. And although his afternoon had been brief and unsuccessful, he had become favored.

The next morning, baseball fans and players across the country would know his name. Wire services sent his story from coast to coast. Joe Nuxhall had become the youngest player ever to appear in a major league game.

A LATER LAUGH—

AS ALL-STARS, THEY WERE FINALLY ON THE SAME TEAM. BUT THE FIRST TIME JOE FACED STAN, HE HEARD THAT MUSIAL SAID HE DIDN'T THINK A KID THAT YOUNG SHOULD BE PITCHING.. THEN HE PROVED IT. AT LEFT IS GENE CONLEY.

In 1944, the nation sought hope and dreams, something in which it could rejoice. Here was a boy at 15 who had made it to the big leagues. His dream had been realized just four days after D-Day when so many others—not much older than he was—lost their lives on the coast of France.

JOE'S EARLY INTRODUCTION TO THE BIG LEAGUES struck a chord of empathy in a game not exactly rife with sensitivity. Baseball was spit, sweat, and cowhide tough. But there was something about this gangly, 15-year-old that made people immediately like him.

"Years later, when Joe and I were both working for the Reds, we became friends," said Litwhiler, the Cardinal outfielder. "He was truly one of the nicest, most humble people I have ever known in my life.

"It's odd, but you get a sense from even that day back in '44, some of us were scared for him. How that one game might affect him. Being so young, something like that would have ruined a lot of people. But Joe, well, Joe was a competitor. That was evident from day one."

Six decades later, the Old Left-hander looks back on the kid who took the mound that day and remembers the sudden and mysterious inability to throw a strike, but the emotions of the moment seem very far away.

He remembers most how hot it was. "Brutal, I'm tellin' ya. I didn't know what to expect, but I sure didn't expect that. To go in a game that quick.

"Funny thing, I was fine warming up. Couldn't throw anything but strikes. Then, something happened. My heart started pounding. My palms are sweating. I can feel my muscles all tightening up. Then, no control. There is nothing I can do about it."

And while his reactions that day seemed normal to most, they never seemed normal to him. Not then, not now. He has never been, or will ever be, a man to rationalize his own performance.

"Things happen, sure," he says. "Guys lose it from time to time. The best pitchers do. But, the fact is they were paying me to do a job and I needed to do the job. I didn't."

Everything had happened so quickly. One day he was in junior high, throwing no-hitters in knothole baseball; the next day he was at Crosley Field, on the mound against the Cardinals. Stan Musial stood at the plate with the bat down around his belt, coiled up and looking at him like lunch had just been served.

The sound of that single off Musial's bat would never leave his memory—a ringing, rifle shot that jolted him into reality.

It was the same game he had played back home on Ford's Fields yet it wasn't.

"I knew," Joe says, "I had a ways to go."

He had been tested against the class of professional baseball—not only Stan Musial, who was well on his way to becoming one of the game's greatest hitters, but also the St. Louis Cardinals, on their way to a third straight pennant and another 105-win season.

McKechnie could have chosen an easier start. The Phillies. The Boston Bees. Brooklyn was bad in 1944.

"Got to start somewhere," Joe would say. "Find out where we stand. We got the Cardinals."

After his big league opener, Joe's earned run average was 67.50. He had learned where he stood.

In the dugout, Joe thought about how close he had come to getting out of the inning. He was not accustomed to failure. "One out away and it all goes to hell," he sighed.

He sat there trying to comprehend what had happened and what the consequences would be. One player after another came by to offer encouragement.

"Hey, kid, first time out," they said. "Gonna be okay. You'll be all right."

He heard, but he didn't hear. Would he get another chance? When? Would they send him home, tear up the contract? Would they send him to the minor leagues and, if so, where?

He had no idea how things worked in the big leagues. He just knew that when he needed to throw strikes, he couldn't.

"If I had just thought about it. You know, been prepared in my mind, things might have been different," he said. "I was watching the game. I should have been able to figure out what their weaknesses were. But I didn't. Didn't think about it."

He was 15, running through life without the companions that come with time and failure. Preparation and deliberation were not yet a part of his life. Over the next sixty years, he would ask himself time and again: *What would have happened if I could have pitched the inning without giving up a run? What if I could have thrown without realizing who I was facing? Just let my natural ability take over. I don't think I will ever stop thinking about that. What would have happened then?*

As he sat in the dugout trying to think through it all, he found his determined self. He would hang on and he would do better. As bad as that first outing had been, he never thought of quitting. Instead, he felt indebted, grateful.

"I was given a helluva opportunity," he said. "You don't just shrug that kinda thing off. No matter what they decided to do with me, I wasn't about to quit. I loved to play. Give up and go home? Ya kidding me?"

Afterward, he talked with the other players and reporters. Giles made a trip to the clubhouse to see him. A big and jovial man, Giles' voice boomed through the clubhouse.

"You did all right," Giles said, smiling. "Did all right until Musial came to bat."

Even though the Reds' 18 runs allowed were the most by any major league team since the Giants allowed 19 in 1906, it wasn't such a bad day.

"I'm lucky," Joe told one reporter. "I never thought at 15 I'd be pitching in the big time. Guess lots of kids would like to do that."

He showered, dressed, and caught the bus back to Hamilton.

"Everybody was talking about what had happened. You know, me pitching and being the youngest and all. I didn't think that much about it," he said. "But it sure did seem like a big thing to a lot of people."

The next day, June 11th, the Reds played a double-header. Joe sat the bench while the Cards won the first game, 3-1. Arnold Carter took the loss.

Game two, St. Louis got to Clyde Shoun and won, 4-1.

Shortly after that, Joe would find out what the organization had planned for him and where he was headed.

McKechnie walked up to Joe in the clubhouse and told him Giles wanted to see him in his office—right away.

As Joe made his way toward the office, he was filled with uncertainty. He had not been in pro ball long, but he sensed that a call to the president's office was probably not a good thing.

Giles welcomed Joe and asked him to take a seat.

"He didn't say anything for awhile, and then he looked at me and said, 'Joe, we have decided to send you to Birmingham. Johnny Riddle is the manager down there and he is very good with pitchers. He'll help you with your control.'"

All the arrangements were made, Giles said. Housing was in place, and the Barons were expecting him. Paul Florence, the man in charge of the team in Alabama, would do everything he could to help him.

"And," Giles concluded, "we expect to see you back here very soon."

He handed Joe a train ticket. There was no time to be anxious. The train was leaving that night. Joe was heading south into a completely different world. His life was about to change again, even more dramatically than it already had.

On the night of June 18th, Joe settled into a boarding house in Birmingham. He located a number two pencil, some stationery, and wrote to his parents.

Dear Mom and Dad,

The train arrived in Birmingham at 7:20. When I got off the train, I didn't know which way to go, so I thought maybe I had better call Mr. Florence the president of the Birmingham Barons. So I went to the phone booth and found that they were dial phones and that I didn't know how to work a dial phone so I was out there. I wandered around for awhile finally ran into some taxi cabs and took a cab to Rickwood Field that's the name of the field. I got there early and there wasn't anybody except the trainer, by the way, this trainer is a colored one, but he is a heck of a swell guy.

I asked him if I couldn't leave my grip there until I got something to eat, he said why sure with a southern accent. I went downtown to a place called Thompson's and

THE SOUTH'S FINEST BASE BALL PARK
RICKWOOD FIELD
BIRMINGHAM, ALABAMA
OFFICIAL SCORE CARD
AND PROGRAM
1944
10¢

HEADIN

SOUTHERN YANKEE——AT BIRMINGHAM, WALTER EVANS,

ALSO A PITCHER, AND JOE TAKE SOME INSTRUCTIONS FROM ONE OF THE

BARONS' COACHES, BOBBY MATTICK.

got some bacon and eggs some milk and a orange. After I got done eating I went back to the ballpark. When I got there Mr. Florence was there and I had to put my name on a Birmingham contract and fill out some kind of question blank which I didn't know much about.

Mr. Florence found a place for me to stay about 4 blocks from the ballpark.

The people where I am staying are awful nice but they have that good old southern accent.

I have one room with a nice, soft feather-bed, two dressers and a chif-o-board.

There are two other boys that play on the team staying here. One of them is a little deaf but he's a good player. He plays regular left field and he is only 18. His name is Dick Sipek. He is from Chicago. The other one is from California. He's a pitcher and his name is Walter Evans and he is 17.

There are a lot of colored people down here. On the street cars, they have the colored people separated from the whites.

Boy you think it is hot up there you should be down here it's really hot down here. Saturday it was 105.

Well, that is about all I have for now.

You had better send me about $30.

My address is 506 West 12th St., Birmingham, Alabama. Also send my rationing book.

Good bye, for awile

Love Joe

BOBBY MATTICK WAS A SLENDER, good-looking 28-year-old out of Sioux City, Iowa, a second-generation ballplayer who began his career with the Cubs in 1938. His father, Wally Mattick, had played outfield for the White Sox in 1912 and 1913 and closed his career in 1918 with the Cardinals. Mattick shared two things with his father. They were both Hollywood handsome and neither could hit.

Bobby was a little better than his father until he was hit in the head by a pitch and a subsequent operation left him with vision problems. After spending parts of two seasons with the Reds in 1941 and '42, Giles sent Mattick to Birmingham, where he would begin his career as a coach and take the first steps toward becoming one of the most respected scouts in the game (his signing of Frank Robinson and Vada Pinson did not harm his early reputation).

"We had all heard about Joe or read about him," Mattick says. "After he got knocked around with the big club, we figured it was just a matter of time before we saw him.

"Like everybody, we were all a little curious. A kid, not even 16, signs a big league contract. We just thought he must be a helluva talent. Mr. Florence and the manager, Johnny Riddle, asked us to do whatever we could to help him out, this being his first time away from home and all."

Mattick, now vice-president of baseball operations with the Toronto Blue Jays, didn't quite understand the fuss. After all, the Barons did have other young players, such as Walter Evans, who was all of 17.

"I met Joe at Rickwood Field shortly after he came down," Mattick remembers. "Gawd! He was green and wild, wild as a buck. He could throw hard but he was absolutely all over the place. Up! In the dirt! Off the screen!

"Batting practice, he had guys looking for the exits. But what a great guy. You couldn't help but like him. Big ol', gawky, lanky kid. Kinda looked at you like he was trying to figure things out all the time.

"Hell, I guess he was," Mattick continued. "Everybody just took him under their wing—players, folks with the club, even people around town.

"You know Joe. How can you not like him? Ever heard anybody say a bad word about him? No, you haven't. Nobody has. He just has this way about him. He had it then. He has it now.

"The thing I will always remember about Joe is that he was just a big ol', overgrown kid. I've known him sixty years. And, he hasn't changed. Not one bit. Not to this day. Talk to him today and it's not that different from talking to him back at Rickwood. I don't think he ever will change. I guess that's what people like about him so much."

JOE'S ASSIGNMENT TO THE BARONS was headline news in the Birmingham papers, *The Post* and *The News*. Sports columnists Naylor Stone and E.T. Bales gave the story plenty of play the week of June 10th, but the attention created an obstacle for Joe.

Within days of his arrival in Birmingham, Florence was contacted by the Birmingham Board of Education and the Child Labor Law Office. The statutes were very strict. Before the 15-year-old could pitch for the Barons, there was a significant amount of paperwork and documentation that would have to be completed and filed.

Florence hadn't bargained for that, but then neither had Joe.

Joe just wanted to pitch and Florence wanted to see him on the mound. Already, Baron fans were asking when Nuxhall would get his first start, and Florence didn't have an answer.

Before Joe could play, he had to file a certificate of age, a birth certificate, an affidavit from his parents, a health officer's statement, an employer's statement, and an examining physician's report.

All this, Joe thought, just to play baseball. Things had not been so difficult back in Hamilton.

In 1944, the mail service was not as efficient as it is today. There was no overnight service. Day after day, wires sailed back and forth from Birmingham to Hamilton, explaining the situation. Days passed and still no clearance.

In the meantime, Joe got to know the other players on the team and quickly became friends with Dick Sipek, whose deafness led to a speech problem.

"He could speak," Joe recalls. "He just had some trouble and he could read lips. Ya just had to be sure when you talked to him that you were where he could see you. I don't know why, we just seemed to hit it off."

On game day, they walked from the boarding house to Rickwood where Joe would lose himself and his boredom in the pre-game rituals of batting practice and infield. But, come game time, he and the other players would part ways. Joe was restricted to the bench by the confounding pile of paperwork.

"All those blanks," as he called them.

Even though Joe couldn't play, Riddle took him along on the team's first road trip after his arrival, a nine-day haul from Birmingham to Chattanooga and then on to Atlanta.

Joe didn't think much of Chattanooga, but he was taken with Atlanta.

June 26, 1944
Dear Mom and Pop,
We are in Atlanta now and if there is a better city I would like to see it. I know why they call the girls here Georgia Peaches now. I have never seen so many good looking girls in all my life. The city is just full of them every where you go there is girls and plenty of them to. It looks to me like there is about 4 girls to every boy down here...

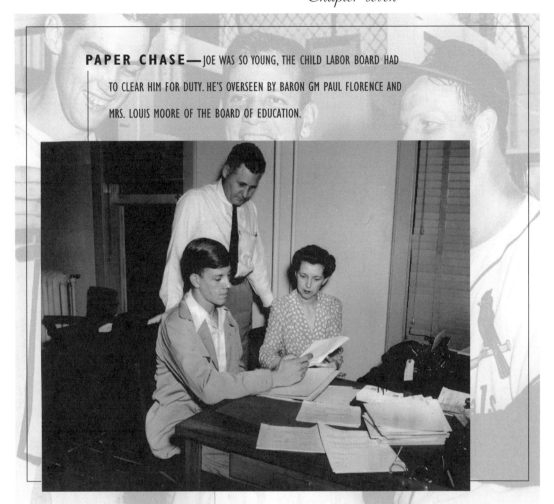

PAPER CHASE—JOE WAS SO YOUNG, THE CHILD LABOR BOARD HAD TO CLEAR HIM FOR DUTY. HE'S OVERSEEN BY BARON GM PAUL FLORENCE AND MRS. LOUIS MOORE OF THE BOARD OF EDUCATION.

During that road trip, Joe learned he would probably be cleared to play against Little Rock on the first weekend in July. On Friday, June 30th, all the required paperwork was successfully filed with the school board and the child labor office. Several pictures of the occasion were carried in the Birmingham papers, Florence and Joe posing with Miss Denise Gravlee and Mrs. Louis U. Moore, representatives of the board.

That day, Florence told Frank McGowan of the *Birmingham News* that Joe would make his debut Sunday in the second game of a doubleheader against Little Rock at Rickwood Field.

McGowan wrote:

Nuxhall is awaiting his first chance on the mound for the Barons and the start of what experts have contended will be a brilliant major

league career...He is very fast and has a nice curve ball. The Barons, who have seen both in action, contend that Nuxhall is faster than George Burpo when he reported to the local ball club...The Ohio boy has the poise of a veteran on the mound and
at 15 is the youngest player to ever appear in a big league game...
A well-mannered youngster, Nuxhall has already proven a big favorite with the Baron players and they will be going all out to help the youngster get started Sunday afternoon.

The crowd that filled Rickwood Field that Sunday was estimated at more than 5,000 people. Birmingham loved baseball and Rickwood Field was a showplace patterned after Forbes Field in Pittsburgh and billed as "the finest minor league ballpark ever."

When Rickwood opened on August 18, 1910, 10,000 people came to the game. Over the years, it served as a stage for players like Ty Cobb, Babe Ruth, Shoeless Joe Jackson, and George "Mule" Suttles, Negro American League home run champ and sensation for the local team, the Black Barons. Suttles was already a legend; he had begun when he was not much older than Joe and became famous for his strength—he used a 50-ounce bat the size of a wagon tongue and tales circulated of his prodigious homers, including one in Cuba's Tropicana Park which cleared a 60-foot fence and landed in the ocean.

In 1944, a box seat cost ninety cents. Kids could get in for forty cents. A Coke cost a dime, a large beer twenty-two cents. Red Hots were fifteen cents. A premium cigar was eleven cents and a cheap smoke was six.

On a blistering hot Sunday afternoon, Joe set about getting his career back on track.

In the late innings of the first game, he started to get loose. He watched as Joe Lease threw a complete-game six-hitter against Little Rock, beating the Travelers, 9-1.

As the second game drew near, Joe was ready. "I don't remember being nervous at all," he says. "I do remember thinking that there were an awful lot of people in the stands."

They had come to see the 15-year-old kid and he started out fine, striking out the first hitter. But then came his demon, riding out of nowhere and with no apparent cause.

One pitch was high, the next outside, and the next in the dirt. The

THE BARONS—JOE'S TEAM PLAYED IN RICKWOOD FIELD, WHICH WAS CONSIDERED ONE OF THE FINEST MINOR LEAGUE PARKS IN THE COUNTRY. AS USUAL, JOE IS AT RIGHT.

more he tried to bear down, the worse things got. He walked the next two hitters he faced.

He picked up a second out on a fly ball to right, but it was deep enough that the runners advanced to second and third.

Then it all came tumbling down upon him, an avalanche of inconsistency. He walked another and another and then—still in the inning—issued his fifth base on balls. Riddle and his coaches were restless in the dugout, seeing no sign that Joe was about to recapture his control.

Joe had forced in two runs on walks, then gave up a single that scored two more.

"And that was that," he says. "Johnny Riddle took me out and I don't blame him. I couldn't throw a damned strike."

Walter Evans came on to finish the inning, giving up a hit that scored a sixth run, which was charged to Joe.

In his second professional outing, Joe worked two-thirds of an inning, allowed six runs—all earned—on one hit, five walks, and one strikeout. He was confused, distraught, mad with frustration.

Why couldn't he throw a strike? Why did everything come off so well, feel so right and then just go straight to hell?

"I couldn't understand," he says, "but I never thought about quitting. I just thought about working things out there in Birmingham."

He assumed he would be given that opportunity. He assumed incorrectly. For the next few days, Joe's activities with the Barons were limited to pre-game tossing, stretching, and running.

One episode of wildness had rendered him invisible to manager Johnny Riddle.

So he ran.

One wind sprint after another, tirelessly chugging from the left field line at Rickwood to center and back again, over and over.

But no matter how much he ran, he couldn't catch Riddle's eye or interest. He was fixed "on the side," and no matter how much Sipek and Joe Talley tried to buoy his spirits, they were failing and fast.

Joe wore the uniform, but he was not really a part of the team. "They even stopped me from throwing batting practice, 'cause I was drilling guys all the time," he says. "I was wild. Hitting guys. They eventually said, 'That's enough of that.'"

When news of Joe's first start reached Hamilton, Papa Joe Gailey thought it was time to make a trip to Birmingham. Together with Joe's Aunt Dorothy, they boarded the Southern for Birmingham.

"We just wanted to see him," Dorothy remembers, "and Papa wanted to see him play. I think, really, he just wanted to see how he was doing.

"We stayed for two or three days, the weekend, and we went to the games there at the field—it was a very nice field—but we never did get to see Joe play. We went out to eat a couple of times. He seemed fine, happy and all. But, looking back, he might have been putting a good face on things just for us."

"After Grampa and Aunt Dorothy left, it started getting to me," Joe says. "I really started to feel homesick."

And the worst times were yet to come. When the Barons were at home, he didn't play. When they went on the road, he didn't travel. He was left alone, back in Birmingham. As days passed into weeks, Joe became more and more forlorn.

"I kept telling myself, 'If I could just play, if I could throw strikes,

everything would be fine,'" Joe says. "But, yeah, it was getting to me
—bad."

There was one saving grace: the people who had come to know him
at Rickwood and those he had met around Birmingham.

"The people were wonderful to me," he says. "I remember at night,
we sat on the porch at the boarding house where I stayed and the woman
who owned the house, I can't remember her name for the life of me,
well, she brought us iced tea and lemonade and we just sat there and
talked. It was peaceful.

"Sometimes, a bunch of us walked downtown to this barber shop
and shoeshine parlor. They told me about this guy that I had to see, 'Peg
Leg Sam.' He had lost a leg. I don't know how. People gathered from all
around and he came out, put a hat down on the ground, and danced.
Danced all over the place on that peg-leg.

"People cheered and tossed money in the hat. I mean this guy could
dance, a real showman."

Joe pauses in reflection, then smiles.

"Real uptown stuff, hunh, partner? Yeah, thank you very much."

As the summer went on and he missed trip after trip and game after
game, Joe found himself slipping further into loneliness, thinking about
his mom and dad, missing his brothers and wondering what the guys in
the neighborhood were doing back in Hamilton.

The people in Birmingham seemed to have an unusual empathy for
his situation and even though he had appeared in just one game for the
Barons, he was a favored young man.

"I met this family," Joe recalls. "They lived out in the country and
they asked me out for dinner all the time. We had these big meals—fried
chicken, mashed potatoes and gravy, apple pie—that kind of thing, and
then we went out on the porch and ate watermelon, or they made
homemade ice cream.

"Their house was near the railroad tracks and in those days the
trains ran all the time. The old man would sit there and tell you when
the next one was coming. He had the entire schedule committed to heart.
He would sit there and say, 'Well, about time for the L&N 721.' Or,
'There she is. The Southern 560. Gonna be late getting to Nashville.'"

He does not remember their names, but he will never forget their
kindness.

"They did things like take me up to Red Mountain to see The Vulcan statue that looks down over the city. It's one of the largest statues in the country.

"You know, I don't think I would have made it that summer without those people. I think I would have been lost. Gawd, I wish I could remember their names. That's embarrassing."

After his debut against the Travelers, a 16-6 loss, Joe was virtually buried by the Barons. He wasn't asked to make many more road trips. "I think I went to Mobile, New Orleans, Memphis," he says.

Space on the trains and hotels was tight in those days, but that wasn't the reason the club left Joe at home.

"It was because I couldn't throw a damn strike," he says. "Why take me, if I couldn't help them?"

Left behind and to his own designs, Joe exhibited the wanderlust he had shown as a child and began to explore Birmingham.

He discovered pro wrestling at Legion Field and the Negro Leagues and the players who filled their ranks.

Rickwood was the dream and realization of Alabama industrialist Rick Woodward. Shortly after the park was completed, Woodward made arrangements to share the field with the Birmingham Black Barons of the Negro League. When the Barons were away on weekends, the Black Barons had the field.

Early one Sunday, Joe was drawn from his boarding house by something that sounded like a carnival, horns and singing and music, a bustle of energy like none he had ever experienced.

"The Kansas City Monarchs were in town," Joe says. "I found out they were like the Yankees of the Negro League. They had Satchel Paige and Buck O'Neill. And I'm tellin' you what, they put on a show. It was more than baseball. It was like entertainment on top of baseball.

"And the people came to see them. From all over and dressed to the nines. Hats and feathers and the finest clothes you ever saw. They outdrew us easily on our best day."

They came by bus and by train. They walked. They came in fine automobiles, as well as wagons. As the famous Buck O'Neill once said, "They would come two-to-a-mule to see us play—because, we were something!"

They came freed from segregation by the presence of *their* teams and *their* people playing at Rickwood Field, and on those occasions a poetic justice was invoked.

When the Barons occupied the park, black patrons entered through a single entrance behind the right field bleachers, and sat on rows of board seats unprotected from the sun. They were not allowed anywhere else in the ballpark. They had their own drinking fountains and their own bathrooms. And all this was based on Alabama law.

By statute, blacks were prohibited from mingling with whites in any public arena, including ballparks.

However, when the Black Barons played at Rickwood, the rules were reversed. The black patrons entered through the front gates and enjoyed the best seats in the house. Whites who wanted to see the game had to sit in the right field bleachers under the withering sun. They were not permitted in the grandstands or box seats. They had to use the outhouses beyond the bleachers. *They* were the ones wondering why a vendor never came their way.

JOE BOUGHT A TICKET THAT SUNDAY and took a spot on the worn bleachers and watched as the mighty Monarchs took on the Black Barons. He doesn't remember how many white people were there with him. It didn't seem to matter. He was too taken with the moment and the masterful Paige, who pitched that day for Kansas City.

"I'm sure you have heard the story and you may have doubted it, but I saw him do it," Joe says. "Satchel took a stick of gum, unwrapped it and stuck it in his mouth. Then, he took the wrapping and put it on the ground.

"He turned around and walked sixty paces and started to warm up. He used that gum wrapper as the plate and he didn't miss. Move it here, move it there. *Pfffft!* Right over the wrapper. Call me a liar! I saw it. He did it every time. Damndest thing I've ever seen."

He saw Paige's whole arsenal: the single wind-up, triple wind-up, hesitation wind-up, no wind-up, step-and-pitch-it, side-arm throw, and bat dodger.

"He was like no pitcher I had ever seen," Joe says, "out there like three wires pitching, skinny as could be, and as good as could be.

"And he wasn't alone. I remember thinking how good these players were and at every position and on both teams."

He was in complete wonder of all he saw. For the first time in his life, Joe was faced with the great divide in the national pastime.

"But back then, I didn't think about it too much—why these guys couldn't play with us—I guess I was too young. I didn't give it a great deal of thought until years later when I got to know Jack Robinson.

Now there was one helluva player and, my God, what he had to go through."

But soon, Joe would run out of diversions. Even the kindness of those who had befriended him in Birmingham couldn't soothe the ache he felt for home. Baseball wasn't going as he had hoped and there were other frustrations, financial frustrations. The monthly salary had sounded like so much, $175.

He had hoped to make enough money in pro ball to buy his parents a farm. So far, he had managed to buy his mother a new rug for the front room. Life away from home was more expensive than he expected.

Ten days after his first appearance with Birmingham, Joe wrote home again:

July 12, 1944
Dear Mom and Dad,
How is every thing up there. OK, I hope. The longer I stay down here the more I hate it. I wouldn't feel quite this way if I got to pitch some batting practice once in awhile or something like that but I never get to do anything except run and I am in about as good a shape as I'll ever be...
We leave for Mobile Friday and then we go all the way from there to Nashville and if we don't have Pullmans we sure won't feel like playing ball the next day because that is a 12 hour ride and grandpa nows what it felles like to sit up all night on one of those trains and it sure isn't comfortable...
Well this is all for now. Tell the boys hello.
Love, Joe
P.S. Send me the softball and Sunday League write-ups.

By August, he couldn't take it anymore. He was dreadfully homesick, completely miserable, and barely clinging to a shred of belief that he could perform in professional baseball.

"Then," he says, "I did a bad thing. I told them my mother was sick and I had to go home. She wasn't sick, but I had to go home."

On August 11th, a month before the Southern League season concluded, Joe was allowed to leave the team.

NEARLY SIXTY YEARS LATER, Joe sits in a restaurant on a sunny, brisk January afternoon, face-to-face with a lie he told as a boy back in Birmingham. He gently places his coffee cup on the table.

"I never should have done that. It wasn't good. Damn it! I should have stuck it out. But, I couldn't and I didn't. I needed to come home."

He looks out the window at a sky rushing from blue to gray and promising snow. He remembered a long summer in Birmingham, the faces, and the friendships.

"I'll never forget. We were in Memphis. Playing the Chicks. They had Pete Gray, the famous one-armed outfielder. Played for the Browns the next year.

"Well, we were downtown, coming out of this restaurant. It was me and Jake Daniels and Sipek, coupla other guys. There were these sailors there and one of them was making fun of Sipek, 'cause he had a little trouble speaking.

"Daniels, pretty good-sized guy, tells him to cut it out and he just starts in again. The sailor is standing on this curb with his buddies behind him. They are all laughing.

"Daniels walks up and *blip!* He gives this guy a shot, right in the chops. I mean he is like prone in the air and flies up against this building. His buddies didn't say anything and neither did he. In fact, it was awhile before he got up. And I'll bet he never made fun of another deaf guy again.

"What a time it was. They were good people there. They did an awful lot for me. I just wish I could have done more."

Deprived of a second chance at Birmingham, he was never angry or bitter. He never raised his voice or challenged Riddle in any way. He never approached Florence, asking for another opportunity.

Joe had been given two chances, and he had failed. The fault was his and no one else's. It was as simple as that.

"Between the Reds and the Barons, I pitched an inning and a third that whole summer," Joe says. "What a line. Eleven runs, ten walks, two hits, two wild pitches, and a strikeout.

"They sure as hell got their money's worth, didn't they? Yeah, boy."

Chapter eight

In just two months, Joe had pitched in a big league game, toured the French Quarter in New Orleans, and seen Beale Street in Memphis. He had experienced the kindness and contradictions of Birmingham and the beauty of Atlanta.

He had made friends with boys from California, Chicago, and the Carolinas, ballplayers from all across the country trying to make it in a game that was more difficult than they had ever imagined, all of them discovering that pro ball was not the game they had played in the parks back home.

Joe had seen the incomparable Satchel Paige and faced realities that had never crossed his mind before. Separate entrances. Separate drinking fountains. He had stood in wonder of this thing called segregation.

He had seen a one-armed outfielder and a peg-legged dancer. He had walked aimlessly through unfamiliar streets looking for something to do, and he had eaten homemade ice cream on a porch in the serene countryside of Jefferson County, Alabama, where he had heard the forlorn whistles of L&N and Southern trains heading back north.

BALL DIAMONDS ARE FOREVER—WHEREVER THERE WAS A TEAM AND A GAME ANYWHERE AROUND HAMILTON, JOE WAS PROBABLY ON IT AND IN IT. THIS IS THE HAMILTON MOOSE LODGE AMATEUR BALL TEAM, WITH JOE AT FAR RIGHT.

AGAIN

And in this game he had always felt was his, he had confronted failure. The game wasn't his. It belonged to no one. It danced out in front of one's grasp like a dream.

That summer gave birth to a notion that Joe would repeat over and over for decades: "This game will humble you in a heartbeat. The minute you think you got it, it's gone."

Faced with frustration and loneliness, Joe was going home, where all things were in place—except his future, far more clouded than when his odyssey began.

The train clattered home across the clay earth of Alabama, through the green hills and valleys of Tennessee and Kentucky, and back to the bustle of Union Terminal in Cincinnati.

His parents were there to greet him and he was thrilled to see them. He hugged his mother and shook hands with his father. It was good to be home. Yet in this happy homecoming he felt an emptiness that went unspoken. He had left his team under false pretenses. While the Barons were clinging to slim playoff hopes, Joe was reaching for the comfort of home.

Sipek and Evans, Talley and Vincent, all the guys—they were back in Birmingham finishing what they had started.

As much as that worked away at his heart and for all he had seen and done, nothing, though, looked or felt better than Hamilton, especially his own bed. And even if dinner was macaroni and cheese, it was somehow more satisfying than any meal in any team hotel.

He reveled in the reunion with his brothers and spent hours telling his mother and father about the time he had spent on the road.

Joe rediscovered the pleasures of home: his father's cherished rose bushes in the backyard, the cherry trees that Orville carefully pruned and tended so often.

BUT WITH ALL THE PLEASURE AND RELIEF that came with his homecoming, there existed a new set of demands and expectations. He was, after all, the youngest player ever to appear in a big league game. He had already been recalled by the Reds for the 1945 season. He was a local legend and no one in Hamilton was about to let him forget it.

The war had given birth to the "The Smokes Game" in Hamilton, the small southwestern Ohio city that had given so many and so much to the war effort. It was sponsored by the Mothers and Dads of Sons in Service and, each year, pitted the champions of the Municipal Hardball

League against a group of All-Stars from other teams in the league that had fallen short of the title.

The games were played at the North End Fields, the very place Joe had made his name.

The price of admission was a cash donation or a pack of "smokes"— Camels, Lucky Strikes, Pall Mall, Chesterfields—which were then boxed up and sent to the servicemen from Hamilton.

Bill McGuire's team, the Micks, had run through the Municipal League that year. They were 18-1 entering the Smokes Game, and they had two excellent pitchers: Bob Brunner and Bob Seeley, both right-handed, both Joe's friends.

In the days leading up to the game, McGuire's team was heavily favored to take the season-ending contest, but when it was learned Joe was headed home, things changed. Hib Iske, the head of all things at North End, asked Joe if he would play for the All-Stars.

"I wasn't sure if I could or not," Joe says. "Birmingham's season wasn't over and I had come home under, well, unusual circumstances.

"But the Reds said I could. I don't know why. I'm surprised they did. But I was allowed to pitch."

It didn't dawn on him then that everyone from Warren Giles to Johnny Riddle knew that Joe was horribly homesick and that his state of mind was probably playing a large part in his failure to improve.

Though Joe never knew it, Giles was particularly sensitive to his situation from the time he signed his contract.

"My father knew how difficult this would be for Joe," says Bill Giles. "He was aware there would be unique challenges. After all, Joe was 15, 16 years old. This was a highly unique situation, and he also believed Joe had great ability."

Consequently, Warren Giles was prepared to allow Joe some latitude. He was aware that Joe was not a quick study, nor was he a candidate for immediate success. Pitching was pitching and maybe, back home, Joe would find himself and restore some of the confidence that had been lost at Crosley and Rickwood.

When news broke that Joe would pitch in the Smokes Game, the outlook for the game immediately changed. The *Hamilton Journal-News* carried one story after another about Joe's appearance with the All-Stars.

The largest crowd of the season is expected to see Joe Nuxhall,

Hamilton boy who was with the Reds and Birmingham during most of the season, pitch against McGuires.

It will be Nuxhall's first game in Hamilton since he pitched the Hack Wilsons to the league championship last fall. His presence makes the All-Stars a slight favorite.

That prediction was made time and again, and Joe's presence gave the game a huge boost.

On August 27th, people from all around came to see the game. While there is no record of the actual attendance, the bleachers were filled and folks lined up all along the foul lines in both right and left field.

The official take: 182 packs of cigarettes and $108.47, believed to be a record in the short history of the Smokes Game.

In many ways, Joe was equal to his pre-game billing. In nine innings, he struck out seventeen batters. He started the game with six shutout innings and was staked to a three-run lead. Much to the delight of Hamiltonians, he was dominant—for awhile.

Then came a lapse. The Micks scored three in the seventh when Joe committed a throwing error, and the overall defense of the All-Stars began to wilt. The Micks added three more runs in the ninth to post a 6-3 win.

Joe pitched nine innings, allowed six runs on six hits, four walks, a wild pitch, a hit batsman, and two errors.

While the paper lauded his seventeen strikeouts and apologetically offered that Joe was a victim of suspect defensive play, he learned something that day—a reality that was not broached in the local press. He suddenly saw the difference in pitching at North End and pitching at Crosley and Rickwood.

What had been so perplexing was immediately clear.

"My problem was that I was always high with my pitches," Joe said. "If I threw, say eighty pitches, sixty of them were high. Back home in Knothole and the North End, guys would chase that stuff. They would chase bad breaking balls, a lot of stuff.

"In the big leagues, no way. They just stood there and looked at ya. And the best guys in the minors, same thing. Just waitin'. Calm in the box, steady, waitin' for a strike, something they could hit.

"Back home," Joe says, "most guys were swinging from the heels, stuff in their eyes, pitches in the dirt. Far cry from Birmingham. And a real long way from the Reds."

Finally, Joe had a handle on a summer that had been little but frustration. He knew what he had to do, but how to do it?

It would take eight years to solve the puzzle, the first of which was, by far, the most difficult.

HE WAS BACK HOME. He was a local hero and a young man of national interest. In a few short months, he had made the handsome sum of $1,527.06 playing for the Reds and the Barons, but all that would separate him from what he loved most.

"When school started that fall, it hit me," Joe says. "No football. No basketball. No nothing. It was hard. Here are all my friends out there playing and I couldn't do anything. I honestly didn't think it would affect me like it did, but I was lost."

He may have been lost, but he was not idle. Joe attended virtually every athletic event involving Hamilton High, lending his active and vocal support from the stands. He even attended junior high games, but it only fueled his desire to be back in the mix.

Eventually, Joe found refuge in the Shop League, playing basketball with men nearly twice his age, some back from the war and some with college experience.

"Now that was a tough league," says Bob Nuxhall. "Rough! I used to go watch Joe play and they let 'em play. Elbows. Pushing. Really physical basketball. All these guys were older and stronger. They played a different game than they did in high school. And what did Joe do? He excelled."

At season's end in 1944, Joe was named Most Valuable Player of the YMCA Shop League, an honor based on voting by players and coaches in the league. He had averaged over 20 points a game and was among the leading rebounders. He was 16 years old and he was the youngest player ever to participate in the Shop League.

"There is something I don't think most people know about my brother," says Bob Nuxhall. "They think of him as good ol' Joe and he *is* good ol' Joe, especially now. But he was the most competitive, the most determined and toughest guy I ever saw.

"Lots of times he wasn't the most talented player out there. But he was tough, whether it was basketball or football or baseball. My brother was a classic over-achiever. He had that determination. He had that will and that great work ethic. He would find a way to win. He got a lot of that from my father, I think, and his example shaped the rest of us boys. We learned an awful lot from Joe, all of us."

Bob still lives in the family home on Vine Street in Hamilton, just blocks from the North End Fields where their father and the Nuxhall boys, each in his own right, achieved notoriety in Hamilton.

"You know it's funny," he says. "That Shop League was tough and Joe got kicked out of a few games. Griping, you know. Pushing somebody a little too hard. The language would get—well—pretty dicey. But Joe never gave an inch to no one and, let me tell you, they tried to push him around, intimidate him 'cause he was younger. He stood right up to 'em, elbow-for-elbow.

"But that same year," Bob continues, "Joe led his Sunday School team to a championship. But that's just Joe. He's always had the ability to walk from one world to another. That's a gift."

THAT WINTER, JOE BEGAN TO FLIRT with a notion that would occupy his attention far more than he liked. At first, he was uncomfortable with the idea but he could not dispel it. It accompanied him every day and every hour and it was strongest when he watched his high school teams play.

Yet he told no one. He didn't dare. The last thing Joe wanted to do was disappoint anyone. He carried this uncomfortable burden around rather than risk the possibility of disappointing his father and family, or those in the community who had supported him for so long.

"There are times," Joe says, "when it is not about you. Take a game, for instance. You are tired, you are struggling, and you don't think you have anything left. What are ya gonna do, just walk off? 'I'm done.'

"No, ya can't do that. You got eight other guys out there. They have worked as hard as you or maybe harder and they are backing you. They are just as hot, just as tired and got all the same problems you do, maybe worse.

"You can't just do what you want to do. There's a matter of respect there. You got to go as far as you can for other people. If you don't, then maybe they are not there for you next time and maybe they shouldn't be.

"You have to give it your all. But sometimes," he adds, "it is harder than other times."

That winter was one of those hard times, yet it seemed to pass faster than he wanted, running toward another spring and another opportunity.

"We were not aware Joe was troubled that winter," his brother Bob

THE SHOP LEAGUE—IN 1944, JOE WAS MVP, AVERAGING

OVER 20 POINTS, A LEADING REBOUNDER, AND THE YOUNGEST PLAYER

EVER TO PARTICIPATE IN THE LEAGUE.

says. "He was never one, and still isn't, to talk about those things—or anything that might be bothering him. We were just glad to have him home. Oh, we knew he hadn't done that well with the Reds or in Birmingham. It was in the papers. But he never talked about it. He was always positive about everything. He talked about the good things. And, I think, deep down, he was determined to make it."

That winter, Joe began to explore other means of preparing himself for the Reds. He discovered Brinkman's in Hamilton, where he lifted weights. He played handball to improve his hand-eye coordination and increase his agility and stamina.

"He worked his butt off," Bob says, "and he would do that for years. In many ways, my brother was way ahead of his time."

That off-season, the Reds were faced with their own set of difficulties. Their roster was shifting and uncertain. After a third-place finish in '44, conscription was reaching deeper into the Reds' ranks. Giles wasn't sure if he would have Bucky Walters, who had led the league in wins with 23, or Ed Heusser, whose 2.38 earned run average was best in the league.

Both pitchers held wartime jobs and it wasn't certain if they would be released from their posts in time for spring training or even the season. And that was just the beginning. The Reds were scrambling for players that winter. Giles spelled it out for Tom Swope, baseball writer for the *Cincinnati Post*.

Less than half of the 39 players who appeared in National League games with the Reds last year are expected to show up at the club's spring training camp which opens at Bloomington, Ind., March 19, General Manager Warren Giles said...

Of the 39 who wore Red uniforms in championship battles last season, 18 carried the load, and of these Giles expects only 10, probably less, to train under Bill McKechnie's management...

Swope showered his readers in bad news that morning. Not only was it quite possible that Walters and right-handed pitcher Jim Konstanty would not be released from wartime jobs that season, but Frank McCormick, the Reds' big hitter at first base, formerly classified 4-F and exempt from the draft, was still trying to pass his physical in order to enlist.

The prospects for the season were not good, but as cloudy as things

HARDBALL HANDBALL—EARLY IN HIS CAREER, JOE BEGAN

A REGIMEN OF EXERCISE, LIFTING WEIGHTS AND PLAYING HANDBALL. HERE,

HE'S WITH WORKOUT PARTNER BOB BARTELS.

were for the Reds that winter, Joe remained squarely in their future.

February 5, 1945
Dear Joe:
Herewith a 1945 contract, specifying the same salary as your last year's contract ($175.00 per month).
I hope you will have an opportunity sometime before spring training starts to come in and see me, as I would like to have a talk with you.
We expect to begin training at Bloomington, Indiana, March 12th or 14th, and I will have definite information on that a little later.
With kind regards, believe me.

Cordially yours,
Warren C. Giles
Vice-Pres. & Gen'l. Mgr.

GILES WANTED TO TALK TO JOE about the coming season.

Without discouraging him, he wanted to make sure Joe had no delusions about his course that year. Giles wanted Joe to know that unless he made dramatic improvements, he would spend the year in the minors. He also wanted to assure him that a minor league assignment for a 16-year-old boy was not a disgrace.

As spring approached, Joe found himself excited about returning to the Reds. Several of the guys from Birmingham would be on the spring roster, and it would be good to see them. Still, he was torn. While he was drawn to the comforts and familiarity of home, he was also lured by baseball. It was not by the money or the notice that came with being a big league ballplayer. It was the challenge.

Every day, he wrestled with the idea of leaving home again and the deep resolve that he could and would make it in big league ball. Each day, he thought back on the Smokes Game and what he had learned.

He could make it in the big leagues, he told himself. If he could only master his control and keep his pitches down. Night after night, he went to bed thinking about the corrections that would have to be made. He had not solved the puzzle, but he was close to finding the key.

"When you are 16, you think you have the answers," Joe says. "It seemed clear. Keep the ball down. Work as hard as you can.

"Easy, right? But, it's one thing to know the problem, see it in your mind, and another to fix it.

"Let's just say," Joe adds, "it took a little longer than I thought it would. It's easy to laugh about it now. Back then, damn! I needed some help."

In March of 1945, the road led west. Whenever Joe sought help, he found it. He was not a particularly religious man, but he often thought that something greater than anything he knew was pushing him forward and paving his way.

It struck him as odd the way things were taking place. He was making good marks in school. His grade-point-average that spring as a sophomore was above 80 percent. While the arcane secrets of the curve ball revealed themselves to his scholarship, algebra may as well have been the Chinese alphabet. Yet Joe was carrying almost a "B" average. Even he did not know how such an unlikely event could be.

Consequently, John O. Fry, the principal at Hamilton High School, cleared Joe to leave school and attend spring training with the Reds.

All winter Joe had felt a little bit like an outsider in his own hometown, unable to be a part of the games and the teams he loved. But, now, for some reason, he was looking at things differently. Nobody else was leaving school in March. No other kid had a big league contract.

FIRST

TWO MEN AND A BABE—JOE IS FLANKED BY THE TEAM'S GRAND OLD MEN, PITCHERS HOD LISENBEE (LEFT) AND GUY BUSH. BOTH OF THEM WERE OLDER THAN JOE'S FATHER.

Yeah, this was pretty good. He had to admit it. No school and making $175 a month.

He was getting another chance.

Now, here he was, cruising out of Cincinnati, riding along with two well-known sportswriters on his way to Bloomington, Indiana, and spring training.

He didn't know what lay ahead, but he liked the feelings he was having. This was a lot different than when he left for Birmingham. He was older now. He had been around. He had an idea of what camp would be like and, most important, he knew what he had to do.

Last year had been rough. Waiting all that time to get in a game with the Reds, then getting drilled by the Cardinals, going to Birmingham, being away from home for the first time and being in a place that seemed so far away and so different from everything he had ever known. And, worst of all, experiencing failure—the inability to throw strikes. It wasn't what he had anticipated.

He had expected to meet success and he knew that was what others expected. He could see it in their faces. He felt like he had disappointed people. He had tried very hard to please everyone, but things didn't seem to fall in place. He couldn't control events, least of all his pitches. Back home everyone seemed to think it was so easy, just an eyelash and a whisper from the games at North End.

A lot of guys back in Hamilton could play: Al Kaiser, Harold Treinen, Bob Brunner, to name a few. But in pro ball, *everybody* could play. There weren't any holes. But he would never say that back home. Who was he to walk over their hopes? Nonetheless, he had learned—in just a matter of months—that the distance between the game at North End and pro ball was like sitting on your back porch and looking at the stars on a still and cloudless night.

They looked so close, shining, right there, as if you could just reach out, scoop them out of the sky, and drop them in your pocket. That's the way he used to see it.

He still lingered over the memory of the glint in Musial's eye when the Cardinal slugger stepped to the plate. He remembered Musial's absolute stillness in the batter's box before he rifled the base hit to right. It was one brief at-bat, but it left an indelible impression. He knew then why they called Musial, "Stan the Man." He remembered the conversations during his first trip to St. Louis with the Reds. The guys were right. No one should make it look *that* easy.

GENERAL OFFICES
307 VINE STREET

REDS

CROSLEY FIELD
FINDLAY AT WESTERN AVENUE

Founded 1869 — The First Professional Base Ball Club in America

THE CINCINNATI BASEBALL CLUB CO.

NATIONAL LEAGUE

Cincinnati
ZONE 2

February 5, 1945

Mr. Joe Nuxhall
1224 E. Vine St.
Hamilton, Ohio

Dear Joe:

    Herewith a 1945 contract, specifying the same salary as
your last year's contract ($175.00 per month).

    I hope you will have an opportunity sometime before spring
training starts to come in and see me, as I would like to have a talk
with you. I am going to be out of the city a lot, so I suggest you
call before you come in, so as to be sure I will be in town.

    We expect to begin training at Bloomington, Indiana, March
12th or 14th, and will have definite information on that a little later.

    With kind regards, believe me

Cordially yours,

Warren C. Giles
Vice-Pres. & Gen'l. Mgr.

WCG/FL
enc.

THE CAR WHIRRED OVER Indiana State Highway 46, a slender ribbon of a road that leads from the Ohio border into the eastern flats of the Hoosier State. It begins as a simple, straight run but eventually turns treacherous as it heads into the hills and valleys. It is a mercurial kind of roadway, lulling motorists before turning upon them with its suddenly devious trajectories. Even today, it demands a certain quotient of care.

The landscape reminded Joe of the farm country around Oxford and Millville back in Ohio. Yet it seemed bigger and wider, stretching at times beyond the eye's reach. Once in awhile, he saw a farmer on a tractor plowing a field, an isolated figure punctuating an endless horizon.

One moment, it appeared to be the flattest land God ever created. But then came a slow turn and another and the landscape began to roll this way and that, dropping into gullies and valleys, pitching high and turning into steep, wooded hills.

When God made Indiana, He was indecisive. One thoughtless move on this road, and Indiana might claim you forever. Consequently, its people would forever be adapting, always careful when it came to sudden turns and unique notions.

This southern part of the state was the last, long arm of the Appalachians, stocked with people who had left the mountains of Kentucky and West Virginia, hoping for a better life in Indiana.

Indiana was clear air and room to find yourself, for those who wished to be found.

"Joe! Joe, look! You have to see this."

He wasn't sure who had spoken.

Frank "Pop" Grayson and Lou Smith were in the front seat. Grayson was a writer for the *Cincinnati Times-Star*. Smith covered the Reds for the *Cincinnati Enquirer*. They were going to cover spring training and gave Joe a ride.

"You gotta see this, Joe," Grayson said. "It's one of the wonders of the world."

They slowed the car in front of the courthouse in Greensburg.

"Look! There it is! See the tree. The tree grows out of the top of the bell tower of the courthouse. Nobody knows how it happened."

Joe thought perhaps it was a trick but if it were no one said anything. He tried to imagine how something like that had happened. He wanted them to slow down, but once they passed the courthouse the car speeded up and he could only stare out of the back window as the courthouse receded behind them.

RECALLED FOR POSSIBLE DUTY—THAT'S HOW THE CAPTION OF THIS DRAWING READ IN MARCH OF 1945 AS JOE SET OUT TO JOIN THE REDS IN SPRING TRAINING

JOE NUXHALL

SO WHAT?

BEFORE HE JOINED THE REDS JOE NEVER HAD ANY PROFESSIONAL EXPERIENCE

Grayson and Smith quickly turned the conversation back to baseball. They told him stories about pre-war camps in sunny Tampa. They had traded the blue skies and gentle breezes of the Grapefruit League for what had become known as the Limestone League, six big league teams knocking around Indiana, from Terre Haute and Muncie up north, to Evansville and French Lick down south.

They laughed at Indiana. It was an odd state. There was an old joke: "You got South Bend in the north, North Vernon in the south, and what the hell is French Lick all about?"

They cursed the wartime travel restrictions and said spring in Bloomington was no treat at all. They told him about training inside the Indiana University Fieldhouse and how hard the ground was, how it transformed every ground ball into a missile.

Having delivered such foreboding information, they assured him he would also have fun. They said that, given the circumstances—with the war going on and baseball's ranks so thinned—he had a shot at making the big club.

Joe listened, but he wasn't sure that everything they said was true. He had adopted a wait-and-see attitude, which he would carry with him for years. He wasn't at all sure he had a shot at making the team.

In 1945, Bloomington, Indiana was a sleepy town huddled around the grounds of Indiana University, and the Graham Hotel—the team's headquarters—was only a few blocks away, walking distance for the players. The Graham was also across the street from the Monon line whose busy tracks provided an almost constant soundtrack for the hotel guests. The regulars became attuned to this railyard symphony, but newcomers usually required a period of adjustment. On one such occasion, one of the sportswriters overheard a sardonic new occupant ask the hotel clerk, "When does my room get to Chicago?"

There were thirty-nine players in camp, and among those, six had been with Joe in Birmingham. Johnny Riddle, his manager with the Barons, was also there, trying to win a major league job as a 40-year-old catcher.

Joe roomed with his friend, Dick Sipek. He was glad to see Sipek. As much as he, himself, wanted to succeed, he wanted success for Sipek. And Sipek, despite his physical disabilities, was on the brink of success, far closer than Joe believed himself to be.

Dear Mom, Dad and Boys,

I guess you read about Sipek hitting that home run that won the ball game for Reds at Fort Knox Friday. They said when he crossed home plate he had a smile on his face from ear to ear so he must have been pretty happy about it...

Perhaps Joe was drawn to Sipek because of the hearing problems his own mother and Aunt Dorothy faced. He didn't think about that. He only knew that he had immediately liked Sipek.

He also liked camp. This time, he was put into a steady rotation, and he liked being able to pitch again. At the same time, he understood that camp consisted of a bunch of kids and another group of guys who, for one reason or another, weren't in the military. *A motley crew*, he thought.

"But for the war," wrote Tom Swope in the *Cincinnati Post*, "pitcher Herm Wehmeier, catcher Bernie Westercamp, and pitcher Joe Nuxhall would be going to school Monday instead of donning Redleg uniforms at Bloomington..."

Along with the boys were the aged ones: Guy Bush, who at 42 was believed to be the oldest man in camp, just months older than Hod Lisenbee, who, like Bush, was a right-handed pitcher.

Bush was asked to pose for pictures, sandwiched between youngsters Nuxhall and catcher Ray McLeod, both 16. He was a small man with dark eyes framed in deep circles. He had the look of one who had seen too much disappointment. But in the early days of camp, he was a man of distinction, a celebrity. He was the sage, the oldest man among all those vying for a job with the Reds. Posed between Joe and the catcher, he was a portrait of age bracketed by the inevitability of youth.

On March 22, Grayson described the scene he saw each day in the Reds' camp:

There are so many youngsters lined up on the benches and basking in the presence of only too few veterans that one feels right away that if a truant officer would barge in someday he would clear the clubhouse of its adolescent population and the Reds would be left without a ballclub.

There are two kids there who, if we are not mistaken, take a sly squint at themselves in the shadowy clubhouse mirror every day to ascertain whether there are any signs of whiskers appearing on their chins. There are several other youths who can proudly point to the fact that they have to shave once a week at least. Ascending the hirsute scale there comes quite a pleasing reaction when we find a few hombres who have six o'clock blue shadows on their jaws every day.

Grayson also scooped his competitors on Lisenbee, the hardened product of Tennessee tobacco fields, as well as a Sunday School teacher and devout member of the Cumberland Presbyterian Church. Lisenbee had been so involved in his family's tobacco business, reported Grayson, that he didn't enter high school until he was almost 20.

By 1927, he was a member of the Washington Senators and won 18 games while losing just nine. In six starts against the Yankees' "Murderer's Row," he was positively saintly, his only sin one loss and a home run to Babe Ruth, Ruth's 58th of the year. Lisenbee had been with Syracuse in 1944, where he pitched a no-hitter.

"A man of compact build," Grayson described him. "His hair is iron gray, his chest is deep and his shoulders are broad…He is one of the game's great nomads. He has been on the rosters of 21 professional clubs."

And, Grayson concluded, while it was believed by all that he was headed toward his 42nd birthday in September, he was actually born in 1901, which made Lisenbee, not Bush, the oldest man in camp.

He will be 44 his next birthday…He neither drinks, smokes or chews and he is not given to the persiflage that usually exists in a clubhouse and which more often than not is interlarded with original profanity.

Lisenbee may have been a Sunday School teacher and he may have been a devout Presbyterian back home in Clarksville, Tennessee, but he was also short of memory or loose with the facts. Records would later show that he was born in 1898 and headed toward his 46th birthday that year. For Grayson's part, he was neither the first, nor the last, to be taken by a subject with a good yarn up his sleeve.

The youngsters did not have much in common with their Paleolithic counterparts. They would not have been surprised had Bush and Lisenbee come to the plate with a bat made of chipped stone. Both were older than Joe's father.

ON THE TOWN—IN 1945, ON A TRIP TO NEW YORK, JOE ENDED UP IN A GAG PHOTO, AND LOOKING NOT ENTIRELY AT HOME IN THE BIG APPLE.

THE BOYS DID NOT LAUGH AT THE OLDER MEN. They kept quiet, unsure of their place. No matter their diminishing skills, the old men had still played in the major leagues.

Dear Mom, Dad and Boys
We have been going outside for the last two days and the sun was shining both days. Today we had a big pepper game and Kermit Wahl and myself went up to 56 before we missed one. Also today we had an inter squad game and I pitched three innings and allowed about four hits and two runs but they didn't have any walks or the bases would have been loaded all the time. The most of the balls I pitched were outside but they weren't high or low but just a little outside. I was at bat once and hit a line drive to the third baseman. I was throwing a little old curve ball today and it was breaking pretty good. In fact I had better luck with it than I did with my fastball.

We have been doing a lot of calisthentics and there is one where you jump and spread your legs and clap your hands over your head at the same time and Guy Bush can't do it at all and boy we really have a circus watching him try to do it.

> *Love to all,*
> *Joe*

Joe's press was mixed that spring, and inconsistent. On March 21, the Associated Press carried a promising report:

No youngster in camp is getting more intensified instruction than Joe Nuxhall...Bill McKechnie and his coaches regard him as a real diamond in the rough, so are making all possible efforts to shorten the process of polishing him...Still, he has a lot to learn.

The following day, the AP carried a different report from French Lick. Johnny Riddle was asked about the seven players in camp whom he had managed in Birmingham. Riddle rated five of the seven as legitimate prospects. Joe was not among the five. Riddle told the reporter he had not used Joe much because he was "trying to cure his wildness."

Meanwhile, Joe filed his own reports home:

French Lick, Ind., U.S.A

April 9, 1945

Dear Mom Dad and Boys,

I am sorry that I haven't written oftener but it's taken about three days to get enough stuff to write a letter.

This is about the deadest place I have ever been in. When the ball team went to Louisville Thursday they left eight of us here and did we ever have a time all we did was sit in the lobby and listen to the music. They have a band in the lobby every night for dancing but none of us ever dance.

John Riddle and I sat down there every night for about 2 or 3 hours listening to the music which was pretty good.

Last night, Gee Walker went to the show and was going to take some pop corn in the show with him but the usher wouldn't let him because the rats in the place are so bad...

The baseball field here is pretty good it is cut out just like a big league diamond and is very pretty. There are trees around the whole ballpark. It is hard to see the ball because of the trees...

I guess you have smelled sulphur water, well that is about all you smell around this place is sulphur water and it makes me about half sick to smell it and we take showers in the stuff...

Today we are suppose to play the Cubs to benefit the Red Cross and I think I will get to pitch a little, at least I hope I do.

Dad, my control is getting a little better and my curve ball I am breaking it down around the knees and it is breaking good.

Well then that is about all for now...

Love Joe

Once, after a game, Joe caddied for Bucky Walters. Walters was a converted third baseman, arriving in Cincinnati in 1939 to lead the National League in both wins and ERA, as well as pitching the Reds into the World Series. It was one of the best trades the team ever made. Walters had been 23-8 in the 1944 campaign, back to his old form.

They went to the Bloomington Country Club, walked the entire course—there were no carts—and talked baseball. Walters shot a 72 and, afterward, Joe asked him to sign the scorecard for him. It was an occasion he would never forget.

THEY PLAYED BALL DURING THE DAY. At night, they sat in the lobby or on the vast porch that fronted the Grand Resort of French Lick. The boys were largely oblivious to the history of the grounds they walked.

French Lick was settled by French traders more than two centuries before Joe arrived, and in the first part of the 19th century, a British fort had given way to a hotel and a stream of customers coming for the mineral waters, which they carried off in any manner of container. Early in the 20th century, an Irish immigrant named Taggart, one-time mayor of Indianapolis, made the hotel nationally prominent by laying a special spur line that connected Chicago to his hotel's front door. It was here, in 1917, the hotel boasted, that famous chef Louis Perrin first served tomato juice, after running out of oranges. Taggart modernized the baths, bottled the mineral water, and in 1931, Franklin Roosevelt gathered support for his presidential nomination at a governors' conference in Taggart's hotel.

The boys were unimpressed and, besides, the water smelled bad. They weren't there for a history lesson. They could get history from Bush and Lisenbee. They just wanted to make the team.

But with each passing day, it was increasingly clear to Joe that he was bound for the minors. Lisenbee and Bush seemed to have a leg up on making the big league team simply because of their experience. But where would *he* go? He would find out very quickly.

On April 10, he was headed to another new place. Giles had given him a $75 raise per month and dispatched him to Syracuse, New York, where he would pitch for the Class AA Chiefs. He had gotten himself a raise to pitch in the minors.

A kick in the butt, Joe thought. Now he was making $250 a month and he understood even less about how baseball worked.

His hometown newspaper, the *Hamilton Journal-News*, carried an optimistic report.

Nuxhall has been with the Reds since the start of spring practice. He is still having trouble with his control and the Reds management figures more regular playing at Syracuse will be better than bench-riding for their prospect.

Nuxhall must have displayed a good bit in camp to rate the option to Syracuse instead of a lower class. Syracuse is in the International League, a Class AA circuit, one step from the majors.

He hadn't done well that spring. He was wild. He gave up a lot of hits. Still, the Reds were not about to give up on a kid with such a live arm. Syracuse, however, proved to be but a brief stop before a precipitous fall. Giles and company was about to face reality. Nuxhall was a talent, but he was raw. And he was nowhere close to being ready for a major league assignment.

April 25, 1945

Dear Mom, Dad and Boys,
Well here I am in Syracuse I got here at 2 o'clock today.
I missed the 6 o'clock train in Cinn. So I had to get the one at 11:50 and change in Cleveland. It wasn't as bad as I thought it would be. I got a seat right away and was I glad because I walked a couple of sailors downtown after I checked my bags and I found out I missed the 6 o'clock train. I went downtown and went to the show and couldn't find my way back so I had to call a taxi and get there that way and I did get there. I haven't much of a look at the town yet but I will let you know how it is after I look around a little.

Love,
Joe

He would see Montreal, Toronto, Newark, and Rochester, but he would not see or remember much of Syracuse. It seemed as if he were on the road all the time, and in one bad ballpark after another. Rocks in the infield. Bad grass. Uneven ground in the outfield. Long trips and sitting up all night.

He appeared in seven games for the Chiefs and he was not effective.

Two months after he was assigned to Syracuse, Joe received a letter from Warren Giles. In the most gentle yet direct words at his disposal, Giles explained what lay ahead. Joe was headed to the lowest ranks of professional baseball.

June 20, 1945

Dear Joe:
I believe it is best if we cancel our right to recall your contract from Syracuse and make your services the outright property of the

Syracuse club. In that way, Syracuse could assign your contract optionally to some lower classification club in case it appears that would be best for your development. We are, therefore, canceling our option and your contract now belongs to the Syracuse Club.

Of course, you realize we have a working agreement with the Syracuse Club and can select players from that club whom we think are able to play in the Major Leagues when we think they are able to do so. The situation, so far as you are concerned, is not changed materially except that your contract and transfers are now subject to the direction of the Syracuse Club rather than the Cincinnati Club.

If you find that you are not getting enough work at Syracuse to justify your development, I suggest you talk to Mr. (Leo) Miller and ask him about the possibility of sending you to some Class D League on option. If they do think that advisable, I believe the Ohio State League would be a good place for you to play and would be near your home, and I think Lima would like to have you…If your control and experience is not such that you can get regular work at Syracuse, I think it would be better for your future if you were out in some small league. While I do not want to dictate that policy, I am suggesting that you talk it over with Mr. Miller and if after a while longer at Syracuse they find that your ability is such that they cannot work you more or less regularly, ask him about the advisability of sending you to Lima.

We will be watching your work with interest and hope some day you will be pitching for the Reds.

Sincerely yours,
Warren C. Giles
Vice-Pres.&Gen'l.Mgr.

Two weeks later, on July 6, Joe was shipped to Lima, Ohio, Class D ball, the lowest rung on the professional ladder.

This was the first of six years in the minors. It was a season that would eventually lead to an interruption in Joe's baseball career. It was also a summer in which he would confront—for the first time—his most dangerous opponent.

OFF TO SYRACUSE—IN NEW YORK HE MET UP
WITH BOOMER GABBARD, ANOTHER HAMILTON STAR. THEY NOTED
THAT THE LARGER UNIVERSE SEEMED, AT THE MOMENT, UNIMPRESSED
WITH THEIR HOMETOWN RESUMES.

Chapter ten

The Ohio State League consisted of six teams scattered across the heart of the state, from Lima in the northwest to Middletown in the south; all cities bound by a history that led to the commercial and industrial success of the state.

Beyond Lima and Middletown, the league included Marion, Springfield, Zanesville, and Newark, towns built on hard labor and innovative ideas. They had grown from frontier settlements challenged by Tecumseh and the native Shawnee to bustling communities that took great pride in their past. These were towns peopled by fighters, survivors, and builders.

In 1945, the lights never seemed to go out in this part of Ohio. The factories churned and smoked, turning out everything from soap to Sherman Tanks. It was a hard, determined land of progress and so was the Ohio State League.

This was Class "D" Ball, the proving ground for unpolished roughneck ballplayers trying to make their way to the major leagues. They came from farms and factory towns, and they were as uneven as the gravel roads and pot-holed streets they

TAKING THE WATERS—THE OLD LEFT-HANDER TAKES
A SOAK IN THE UP-TO-DATE EQUIPMENT OF THE DAY.

NOT QUITE

PARADISE

left behind. There were no retread ballplayers here. This league was populated by young men, boys who had come from sandlots and high schools who knew little, if anything, about the pleasures of Pullman cars, big league parks, or fancy hotels. To them, Vander Meer and Musial were only names in the newspaper.

They were kids, scrubbing along, surviving in the game day-to-day, all hoping to do well enough to get a glimpse of the good life, and in "D" Ball, the odds against the good life were staggering, 10-to-1 at best, and the imminent end of the war would worsen their prospects.

Yet one would never have known their chances were so slim, for they were a happy and excited bunch, glad not to be digging ditches or topping tobacco. They were playing ball and dreaming of being the next Ott or Alexander. They were old enough to ponder their dreams but young enough to ignore their realities. They were healthy, growing lads who didn't seem to have a care in the world until they lay down at night, trying to sleep in another strange town and another strange bed in yet another hotel with a name most of them had already forgotten.

In the dark, when the streetlights peeked through the blinds and city sounds seemed to float on their narrow beams, doubts and loneliness relaxed the daytime bravado. The boys wondered if they belonged, and in the interminable spaces of the night the simplest thing might torment them: a missed ground ball, a called third strike, an anemic batting average.

Would it mean a ticket home?

And so they tossed and turned and worried.

THIS WAS "D" BALL, where it took more than hitting the curve ball to make the grade. They tested your arm, your bat, and your heart. Perseverance was required, for this was baseball's boot camp.

The Ohio State League was an old league that traced its roots back to 1908. While the cities were connected by a thriving Ohio commerce, that very connection led to fierce competition. The teams were affiliated with the Browns, Reds, Dodgers, Giants, Cubs, and Cardinals, but the crowds cheered for their towns, not the colors and not the names. It was not uncommon for 1,500 people to attend a game and often more.

The towns were blue-collar industrial communities and whether one played in Lima or Springfield, life was pretty much the same. At home, the players stayed in boarding houses with friendly proprietors who had struck a deal with the teams in their towns. They were older folks, for the most part, glad to have the company and the extra income, proud, in fact, to house the players who represented their town.

They provided rooms, beds, fresh linen, and anecdotes about past players and teams. They did not provide meals. Consequently, the players in the Ohio State League held two pursuits above all things: baseball and food.

The best of them made $250 a month—some as little as $150 a month—and no matter how much they made, it always seemed to go faster than expected. In the straits of their circumstances, most of them had one thing in their favor: a lack of culinary discernment. A meal was ruled highly satisfactory by two criteria: (1) if it was filling and (2) if it was cheap.

They pried information from "clubbies," landlords, and people they met on the streets. They looked for diners, dives, and truck stops—anyplace a ballplayer could get a solid meal without spending a fortune. When such a place was discovered, it was given unswerving patronage.

By the time Joe arrived in early mid-July, the reconnaissance of Lima was complete. Other members of the Lima Reds told him about the Regal Room. At first, Joe had his doubts. The very name suggested food fit for a king and prices to match. His fears proved unfounded.

"It was a pool room on one side and a restaurant on the other," Joe says. "They had the best cheeseburgers and chocolate milk shakes you have ever had in your life. I can taste them to this day.

"The shakes, they were thick and cold," Joe says. "So cold the sweat ran down the sides of that silver blender. When you poured it into the glass, ya got these big chunks of ice cream at the bottom. So big and thick you had to eat 'em with a spoon."

WHEN THE LIMA REDS WERE AT HOME, the Regal Room was their hangout. The boys shot a few racks of Eight Ball, had a burger or two, and headed back to the boarding house to rest up for the next game.

Road trips meant bus rides. Cap Crossley, the manager of the Lima Reds, would climb behind the wheel and head toward the next stop on the schedule. No one really liked the bus, least of all Crossley. It rattled. It creaked. It gasped and wheezed and left every one of its passengers with the deep and abiding sensation that they would never make the next mile, much less the next town.

"It was this old school bus," Joe says. "Bad transmission. Bad exhaust. Smokin' all the way down the road. Thing would hardly run.

Straight-back seats. No leg room. We're bumpin' and bouncin' down the road. Thing needed shocks real bad."

One of the highlights of the summer came when the old school bus coughed and sputtered and appeared to turn its cylinders for one last time. It groaned and smoked and slowed to a stop on a highway somewhere in the middle of central Ohio. The Lima Reds didn't shed a tear. They cheered the apparent passing of the big yellow bus.

"We thought it was a goner, done for sure," Joe says. "They got us this new bus. Shiny. Big. We were ridin' in splendor. You could stretch out and relax and pretend you were actually somebody. But guess what? Next trip, the old school bus was up and runnin'. Gawd, were we disappointed."

The old bus was back. The shocks were still bad, the seats were still too small, and something was amiss with both transmission and the exhaust system. But in 1945, it was good enough for "D" Ball.

The big league teams saw no purpose in spending more money than necessary on their "D" Ball clubs and didn't particularly care if their players traveled in comfort.

"And why should they?" Joe asks. "From their perspective—and they were right—so few of us were going to make it. We were low men on the totem pole."

THE TOWNS HAD DIFFERENT NAMES BUT SIMILAR FACES, and every bus trip seemed to end in the same place. The fields were rough, the clubhouses were tiny and sometimes, as the boys prepared for a game, tempers grew short.

"We got 18, maybe 20 guys trying to get dressed in a clubhouse not much bigger than, oh, a small kitchen," Joe says. "You are bumping around, falling into one another. It's hot. It's crowded. You've just come off a bus ride. Nobody can move. We got to go play a game and everybody is tired and getting ticked off. Not the best way to go into a game.

"Worst part about it—you were lucky if you got your uniform washed once a week and if you were a catcher or a pitcher, you were in a world of hurt. You can't *imagine* the smell."

Following a game, the wet, wool uniforms were either placed on hangers to air-dry or, worse, folded and packed away in footlockers until the next stop on the road.

"Next day, they would get 'em out," Joe says, "we put 'em on and we are one sour bunch. Rank, I'm tellin' ya. Thank God, we were all in the same boat."

Joe seemed to fit in perfectly with this crew. These acrid days in "D" Ball were the first of many he would spend in the minor leagues, but they were among the most pleasant.

"Especially in those early days," he says. "It was like Mr. Giles said—maybe the way he planned—I was close to home. I was finally getting to pitch and I was having some success."

Joe was hungry to perform and starving for home, and with Lima, he had a taste of both. As soon as Joe arrived, Cap Crossley placed him in the starting rotation.

On July 9, he struck out fourteen hitters in a 5-1 win over Marion. It was his first victory as a professional player. Four days later, he struck out thirteen in a 15-5 win over the Springfield Giants. Each outing restored his confidence.

"I was starting to believe I could play and that I would eventually get back to the big leagues," he says. "Now, granted this was a whole lot different than pitching in the Southern Association with Birmingham or at Syracuse in the International League.

"The players in Lima weren't, well, how should I put it, as *polished*. Hell, it wasn't a lot different than pitching back home in the Sunday League. But at least it was a step in the right direction. First one, too. So, I was beginning to feel pretty good about things."

This was familiar ground, far away from places like Montreal, Toronto, and New Orleans, where he had often felt so much anxiety about pitching and so completely removed from everything he knew. No one had said anything or done anything, but in Birmingham and later with Syracuse, Joe felt the pressure to do everything perfectly. There was no room for a mistake, no room for failure. In that confined space and state of mind, Joe felt like he bungled every opportunity.

He felt tight, nervous, as if somehow he had lost touch with his own identity. Throwing strikes wasn't that difficult. He had done it all his life. Why, given such an opportunity, did he feel so fettered and incapable? He didn't know.

IN THE OHIO STATE LEAGUE, Joe made new friends, like Dale Long, a left-handed hitting first baseman from Missouri, who everyone felt was on a fast track to the majors. He was also reunited with friends from his childhood. Bob Brunner and Al Kaiser were products of the playgrounds and ballparks in Hamilton. Both had signed with the Browns and were playing for Newark.

"When we played Newark, it was like old home week," Joe says. "We talked about home and Hamilton. How things were going. What our chances were."

They shared newspaper clippings from home and stories that had been passed along from family and friends. As time passed, riding around the Ohio countryside in a ramshackle school bus didn't seem to bother Joe, and neither did the rancid uniform. His spirits climbed and so did his hopes. In less than a month in the league, he had established himself as a star. Two days before his 16th birthday, Joe was in a restaurant in Newark, where he found a notepad left behind by a salesman for a coffee company. He used the pad to write home:

Sat July 28
Dear Mom Dad and Boys,
I hope you don't mind me writing on this paper.
I am working for the Continental coffee company and I have to help there advertisement a little. Ha Ha.
We are in Newark now. We stay in Granville about a mile from Newark. Denison University is located here but the school isn't open right now and that makes the town kinda dead about all you can do around here is eat and sleep.
Well, we won the first game of this series Fri nite 6–5 in 13 innings but should have won it easy except the pitcher gave up a home run ball in the eighth with one on and two outs.
I saw Bob Brunner and Al Kaiser and they said they were geting along alright. As you probably know Kaiser is leading the league in hitting something like .360, that isn't bad is it. I am supposed to pitch tomorrow and so is Brunner so I hope him and I get to tangle horns.
I beat Middletown Wed night 5-4. I scored the tieing and wining runs. I only walked three and struck out 10 so my control is getting a little better as you can tell.
I wrote Grandpa a letter and mailed it a couple of weeks ago and I just remembered that I didn't put a stamp on it or any return address so I am going to write him another one tonight. I bet he is really mad at me. Well, that is about all for now.
Love to all,
Joe

The next day, facing Newark and his friends from Hamilton, Joe was nearly unhittable. A pop-single over second by Tommy Caciavely cost him a no-hitter. He still managed a 1-0 shutout. He followed that with another shutout, 3-0, over Marion. Joe was loose on the mound and comfortable. It added up to more strikes, more wins, and promising progress reports to the Reds' front office.

Warren Giles was not surprised. Joe was close to home and closer than Giles knew.

"A lot of Sundays, 'specially when we were in Lima," Joe says, "as soon as our game was over, I would dress and hitchhike to Dayton. From Dayton, I could catch a bus to Hamilton and see Mom and Dad and the boys. The buses ran every hour so it didn't matter what time I got into Dayton, I could get home for the night. I think it cost a dollar."

The money didn't seem important to Joe. The time with his family did.

"Sometimes I wouldn't get to Hamilton until 8:30 at night, but Mom would always cook me a little something to eat. I could talk with Dad and the boys. Next morning, I'm back on the bus bright and early, off to Dayton and then hitching to Lima or wherever we were playing.

"I know it sounds crazy and—looking back—it probably was. But no matter how little time I had with the family, it was important to me and I think they knew that."

SOMETIMES, GETTING BACK TO THE BALL CLUB was a difficult and hurried trek. Lima was over 150 miles from Hamilton.

Sometimes he thumbed through the rain; often he walked along the roadside under a stifling sun, listening for the next car to come along, hoping the driver was friendly and headed his way.

In 1945, hitchhiking was an acceptable means of travel. Thousands of boys were making their way home from the war and often home was a village or town far from the nearest bus stop. Most of the time, they would get a ride. The country was at a different juncture in those days, less suspicious and far less fearful.

"I never missed a game," Joe says. "I was never late for a game. I always managed to get a ride. 'Course, I always tried to give myself plenty of time. I will say—there was a time or two—when it was close, real close. But I was always there when the bell rung."

The more success Joe enjoyed in the Ohio State League, the more his competitive spirit awakened. He played with an edge that made an impression on everyone he encountered. People began to see the player Brunner and Kaiser knew from Hamilton, the kid who dominated the Shop Leagues in basketball and the Sunday League in baseball—the kid who would split your face with a forearm in a pick-up football game.

Stories began to spread. One day during batting practice in Newark, a hard-hit line drive caught Joe on the left elbow. It hit him cleanly, spun him around, and knocked him down. The shot left him without any feeling in his arm for several minutes, and he was scheduled to pitch that day.

And so he did, striking out twelve hitters in eight innings and allowing just four hits. Lima won, 10-1.

In a short period of time, Joe gained a reputation as a fierce and determined competitor. He was only 16, but he was tough and given to one pursuit. He was there to succeed. He wasn't mean. He wasn't dirty. He was, however, given to legendary fits of temper.

Two of the best teams in the league that year were Lima and Zanesville. Every game seemed to be hard-fought and hard-won. As the season was winding down, they met in a double-header in Zanesville on August 15.

Zanesville won the first game. Joe warmed up for the second game, knowing playoff positions hung in the balance. The game followed the script of the season. Lima and Zanesville were tied, 2-2, in the bottom of the seventh. Lima couldn't afford to lose this game, and at this critical point Joe had a runner at second base, in scoring position. Two were out when a ball was hit to the outfield. Hope wasn't lost, however, because the Reds had a play at the plate. Fans stood and screamed.

On the field, the roar from the crowd disappeared in the moment. There was nothing but silence. All that existed was the sound of runner, his spikes digging into the clay as he cut third on the inside of the bag and raced toward the plate. The throw came in straight, catcher Isaac Seoane fielded it cleanly, blocked the plate, and made the tag—or so he thought.

"*Safe!*" yelled plate umpire H.L. McDowell. The crowd was jubilant. The Zanesville players jumped and cheered. They had swept the doubleheader.

Seoane turned on the umpire. He bumped him once. He bumped him again. Joe was backing up the plate on the play. He saw it clearly and rushed into the argument, protesting the call. Accounts differ, but some suggest that in the scuffle, Joe restrained McDowell while Seoane threw a punch at the umpire.

"I don't know about that," Joe says, bristling at the memory. "I do know that guy never touched the plate and hasn't touched the plate to this day. The guy missed the call. It was a horrible call, a ridiculous call."

McDowell made another call that day—this one to the league office. McDowell reported that Nuxhall and Seoane had assaulted him, both verbally and physically. Both players were suspended indefinitely, pending a hearing before league president Frank M. Colley. The actions were viewed as so egregious that Judge W.G. Bramham, President of the National Association, was notified.

Three days after the incident, Nuxhall, Seoane, and McDowell were called before Colley at the Bancroft Hotel in Springfield and oddly enough, the umpire amended his charges. The indefinite suspensions were dropped, but both players were fined $50 for disorderly conduct.

Dan Hoyt, a reporter for the *Springfield Sun*, covered the hearing. His story of the following day raised considerable doubt about Colley's ruling, as well as the specter of influence peddling.

Hoyt referred to Nuxhall as a "hot property of the Reds...a $15,000 investment." Colley's finding, he reported, was that Nuxhall's only offense was rushing McDowell and saying, "I oughta pop you right in the nose."

Hoyt wasn't nearly so kind to Seoane, a native of Cuba.

Seoane is one of the most colorful players in the league and is one of Lima's two most dependable hitters, currently sporting an average of .340. The little catcher cannot speak English and is sometimes a trial for the umpires. He was tabbed early on as a hot head and as light heavy-weight Golden Gloves Champion of Cuba he is said to hold his own with his hands.

"Horse hockey," Joe says. "Seoane was a helluva nice guy, a good catcher, too. And I don't think I said, 'I oughta punch you right in the nose.' I think I said something like, 'You missed the call!' And it was probably a whole lot more colorful—if you will—than that. There were all kinds of players around the plate and Seoane was in the middle of it. I was trying to get him outta there and I had a few words to say myself. Did I push a guy or two? Probably. Did I hold the umpire while Seoane hit him? No! I never did anything like that. Did I have a case of the goos? Yes! And that's the regrettable thing.

"That was the first time—as a professional player—I let my temper get the best of me. Wasn't the last, by any means. That was always a problem. I could get real riled up and over the smallest thing.

"It hurt me, no question about that. Held me back. You know," he continues, "I have always wondered—and I guess I always will—how many games I could have won, how much better I could have been, if I could just have learned to control my temper."

AT THIS MOMENT, he is an old man wishing he could alter the young man he once was—but the young man is gone now and didn't learn the lessons of an even temperament until late in his career, when the arm wasn't as strong, the legs not nearly as loose, and time was running down.

"Damnit, it was so stupid," he says.

"Today, when I talk to kids at schools, I always tell them that temper and anger are horrible enemies. You hurt other people and you end up hurting yourself more than anybody else. That I know for a fact."

Joe was ashamed of the incident in Zanesville. The charges made headlines. The resolution did not. Throughout his career, he tried to make people proud—his family and friends, the people back in Hamilton. Sometimes he felt like he did his job, but there were times when he felt he failed.

"There are things I am not particularly proud of," he says, "and usually it came down to one thing—me getting the ass about something that wasn't all that important."

Now, it is easier for him to see things clearly. So much has been distilled by time. Then, every day was a dance on an open nerve.

He was 16 and for the better part of three years, professional baseball had been calling him. He listened, but he still wasn't sure he could answer. There was something else he was driven to do.

Would anyone understand?

The afternoon shadows were growing long across the heart of Ohio. Summer was still settled in, but the sun was making its slow descent toward autumn, yielding to nightfall earlier each day and leaving behind the brush and whisper of cool breezes that presaged fall.

All through the season of 1945, Zanesville and Lima had distinguished themselves as two of the best teams in the league, and when the playoffs began in September, they were paired again.

Joe was no favorite of Zanesville fans. He had pitched well against their team most of the season and the confrontation with plate umpire H.L. McDowell in August cast him in an unsavory light. The attendant press didn't help. Most fans in Zanesville believed him to be a high-priced, hot-tempered thug whose talent far outweighed his judgment.

But even the most critical among them doubted neither his ability nor his fastball. In the opening playoff game, Joe was showered with boos and catcalls. He withstood it all, winning 5-4 in a game that was primarily a testament to his team's defense and his own ability to pitch himself out of trouble.

HIGH

MOST VALUABLE, YES—IF HAMILTON HIGH

HAD PLAYED HOCKEY, JOE MIGHT HAVE BEEN MVP THERE, TOO.

THIS HAPPENED TO BE FOR BASKETBALL, THE HARDWARE PRESENTED

BY HIS COACH, HARVEY SOLLENBERGER.

T I M E S

He allowed only six hits but walked eleven. Still, he had beaten the biggest name in the league that season, Joe "Red" Bielemeier, a 23-game winner for Zanesville.

But soon Cap Crossley's Reds were heading home, eliminated from the playoffs in an 8-0 loss charged to Nuxhall. Zanesville, part of the growing Brooklyn farm system, went home with the league championship. The Lima boys went home with their memories.

They had spent their summer on rag-tag ball fields, coursing the countryside in the decrepit yellow school bus, and—for the winter at least—they were leaving behind the Regal Room cheeseburgers. But every player packed a story to take home, and they had seen things they had not seen before—Dale Long's effortless power, the movement on the Nuxhall fastball. And they had seen the burning field in Muskingum County.

It happened during the dog days of summer when a hot sun smoldered behind a cloud-filled sky. Every afternoon a thunderstorm blew in from the west, tumbling and rattling and throwing steamy rain their way. And once again Joe and his teammates were in Zanesville, facing another rained out game and the prospects of yet another doubleheader.

They were bored and tired, pondering an idle day around the team hotel when the rain stopped and the Zanesville grounds crew began a determined attack on the field. The first wave involved rakes and shovels but only succeeded in moving the standing water from one place to another. Seemingly defeated, they made a quick retreat, emerging minutes later behind wheelbarrows filled with sawdust. The sawdust was dumped on the field in large piles, then raked all about.

Once more they raced off the field, returning with five-gallon oil cans, each crew member wobbling back and forth while laboring under the weight of the task. The players watched from their dugouts as the contents of the cans were dumped on the field. The smell was unmistakable: kerosene.

When the field was doused, the crew chief gave the signal, and the field was torched. The players looked on incredulously as the black smoke rolled skyward. It stunk as only burning kerosene can, thick and acrid, taking up residence in the nose and throat. They coughed. They spit. But they also played that day.

The field, however, was black and burned, and by game's end the players resembled coal miners and chimney sweeps. It was a good day, someone decided, to wash the uniforms.

Twenty young men had built a bond around such memories. As they said their goodbyes, they wondered who among them would be back the following year, and who would never be seen again.

They were boys without answers, reluctant to part with this life in professional baseball—even for the winter.

JOE FELT DIFFERENTLY. He loved the game, but he didn't like the road. He didn't like the rented room on Wayne Street. He didn't like the hotels and meals taken from one diner after another. Where others found freedom, Joe longed for time with his mother, father, and brothers. He didn't feel confined at home.

While his teammates packed slowly, Joe left Lima quickly. He put his personal belongings in a small satchel: glove, spikes, a few suits of clothing. He hit the road again, hitching his way back to Dayton, where he would catch another bus to Hamilton.

Back home he could finally walk down the street with pride. When people asked him how he had done that season, he could smile and say—honestly—he had done well. In 16 games with Lima, Joe won 10 and lost five. His earned run average was 2.57. He had pitched 11 complete games and struck out 135 hitters in 126 innings. In his first five games, he had 60 strikeouts.

No one was really surprised. In Hamilton, they all believed Joe would be a success in whatever he chose to do. Everywhere he went, he was gracious, thanking those who praised him, then turning the conversation to other players from Hamilton.

He told them about Al Kaiser, who led the league in hitting. Hit almost .370. Twelve homers, nearly180 hits. He asked if they had heard about Bob Brunner, who won 12 games for a last place club.

Joe made everyone he met feel good. He made them smile and they weren't always sure why. Because of his extraordinary physical development, even his neighbors sometimes failed to notice that he was still a boy. Therefore, none of them was particularly surprised when he struck out 13 or 14 batters.

But Joe had a surprise for them. He was prepared to give it all up— money, celebrity, the big leagues—to do something else. He had been given the opportunity to join a man's world—a very *particular* world— when all he wanted was the chance to be a schoolboy.

He remembered a time that seemed long ago. He was perhaps 12 years old. It was the afternoon of an endless summer, and he was roaming the playground, looking for something to do. In the distance he saw a tall, lean man running sprints. After the sprints, the man fell to the ground and did push-ups, then sit-ups. Each exercise was done quickly and without labor. He ran around the field carrying a football, shifting it from one arm to another and lifting his legs higher and higher with each step. He never seemed to tire.

Joe drew closer and when the man finally stopped for a breath, Joe said hello. The young man looked up, his face bathed in sweat, and Joe suddenly recognized him. It was Paul Sarringhaus, a football legend at Hamilton High School and an Ohio State All-American.

Joe was face-to-face with a man whose image would soon land on the cover of *Life* magazine. Sarringhaus was part of Paul Brown's national championship backfield in 1942 when his 72 points had made him the second leading scorer in the Big Ten. Sarringhaus and his compatriots scored 337 points that year, a record that would stand until 1969, and their only loss of the season—to Wisconsin—came after players and coaches were laid low by a devastating virus caught from a drinking fountain on the train.

Joe didn't know what to say. This was his first brush with fame. No one he knew was as famous as Sarringhaus.

SARRINGHAUS SHOWED JOE how to run pass routes. The footballs were like bullets, burning his hands. Sarringhaus laughed, then showed the boy how to gather the ball with his hands and bring it into his body. Finally, he began to catch a few of them.

When they rested, Sarringhaus talked to him about playing at Hamilton High, and what Saturday afternoons were like in Columbus when Ohio Stadium was filled with what amounted to the entire population of Hamilton.

Sarringhaus marveled at Joe's size and complimented him on his speed. And so the afternoon went gloriously by. When Joe left the playground, his legs were heavy and tired, his hands were red and swollen, but his mind was filled with determination. He would play at Hamilton High and, maybe, he could be as good as Sarringhaus.

By late summer of 1945, Joe had already secured a place in sports history, and it seemed only a matter of time before he was a mainstay in the major leagues. But it was not enough.

Every trip Joe made back to Hamilton that summer, he raised the topic with his parents. At first, he treaded softly, trying to gauge their

LARGER THAN LIFE—JOE'S BOYHOOD IDOL,

PAUL SARRINGHAUS, REENTERED OSU AFTER SERVING IN THE ARMY

AND SCORED FOUR TDs IN HIS FIRST GAME, AGAINST MISSOURI.

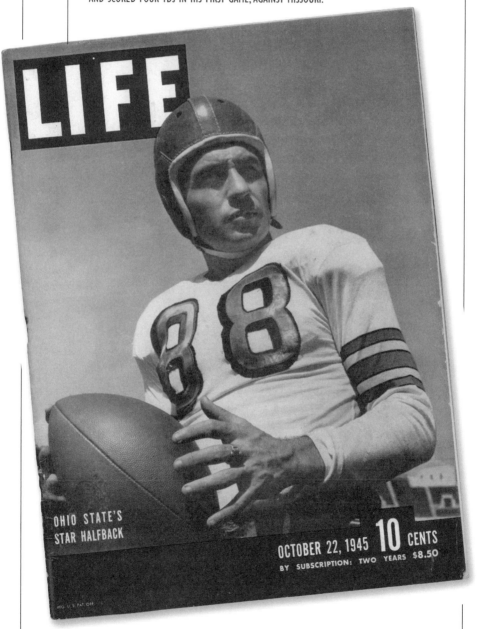

LIFE

OHIO STATE'S
STAR HALFBACK

OCTOBER 22, 1945 **10** CENTS
BY SUBSCRIPTION: TWO YEARS $8.50

feelings. He thought his mother would back his decision. He wasn't sure how his father would react.

Joe repeatedly raised the question: What would it take to regain his amateur status and eligibility to play high school sports?

His parents weren't sure. They also wondered if this was a wise choice. The Reds had been good to Joe and paid him handsomely. Orville told Joe he was relatively certain he would have to give up big league ball.

GENE NUXHALL IS THE TRUE WANDERER of the family, two years younger than Joe, a retired engineer, the sole college graduate among the four brothers, and the only one who does not live in Butler County.

"Business took me away a long time ago," he says. "When I go home now, I feel like a stranger in town."

But distance often leads to perspective. He is home and alone in Fort Wayne, Indiana, just five months removed from burying his wife of nearly fifty years.

He lives in a pleasant home in an affluent part of the city and nothing pleases him more than talking about his brother.

"It was a different era," he says. "Today, it sounds so odd that someone would give up a professional contract to play high school sports. It is contrary to everything we witness today. We live in a time when everyone wants everything now, and they think they can have it. You have to understand what it was like back then. Today's culture is so alien to the life we knew."

The Nuxhalls were disciplined Dutchmen who believed good things came with time, patience, and hard work. The greatest obstacles could be overcome if one simply shouldered the task. The burdens that beset even the most well-intentioned were simply God's will.

Gene remembered when his father was out of work for over a year. He remembered the family's struggles and how his father, a man with a 10th grade education, completed a correspondence course so he could get a better job.

The Nuxhalls were a product of the Depression, a harsh moment in history that bound families and communities together with values that would be largely mothballed by the post-war decades: unlocked houses, kids playing outside for an entire day, people walking everywhere, and trust born of their shared vulnerabilities.

"About 1935 we had moved out in the country along Route 27,"

Gene said. "We were on a little farm. My dad had a garden and he hunted some. So we were doing okay. Route 27 was a major north-south artery back then and once in awhile a complete stranger would come up to the front porch, knock on the door, and ask if they could possibly have something to eat.

"Mom never turned them down. She asked them to sit on the porch. She went inside, cooked them some eggs or something. They ate and went on their way. Can you imagine something like that happening today?"

Gene recalled a Christmas when the family lived at Ninth and Vine in Hamilton. It was especially cold that winter. The house was small, but it was all Orville could afford.

"It didn't have one thread of insulation. You could feel the wind come through the walls. Christmas that year my grandfather gave us a crate of oranges. At night it was so cold in the house the oranges froze. The crate of oranges was all we got for Christmas that year.

"I swear to God, I don't know how my parents made it. Feeding five kids. Keeping things together. Sometimes I am surprised they made it at all.

"These were not the good old times, far from it," he says. "My God, no! These were difficult times. But this is what shaped our family.

"No matter how hard my dad worked, we had just enough to get by. But, as corny as this sounds by today's standards, we always had one another. That's why it hurt so bad when our sister died."

EVERY DAY, ORVILLE WALKED HOME FROM WORK and on the way, he stopped and bought a six-pack of beer. He sat on the back step and drank his beer until Naomi called him to dinner.

After supper, he clapped his big hands against his thighs and said, "Who wants to play ball?"

The boys and their father played until it was too dark to see. When the games were finished, they went inside and gathered round the radio.

Sometimes they listened to the Reds' game, but more often it was *Hermit's Cave*, *Hopalong Cassidy*, or *The Lone Ranger*.

And that is what Joe missed. It is why he wanted to stay in Hamilton and play high school ball. At home, he was perfectly at peace and perfectly secure.

"He had been forced to grow up so fast," Gene said. "I don't mean mature. I mean he had been led to do things well past his years. Think about it. He's 14 and he's on a road trip with the Reds. The following year, he's pitching in a big league game and then they send him to Birmingham, hundreds of miles from everything he knows.

"He comes home and he can't do anything he really loves to do or participate in any of the sports at school that are so important to him. Then, it's spring training and Syracuse and Lima. Hotels. Road trips. And all before he is what, 17?

"That's an awful lot to absorb at such a young age, maybe too much. Who could blame him for wanting to come home?"

For his brothers, there is no mystery in Joe's desire to return to Hamilton.

"He was asked to be a man before his time came," Gene said. "Joe just wanted a chance to be a kid and he deserved that chance."

That fall, Orville set about the task of clearing the path for his son's return to high school sports. Initially, he turned to Warren Giles and, once more, the Reds' general manager expressed his empathy.

Giles assured Orville he would do all he could to help Joe regain his amateur status. His largess, however, was two-fold. Joe clearly needed more time to develop, and with the war winding down, players were beginning to return to the major league ranks.

Orville's next step was to contact John O. Fry, the principal at Hamilton High School. Fry promised he would take the matter to the Ohio High School Athletic Association.

Fry quickly delivered a list of requirements. Joe had to stop playing professionally for one full year. He could not play high school sports for a year. During that time, he could not accept payment of any kind for any athletic endeavor.

It sounded simple enough, except for one thing.

Joe had never been patient. It was almost impossible for him to remain still.

And so he didn't.

From the fall of 1945 until school began the following year, Joe prepared himself for what would be one of the greatest sports seasons ever achieved by any athlete in Ohio high school history.

In the fall of 1945, he played sandlot football. It was an all-out, full-contact game. They abided by the rules—as they knew them—which were few. The games were spirited and reckless, the only equipment being the ball itself.

Joe excelled in sandlot football, although he took his share of blows.

There was a time when Jeni McCullough's teeth opened a large cut in Joe's head. He remembered a particular Sunday when a tough kid named Snip Huey joined the game.

"He was running all over the place," Joe recalled. "Well, I'm trying to tackle him and somehow I end up down and he just stomps all over my face.

"As you might expect, I was a little ticked off. I'm bleeding a little bit. I'm all scratched up. So we run him down and guess what he's wearing? He's playing football in Australian lumberjack boots! Got these long spikes on the soles. The guy stepped on my face in boots and ground it in and I don't think to this day it was by mistake."

Snip Huey was relieved of his boots, and the game went on.

THERE WERE A LOT OF WOUNDS THAT WINTER, and some that helped him mature. Ineligible to play high school basketball, Joe went back to the YMCA Municipal League. Once more, he played for the North End Merchants. The previous year, he had been MVP of the league, which was predominately composed of boys, older men, and those who, for one reason or another, were exempt from the draft.

In the winter of '45 and '46, things had changed considerably. While Joe was good enough to retain his spot in the Shop League, others were not. Most of the rosters were filled with battle-hardened veterans back from the war. Joe remained a dominant player, but the points came harder and for every bucket there was a bruise.

The veterans in the Muni League used every means to intimidate Joe. But nothing worked. The Merchants finished second but Joe remained one of its top scorers, averaging over 20 points.

In the spring, Joe suited up for baseball with the Moose Lodge. He tied a league record with 22 strikeouts in one game, and he struck out 21 batters against the American Legion. The numbers became routine, 18 strikeouts here, 19 there—all this coupled with three- and four-hit outings.

That year his name appeared in the Hamilton press with a frequency matched by Marshall and MacArthur, and few headlines were bigger than the one that ran in late summer, 1946:

Nuxhall To Be Eligible For High School Sports

H.W. Emswiler, commissioner of the Ohio High School Athletic

Association, recommended Joe's re-instatement. The OHSAA board approved Emswiler's recommendation in late August, and for the first time, Joe put on a Hamilton High School football uniform.

The coach found him wearing the shoulder pads like a chest protector. He looked at Joe and began to laugh.

"That's not the way it goes, Joe," he said.

Coach Mather didn't laugh much after that. He was too busy applauding Joe on the field where he was linebacker, fullback, and eventual captain on a team that won six games, lost two, and tied one.

Joe thought they should have won the tie, too. With the score 6-6, time running out, Joe threw a pass to Boxcar Bailey without an Elder defender in sight, and the ball went through Bailey's hands.

By midseason, before the Springfield game, Dan Hoyt of the *Springfield Sun* asked Mather what he thought of Nuxhall. Mather, schooled under Hall of Famer Paul Brown at the Great Lakes Naval Training Center, called Joe "the finest back I have ever seen in high school circles."

In 1946, Hamilton outscored its opponents 185-58. Joe accounted for 68 points himself, scoring 11 touchdowns and two extra points. He also sustained what he insists today were the only significant injuries of his entire athletic career.

In the second game of the season, Hamilton played Lorain Clearview, a small school from the Cleveland area. The contact was fierce throughout the game. Although Hamilton won, 31-0, two key players were knocked out of the game, halfback Eldon "Red" Grathwohl, a team captain, and quarterback Bill Zimbleman.

Joe's nose was broken, but he continued to play. Lorain's boys didn't average more than 170 pounds, but they were pineknot tough. Joe heard they were Hungarian. Whatever they were, they played with an intensity foreign to even the Hamilton boys.

Six weeks later, he hurt his knee in a seven-point loss at Toledo-Libbey. He was injured again playing Middletown when, in the first quarter, someone knocked him into the tuba section of the Middie band.

He came back on the field to punt, however. Backed up into their own territory on four different occasions, Joe limped on and kicked his teammates out of trouble. He averaged nearly 40 yards a punt. In a game largely decided by field position and Red Grathwohl carrying the ball, Hamilton won, 13-7, breaking a three-game losing streak to the Middies.

THE BIG BLUE—WHEN JOE PLAYED FULLBACK AND LINEBACKER FOR THE BIG BLUE, THEY CONSIDERED CHANGING THE SCHOOL COLORS TO BLACK AND BLUE. JOE IS KNEELING JUST TO THE RIGHT OF THE BALL.

The healing process was helped by the honor that followed. Joe, along with teammate Harry Phillips, was named Third Team All-Ohio.

IN THE BASKETBALL SEASON OPENER, the former MVP of the Shop League scored 16 points and Hamilton defeated Xenia, 48-26. Wrote John P. Heinz in the *Hamilton Journal-News*:

Nuxhall, playing his first basketball game for the Blue, was a demon under the hoop. His clever southpaw shots had his opponent completely baffled and his follow up play gave his teammates added confidence in shooting from longer range.

Coach Harvey Sollenberger's team, which began the year with no returning starters, opened the season with seven straight wins. Early in 1947, Hamilton fans were talking about wresting the state title from Butler County rival Middletown. Those hopes were tested when the two schools squared off on January 24th. The game drew such local interest that it was played at Withrow Court on the Miami University campus in nearby Oxford.

Hamilton did not play well. With just five minutes left in the game, Middletown led 31-19, its 6-foot-6 guard Shelby Linville doing most of the damage.

But in the last five minutes, with Joe dominating the inside action, Hamilton outscored Middletown 17-to-5. Charley Dininger's basket tied the game, 36-36, sending the crowd of 3,500 into hysterics and the game into overtime.

Hamilton won in overtime, 39-38. The teams would meet again in the last game of the regular season, again played at Miami and, again, Hamilton won by a point, 30-29. Joe scored 17 points in that game, but it was Jack Browning's two baskets in the final seconds that secured the victory.

Middletown, though, extracted a final retribution, which ended Hamilton's hopes for a state title and secured its own. The Middies defeated Hamilton, 36-34, in the district championship. Joe scored 13 points but Middletown's George McChesney made the difference. He scored 12 points, 10 of those in the final quarter, including the game-winning basket. Hamilton ended the season 19-3. Middletown claimed its fifth straight district championship and went on to claim a second consecutive state title, beating East Liverpool, 47-29.

Joe was named first team All-Ohio and captain of the team. He was the second player in Hamilton High School history to earn distinction as Ohio High School Player of the Year and the first in basketball. The other was the young man who had inspired Joe on the playground, Paul Sarringhaus, who was Ohio High School Player of The Year in football in 1939.

Joe's performance that school year established him as the most accomplished athlete in the history of Hamilton High School, a status he holds in most circles today.

In the spring, he played baseball. He threw a no-hitter in the first game of the season, beating Monroe, 2-1. He struck out 12 and walked four. Monroe scored its only run on a wild pitch.

AUTUMN'S REWARD—JOE WAS NAMED ALL-STATE
FOR THE FIRST TIME IN THE '46-'47 SCHOOL YEAR, BUT THE YEAR WASN'T
OVER. THAT'S COACH CHUCK MATHER HANDING OUT LETTERS.

1946 Football Banquet

Principal John Fry *Caoch Sid Gillman* *Capt Eldon Grathwohl* *Capt Joe Nuxhall*

Days later, he faced Monroe again and lost badly. Joe couldn't find the plate. Though he pitched Hamilton into the state tournament, Joe experienced similar lapses throughout the season, which didn't go unnoticed.

Wrote Bill Moeller in the local paper:

Until Big Joe develops control, he will have no hopes of attaining the major leagues…a fact known for some time by local diamond experts and Redleg bigwigs. A couple of years in the minors could do the trick.

Chapter twelve

Nearly three years after his major league debut, Joe returned to the place that gave him a name in baseball history. His celebrated homecoming and unprecedented high school season ended on May 23, 1947, at Crosley Field, where he pitched his final game in a high school uniform.

He had come full circle, from his appearance with the Reds at the age of 15 to an Ohio high school regional semifinal game against Cincinnati Withrow. He was almost 19. He had experienced so much more than anyone else on the field. He had, for instance, stood on the same mound and seen Stan Musial looking back at him.

From that mound and that park, he had gone off on a sojourn that had, almost eerily, brought him back to exactly where he started. Joe pitched better against Withrow than he did against Musial and the Cardinals, but not well enough.

For four innings, he didn't allow a hit yet an error and two passed balls in the fourth put Hamilton behind, 1-0. The next inning, Withrow got a hit, and two more passed balls

POSITIVELY SENATORIAL—COACH JOE BEGGS INSTRUCTS JOE AND BOB NUXHALL, WHOSE BASEBALL CAREER WAS INTERRUPTED BY BOTH INJURY AND THE SERVICE.

A MINOR

set the stage for two more runs. Joe didn't think about the day he pitched against the Cardinals or the unsettling nervousness that fell over him when Musial rifled his base hit to right field, putting him on a train to Birmingham.

"It really didn't cross my mind, being back there," he says. "I was so intent on doing well and being with my team in the tournament. I was very proud of that, all of us playing there at Crosley."

While he was not vulnerable to reverie, he was subject to the same problems he faced on June 10, 1944. He was wild.

"They may have scored all those pitches as passed balls," he says, "but none of them were, shall we say, catchable."

The first two errant pitches sent him into a downward spiral, his emotions eroding his ability to throw strikes. He lost his temper, his control, and eventually the game—3-0.

His brother Gene, the smallest of the Nuxhall brothers, played third base in the loss to Withrow. He was a smooth infielder with soft, sure hands, the only member of the Nuxhall clan who was not a pitcher.

"It was a problem for Joe," Gene recalls. "He had such a great arm and such great stuff, but one little thing would happen and he would just lose it. He would get so angry, so out of control, and the odd thing is he never took it out on anyone else, never blamed anyone else. All his anger was self-directed. He couldn't accept a single mistake or flaw or failure. He was so damned competitive that it diminished his very ability to do what he loved most—to succeed."

In football, Joe's anger made him a determined running back and ferocious tackler. In basketball, it sent him after each rebound with more intensity. As a pitcher, his anger was a thief. It jimmied through the doors of his concentration and stole his composure.

He would grimace and grind his teeth. He would try to throw harder, and the more he tried, the more he forced his pitches. Pitching is peace of mind, flawless rhythm, and—at its best—the art that defuses all else in the game.

Joe had both arm and ability. His father had taught him technique. But he had yet to learn composure.

Perhaps he was more suited for basketball or football. He received offers in both sports from several universities, including Indiana, Purdue, Kent State, Miami, and Xavier. But he never gave their attentions serious consideration. He wanted to prove himself a legitimate major league ballplayer.

Shortly after graduation, Joe was preparing to return to Syracuse and the International League, but Leo Miller, the Chiefs' general manager, had other plans. Joe was re-assigned to "D" Ball, this time to the Muncie Packers, the Reds' new affiliate in the Ohio State League.

Miller's explanation was terse. Joe had been away from professional baseball for nearly two years. He wasn't ready for the International League's caliber of play or competition. Joe bristled at the slight but accepted the assignment.

He wondered, though, if this was not punishment for walking away from the game, turning his back on the Reds to play high school sports. He wasn't sure what they were thinking in the Reds' front office, but he was determined to prove they were making a mistake.

HE FOUND "D" BALL IN 1947 not that much different than it was in '45—largely unregulated and generally unpredictable. During his first season in the Ohio State League, three out of six clubs finished with the same manager who began the season. Zanesville had four managers and a fifth who served on an interim basis. Three games were forfeited because of fights and another because a team used an ineligible player. One game was thrown out because it wasn't scheduled. Having no other commitments and nowhere to go, they merely began another game. Another was postponed because the home team, Middletown, didn't have any baseballs.

Then there was Eric McNair, one of the Zanesville managers, who took a poke at an umpire in each game of a doubleheader. The blow he delivered in the second altercation knocked out the umpire's gold tooth. The game was delayed a half-hour while the search continued—in vain— for the umpire's lost tooth.

It was tough and unruly, and word of every event spread from one town to the other. Maybe that's why an umpire on the league staff ran away, seeking safer ground. He was AWOL for two days before the league office knew he was gone.

Players still had their uniforms washed only once a week. Money was short, and players continued their prowl for inexpensive food and forms of entertainment. They lay down at night in cheap rooms, idleness and boredom their constant companions.

"One night, it was hotter than hell," Joe says. "A bunch of us had walked downtown, went to a restaurant, and were on our way back to this place where we were all staying.

"We sat down on the steps outside the theater. We're just sitting there talking. Well, this cop comes along and he runs us in for loitering. Now here is the thing. From where we were sitting, we could see the police station down the street. We could see it!

"He makes us all get in the patrol car and ride down to the station house. Six of us and the cop in one car, seven people! Couldn't have been more than a block or so. We're crammed in like sardines, trying not to laugh.

"They never arrested us. Just talked to us. Told us about some curfew or something. When they found out we were ballplayers, they let us go."

There was no statute in Muncie forbidding sweating in public or seeking a midnight breeze. And besides, the city fathers were glad to have the Reds' minor league affiliate in town. Arresting six Packers was a misdemeanor in itself.

THE TOWNS WERE SMALL. The crowds were rowdy. Nothing had changed, including Joe's performance. In his first outing for the Muncie Packers, Joe faced the Dayton Indians, a Cleveland farm team. He held them hitless for eight innings, allowing just two runs.

Muncie won the game, 11-4. Joe struck out eight hitters. But he walked 14, a substantial number of those coming after a broken-bat single ended his bid for a no-hitter.

"It was about that time," Joe says, "the Reds came over and we played an exhibition game, and I'm sure I determined my fate for that season. I walked, oh, about 71. If there was any doubt in anybody's mind where I belonged, that kinda cinched things."

Plagued by inconsistency, Joe took the demotion to "D" Ball in stride. Muncie put him closer to home. The Ohio State League loop would take him to Dayton; Richmond, Indiana; and Springfield, all reasonably close to Hamilton.

On June 12, 1947, Joe graduated from high school. He was the second member of his family to receive a high school diploma. That night, after all the pictures were taken and the gowns and caps put away, while his parents and grandparents tipped a beer and cheered the occasion, Joe and his high school sweetheart, Donzetta Houston, took a walk. He was anxious about leaving home and returning to professional baseball. At the time, he thought he was going to Syracuse.

Donzetta was a statuesque brunette who bore a striking resemblance

THE MUNCIE EXIT—JOE LIKED MUNCIE BECAUSE

IT WAS CLOSE TO HOME. BUT THEN HE WAS WHIPSAWED AROUND

THE MINOR LEAGUES, FIRST TO TULSA, THEN TO COLUMBIA, S.C.

to Hollywood's Barbara Stanwyck. Her family had come to Hamilton from Bon Jellicoe, Kentucky. She had a sincere smile and she was utterly devoid of ego.

They had met the previous summer on a balmy night at LeSourdsville Lake, an amusement park not far from Hamilton. Donzetta was there with friends to hear the bands and learn the newest dance-steps.

"I knew who Joe was because of all his athletics, but we had never met until that night," Donzetta says.

"I had been playing softball and me and a buddy just decided to go on over and just see who was there and what was going on," Joe recalls. "I met Donzetta and we talked and it started getting late. She told me she had to go, that her friends were leaving. So, I told her if she wanted to stay a little longer, we would give her and her friend a ride home."

Joe was still in uniform, hadn't bothered to shower, and clearly wasn't there to impress anyone. Donzetta was taken with this big man. He was handsome and charming and his modesty was refreshing. His name was the biggest in town. Everyone knew Joe Nuxhall. Yet, with her, he talked softly and laughed at himself and was embarrassed to dance.

Immediately, Donzetta trusted Joe, feeling assured he would get her home safely. And he did. They rode home in the back of a pick-up truck.

ON GRADUATION NIGHT, she made a suggestion.

"He was standing there talking about how much he was going to miss me, and how he had to go back to baseball," Donzetta remembers. "So I proposed to him. I said, 'Well, you could take me with you.' He looked at me. He said, 'You mean get married! You would marry me?' I said, 'Yes, I will marry you.'"

They were engaged that night. The memory makes her laugh. She wonders, too, if Joe would have had the gumption to propose himself. "He was kind of shy about some things," she says.

The summer of '47 was Donzetta's introduction to a lifetime in baseball. In effect, it was her spring training. She was working at Ohio Casualty Insurance Company as a keypunch operator, but on weekends she traveled to see Joe play. Several times, she took the bus to Muncie and when the Packers were in Dayton, she went with Joe's family to see the games.

On one of her trips, Joe introduced her to Wally Post, another pitcher on the team. Wally was a big, strong, right-handed pitcher from St. Henry, Ohio.

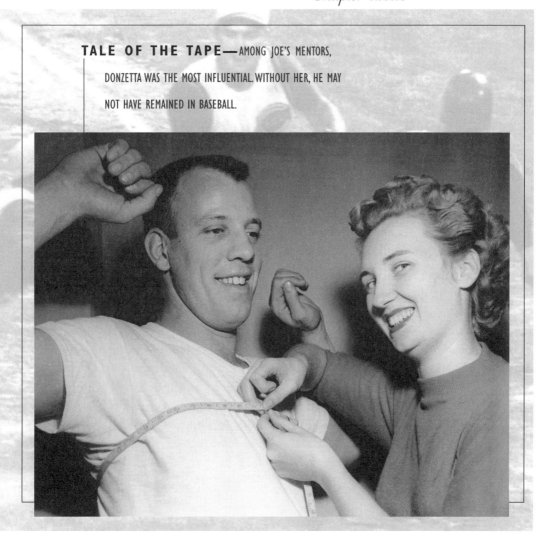

TALE OF THE TAPE—AMONG JOE'S MENTORS, DONZETTA WAS THE MOST INFLUENTIAL. WITHOUT HER, HE MAY NOT HAVE REMAINED IN BASEBALL.

"They had so much in common," Donzetta says. "Wally and his wife, Pat, became our dearest friends, like family. I guess it was because we were so young and went through so many of the same things together. Traveling so much, being here and being there, being apart from our husbands so much. It was not an easy life, believe me."

Post was a big kid from the farm fields of Mercer County. There was nothing complicated about Wally. He was as straight as the rows in a Mercer County cornfield.

In 1947, the essential difference between Joe Nuxhall and Wally Post was their records. Joe closed the season at 7-7. He walked 145 hitters in 100 innings. His earned run average was 3.78. Wally went

17-7. Joe was certain his friend was destined for big things. He wasn't so sure about himself.

On October 4, 1947, Donzetta and Joe were married. For their honeymoon, they went to Punta Gorda, Florida. To save money, they took a bus, which seemed to stop in every town along the way.

"We left on Monday morning and got there late in the afternoon on Tuesday," Joe says. "We were on that bus nearly thirty-six hours. They called it The Sunshine Express, but it wasn't what you would exactly call express. Wasn't so bad though. We talked all the way and we were, you know, together."

They stayed at Joe's grandfather's home in Punta Gorda. Everybody in the family liked Donzetta and felt that Joe was lucky to land such a girl. They thought she would be good for him.

After a short stay in Florida, Joe and Donzetta returned to a small apartment in Hamilton and the first of Joe's winters of free agency. Like all ballplayers of his time—especially those in the minors—Joe had to take an off-season job to make ends meet. Over the years, he worked for the Estate Stove Company, the Bendix Corporation, the Mosler Safe Company, and Fisher Body Plant.

He worked jobs that paid $1.25 and $3 an hour. One year, he made $5 an hour. He worked in the plants, loaded boxcars, and punched a clock. He did not yet have a vocation, but he had a craft.

"My brother was one helluva basketball player," Gene says. "Everybody wanted him for the Shop League teams."

"He worked," Donzetta says, "for whoever had the best basketball team. It didn't matter what he had to do. If they had a good team, he went to work for them."

Joe was a prize recruit for the industrial captains around Hamilton, who, with each year, grew more attentive to a basketball league that soon gained statewide recognition.

Joe was popular with his teammates and prized by his employers, and his success on the court led to other opportunities. The Syracuse Nationals of the fledgling National Basketball Association invited him to a tryout. For two years, the House of David basketball team, the legendary traveling pro team—the Jewish equivalent of the Harlem Globetrotters—recruited him.

While he rejected the Nationals, he briefly entertained the thought of playing for the House of David. But when he was informed wives were not permitted to travel with the team, he politely declined.

FRIENDLY FIRE—WALLY POST AND JOE WERE FAST FRIENDS FROM THEIR DAYS IN MUNCIE, WHEN THEY WERE BOTH PITCHERS. SOON, HOWEVER, POST WENT TO THE OUTFIELD AND BECAME ONE OF THE GAME'S TOP SLUGGERS.

Joe was devoted to Donzetta, but he was young and he didn't adjust to marriage easily or quickly.

"Oh, man, there were times," Joe says. "I don't even like to think about it. I would work all day. Then go play basketball and after that a bunch of us guys would go over to somebody's house, have a few beers, and play cards and gab until all hours of the night. Then we would do it all over again. That went on for a long time.

"I wasn't exactly Little Lord Fauntleroy in those days. Finally, Donzetta got tired of it and she let me know about it in no uncertain terms. I was stubborn, like my dad, and I had that damned temper. I wanted to do what I wanted to do. What she said didn't take for a while, but she finally got through to me. So, I started doing things differently. Well, trying.

"She had, she has—the patience of a saint. She *is* a saint. I have no idea why she has put up with me all these years."

WHILE JOE TRIED TO FIND HIMSELF on the field, Donzetta became acquainted with a world she had never even imagined.

In 1948, Joe was assigned to Columbia, South Carolina, of the South Atlantic League. Spring training was held in Alexandria, Louisiana. The club suggested that wives not accompany players to camp. The work was hard and the travel rigorous. Beyond that, the organization didn't want its players to be distracted.

Joe thought it over, then asked Donzetta to go with him to Louisiana.

"He said he couldn't bear to be without me," she says. "So I went and I was the only wife there. I had no one to talk to when they were off playing ball. I didn't know anyone. I didn't know what to do."

One day, while attending a spring game in Alexandria, Donzetta saw another woman in the stands at the ballpark. It was difficult *not* to see her. Donzetta had never seen a woman in a ballpark who was dressed so well. It was the middle of the afternoon, yet she looked as if she were heading out for an evening on the town.

The woman's dress was clearly expensive. She wore wonderfully white gloves and a large hat, and while it was impressive, it was not ostentatious.

"We talked and eventually we became friends," Donzetta says. "She was very nice, very cultured, and I was just so happy to have someone to talk to."

In the days to come, they would have lunch and walk around town window-shopping. Donzetta was grateful to have found such a friend, but she also began to notice unusual things about her. She had a checking account, which was uncommon for a single woman in those days. She also seemed to have an inordinate amount of cash.

"We were staying at the Bentley Hotel in Alexandria and one day I was in her room visiting," Donzetta recalls. "There was a knock at the door and I noticed it was the hotel security officer. He called her by name, looked at me, and then went away. I thought that was kind of odd but I didn't think any more about it."

Sometime later, the ball club made a trip to New Orleans for a game.

Donzetta's new friend, Jo Rene, suggested they take a bus to see the game and visit some of her girlfriends who lived in the city.

"We get there and we go to this very nice hotel," Donzetta says. "Some of the girls were dressed very well and standing around, but most of them were in nightgowns and bedclothes—and yet it was the middle of the day. Some were lying around in bed.

"I was so young and naïve, I had no idea what I was seeing or where I was. But that day at the game, I became somewhat curious. I noticed that she seemed to know an awful lot of the older players."

A few days later, Al Vincent, the manager of the team, told Joe that it was probably not a good idea for Donzetta to be seen with Jo Rene. Jo Rene, he told Joe, was the most notable Lady of the Evening in all of Alexandria, Louisiana.

"So," Donzetta says, "I lost my friend. Today, I have to laugh. There I was in what I'm sure was a bordello, and I had no idea what was going on."

WHILE DONZETTA WAS DISCOVERING a new world, Joe was learning how demanding life in pro ball could be. At the close of spring training, he was assigned to Class AA Tulsa and the Texas League.

Joe appeared in six games with Tulsa. He didn't win a game, he didn't lose a game, and his ERA was 2.25.

"I guess," he says, "they didn't like what they saw. The worst part of it was that Donzetta had just arrived and was settling in when they told me I was going back to Columbia."

They packed up again and set out from Oklahoma to South Carolina, where they would be re-united with Gee Walker.

Gee was there when Joe made his major league debut, and he had been there when Joe and Donzetta needed a tip on who was who in Alexandria. Walker was popular with players and fans. But he wasn't able to help Joe improve as a pitcher.

In those days, minor league managers had no time for individual instruction. It didn't matter if they had the expertise or the inclination.

"We were too busy," says Sheldon "Chief" Bender, who managed in the Cardinals' minor league organization from 1949 to 1952. "You made out the lineup. You handled the travel plans. You hit infield. You tried to keep these guys on a positive path and sometimes you were driving the bus, looking in the rear view mirror and wondering what you might be missing."

Generally, minor league managers were former players whose major league experience had been limited because of their modest skills. Minor league instruction didn't come along until the '60s. "Up until then," Bender says, "the players were pretty much on their own. Oh, we tried to do what we could, but you had eighteen, maybe twenty guys on a team and you had to keep your main purpose in mind. You were expected to win ball games."

That was a problem for Joe. "No matter where you were or what level, there was no one there to help you," Joe says, "no coaching to speak of. Your mistakes compounded and instead of correcting them, you got into bad habits that you just repeated over and over."

That was the path Joe followed, from Columbia, South Carolina to Charleston, West Virginia, and Class "A" Ball in 1949 and 1950.

CHARLIE WOLF WAS A NOTRE DAME MAN who walked away from South Bend and a scholarship in football and basketball in order to pursue his lifelong dream of playing professional baseball. The Reds signed him for $2,000 in 1947 and by '49 he had advanced to Charleston. Growing up in Fort Thomas, Kentucky, just across the Ohio River from Cincinnati, he knew all about Joe Nuxhall.

"When I first met him," Wolf says, "I was kind of surprised. Here was this big, happy-go-lucky guy who had so much ability and not one ounce of presumption in his soul.

"The minors, back then, could humble you real quick. It's difficult to be cocky when you are getting dressed in some cramped clubhouse or trying to sleep in some little hotel and mice are running across the foot of the bed. Joe was just like the rest of us. Just another guy trying to make it."

Wolf marveled at Nuxhall's fastball, but like the rest of the players with Charleston, he was well aware of Joe's problem: In 1949, Joe walked 151 hitters in 186 innings.

"He was a lot like another pitcher we faced in the Central League, Ryne Duren. Ryne's eyesight was horrible. He wore these glasses with Coke-bottle lenses. He warmed up by putting three or four into the backstop. You didn't even want to step into the box against him. Ryne might walk the bases loaded, then turn around and strike out the side. You never knew what you were going to get. Joe was very similar."

Joe's distinction at Charleston—and throughout the minors—was his strength and endurance, his ability to hit and field his position.

"No one worked harder," says Wolf, who later coached the Cincinnati Royals in the NBA. "No one was in better shape. He always gave you innings, and he could hit. You never had to take him out for a pinch-hitter, and he was a great asset in the field.

"It was just that Joe knew one speed: as hard as he could throw it. I've often wondered what kind of career he would have had if he could have learned to keep it over the plate and change speed."

Jim Greengrass was a Yankee prospect in '49, playing with Muskegon in the Central League.

"Joe had that fastball and a hard curve," says Greengrass. "But, because he was so wild, he was always falling behind in the count. Then when he tried a let-up, you usually got something over the plate you could hit. His fastball went flat, and he lost something off the curve. Everybody who faced him would get one or two pitches to hit. Then, if you did get a hit off him, he'd blow up, get mad at himself, and it was generally over. Joe was his own worst enemy. It was too bad someone couldn't help him get over that, because there is no question the man had great ability."

Joe Beggs tried to help. Beggs was Joe's manager at Charleston in 1949 and '50, and he felt a certain kinship with the young pitcher. Beggs was a reliever with the Reds when Joe made his first trip with the club to St. Louis in '43.

Beggs borrowed some of his managerial style from Bill McKechnie. He valued good pitching and tried to cultivate his players' mental approach to the game. Joe had all the ingredients: the work ethic, the drive, and the stuff. The only thing he lacked was control over his emotions. For two seasons, Beggs talked with Joe about his mechanics. He refined his wind-up, and he talked to him about developing a consistent release point.

Beggs, a former schoolteacher, preached control and warned Joe that until he learned to dismiss a bad pitch or a bad inning, he would never reach his potential. "Master your temper," Beggs said, "and you will master your control."

"He was my first real pitching coach," Joe says. "He was the first person in pro ball who ever spent any time with me on technique. But, like I say, I was stubborn and I wasn't a very good student."

In 1949, Joe pitched in 28 games for Charleston. He won eight games, lost 10, and posted an earned run average of 3.24. It wasn't a horrible performance, but it certainly wasn't good enough to earn advancement.

The following year, Joe's control was better. He walked 98 in 138 innings. Joe had a better record with Charleston (10-9), but he gave up far too many hits and runs. His ERA was 4.83 and he was beginning to get frustrated.

"I was giving serious thought to quitting," Joe says. "It just didn't seem like it was working out and I didn't feel like I was getting any better."

Joe figured he could make a good living in Hamilton. He could play in the Shop Leagues and wouldn't have to worry about the travel and all the headaches that seemed to come with pro ball.

He is certain, left to his own inclinations, he would have given up. But one person intervened, the person who had become the most important influence in his life.

"Donzetta," he says. "Donzetta talked me out of it. She just said things were beginning to get better and the money was improving and if we just hung in there awhile longer, it would all work out."

"It just seemed crazy to me that after all the work he had put in to just walk away," Donzetta says. "Besides, Joe had never been a quitter. There was no sense to start then, not when he had gone so far."

"At first, I didn't want to listen to her," Joe says. He pauses and smiles, as if embarrassed. "Kind of glad I did though, 'cause things did work out pretty well. She's always been the one with the brains in the family."

Apparently, she was also the motivator. Not only did Joe go back to spring training in 1951, he demanded more money. He had been assigned to Tulsa, moving up the minor league ladder. The general manager was Grayle Howlett.

"He was offering me $500 a month and I wanted $600 and I wasn't about to bend," Joe says. "'Well,' he says, 'come on down and I'm sure we can work this out.' I told him I would, but I had to have $600 a month. Ten wins and I'm crying for a raise, and just months ago I was ready to quit.

"Now the thing is—I have just enough money to get down there," Joe says. "Wasn't a good winter, financially. 'Course, few were. So, I take off. It's a two-day drive. I got this '42 Buick. I make it to Memphis the first day, sleep awhile, and take off the next day. By the time I get to Alexandria and walk into the Bentley Hotel and my meeting with Mr. Howlett, I don't have a dime to my name. I'm playing the biggest poker game of my life.

"He's sitting there saying he doesn't see how he can pay me $600 a month. I'm saying I can't stay for anything less than that, and all the time I know I don't have enough money or enough gas to even go down the block.

"I'm sweating BBs and trying not to let him know. He's talking about me being barely a .500 pitcher and having that big ERA. I'm thinking, *What the hell am I gonna do?* I'm just about to throw up, when he says, 'Okay, let's compromise. I will meet you halfway, $550.'

"I acted tough and begrudging," Joe says. "But I was never more relieved in my life. I had a job and I had a raise."

THAT SPRING, JOE WAS ASSIGNED TO TULSA. This time he would stick, and he would get a little more help. The manager there was more demanding than Beggs.

"Al Vincent, one tough son of a gun," Joe says.

Vincent was perfect for the rough run of the Texas League. "Kind of a no-nonsense guy," Joe says. "And he let me know about it right now. He helped me get my act together. I remember him yelling one day, 'Damnit, Joe, I don't care if we got a 10-run lead in the fifth inning. You start losing it and I'm pullin' ya out of the game. I don't care if ya got a 10-run lead with two outs in the ninth, lose your temper and you are coming out of the game.'

"He was true to his word, too. He definitely got my attention. But that didn't exactly cure the problem. No, sir. That continued for quite awhile."

Vincent ran Joe to the mound regularly and yanked him at the first sign of his temper. Joe had damaged dugouts and clubhouses throughout the league, kicking and slamming his way through the season. But Vincent's tactics led him to his most productive year in the minors. Joe won 13 games—more than he had won at any stop from Birmingham to Oklahoma, and he was named to the Texas League All-Star team.

"I remember coming back home after that season and walking down the street," Joe says, smiling. "Finally, I could hold my head up high and when someone asked me how I had done that year I could say, 'Won 13 games!'

"Yeah, 13 games. I didn't tell them I lost 22. Real good year, hunh?"

But something else had been achieved that season. It wasn't apparent in the statistics, and it escaped Joe's attention entirely. And no one involved felt the need to tell him anything about it.

By mid-season 1951, Joe's name was coming up frequently in the intelligence reports Gabe Paul received from the minor leagues. Everyone who saw him pitch at Tulsa was impressed. Control was an issue, but Joe had improved. Enough, in fact, that other clubs were sending scouts to see Joe play, and their numbers were mounting. Nothing warmed a ball club to a player more than another team's attentions to his ability.

Paul was in his first year as GM. Warren Giles, passed over as commissioner, had been named National League president, paving the way for his longtime friend's promotion.

Paul's career had begun as a teenage bat boy with the Rochester club in the International League where he tended rabbits for the third baseman, kept all the bats uncrossed so as to assuage the manager's superstitions, and secured frozen baseballs for the team. The balls were then worked opportunely into play, the manager happily watching on as the lifeless cowhide died quietly in the infield or fell inertly into the waiting gloves of his outfielders.

JOE NUXHALL
pitcher CINCINNATI REDS

STAR TREATMENT—IN 1952, JOE MADE THE BIG TEAM,
THEN IN HIS FIRST OUTING, HE PITCHED THREE SHUTOUT INNINGS, THUS
OFFICIALLY ESCAPING FROM TULSA.

Paul had been hired in Rochester by Giles, who had brought him to Cincinnati as his Man Friday. They were, as Lee Allen pointed out, "an admirably efficient pair," the baseball equivalent of, say, Butch Cassidy and Sundance.

Paul was a tall, impressive man with an easy, engaging smile. In conversation, he often adjusted his shirt sleeves, making sure that just enough silk showed beneath his suit jacket, his hands gracefully moving to his cufflinks or his watch, all tasteful in selection.

Much of this had been inspired by Giles, who, though portly in stature, always prided himself on appearance. Now Giles had moved on. The difficulties they once shared would belong largely to Paul. And Paul had not inherited much of a club. The burden of leadership was assuaged by his guiding maxim. "The great thing about baseball," he would say, "is there's a crisis every day."

The Reds won 68 games in 1951 and finished sixth in the National League standings for the second straight year. Though Ted Kluszewski was a rising star, the team didn't have a .300 hitter in the starting lineup. Four pitchers lost 14 or more games. Willie Ramsdell and Ken Raffensberger lost 17 each and Ewell Blackwell dropped 15.

Attendance wasn't good. Fans were weary of losing and sportswriters clamored for change. Paul entered the off-season determined to put new life into the team.

"Something had to be done," says John Murdough, the Reds' traveling secretary in '52 and later the club's business manager. "We were just scuffling along. Klu and Grady Hatton were about the only players we had to hang our hats on, and our pitching was awful."

The club was short on left-handers. The Reds had Raffensberger and Harry Perkowski, and that was about it.

"So, Joe's name kept coming up in our meetings. Gabe liked him, he always had," Murdough says. "Everybody liked Joe's velocity but there was always that concern about his wildness and his temper. Had the damnedest temper you have ever seen."

While some hedged on Joe, Phil Seghi, director of scouting, raised a critical point. Seghi reminded Paul that Johnny Vander Meer had suffered similar problems early in his career and had gone on to pitch back-to-back no-hitters for the Reds in 1938. From '38 through '48, he won 108 games and had a losing season just three times.

"That kind of sealed it," Murdough says, "that comparison to Vander Meer. They decided to get him back on a Reds contract for the '52

ARMS AND THE MAN—IT HAD TAKEN JOE FOREVER
TO GET BACK TO THE MAJORS. HE WOULD NOT CONTEMPLATE ANOTHER
RETURN TO THE MINOR LEAGUES.

season. Gabe and Phil thought if they could get him into camp and maybe smooth out the edges, he would be an asset."

In October of 1951, Joe was given a big league contract and an invitation to spring training in Tampa. Still, nothing was guaranteed.

"I wasn't really surprised to be invited to spring training," Joe says. "I'd had a pretty good year with Tulsa and I knew some other teams were interested in me. But I still had to make the team."

MAKING A TEAM IN SPRING TRAINING involves many things: skill, opportunity, and team needs. And it never hurts to have a friend in high places.

Major league baseball teams have forever claimed to be impervious to the press, but nothing is further from the truth and that was particularly so in the 1950s. Radio reporters were not yet aswarm in the clubhouse, and television was in its infancy. The daily press and *The Sporting News* brought the game to the people.

In the '50s, baseball writers began to abandon the distant, eloquent approach of Damon Runyon and Grantland Rice, forging their way into the clubhouse for first-hand comments on what had taken place in a game. For the first time, players were confronted with a scrutiny that had never before accompanied their celebrity.

Among the practitioners of this new reporting was Earl Lawson, who began his career with the *Cincinnati Times-Star* at the age of 17 as a copyboy. Two years later, at the height of World War II, he enlisted in the Army.

He was sent to the Pacific Theater, where he won the Bronze Star for valor in battles at Leyte and Okinawa. He returned to the *Times-Star* in 1946 as a member of the sports department. Five years later, he was covering the Reds full time, replacing "Pop" Grayson.

Lawson was a feisty sort, dogged in his pursuit of a story, a quality that eventually earned him the nickname, "Scoops." Some players liked Earl, others did not, and usually the delineating line was performance. To Kluszewski and Hatton, he was a welcome friend. To those who struggled and failed to meet their potential, he had another nickname: "Poison Pen."

After the Philippines, he feared nothing and no one in baseball. He had crawled though mud and carnage to emerge in what he viewed as a wonderful life.

He had a talent for describing the game and its people. He took his readers into that living room of privilege, the clubhouse. He was not quick to criticize. In fact, he was especially sensitive to the tests players faced. But he was always analytical and honest.

"Earl was a good man," says Ed Bailey, a catcher who joined the Reds in 1953. "Good writer, too. I always got along with him—for the most part. But I'll say this about him. He wanted to be the manager and the general manager. He was always politicking. We should do this. We should do that. This guy should be playing and this guy shouldn't. That was just Earl. Most of the time, we let it go in one ear and out the other, but management listened to him—not all the time, but often. He had their ear. No question about that."

ONE OF THOSE TIMES was the spring of 1952 when young Nuxhall showed up in training camp and barreled his way through every workout. If there was one thing Lawson loved, it was effort and those who stretched the limits of their ability.

He watched Joe closely. He watched him in games and workouts. He noted his intensity in drills. He saw Joe do extra running when others had called it a day. Earl wrote about Joe's long road: from his major league debut in 1944, his demotion to the minors, his high school heroics, and his return to the big league camp.

They talked at the ballpark and the team hotel, The Floridan, in downtown Tampa, which was not far from the river and Ybor City, where they rolled some of the finest cigars in the states and you could find the best black bean soup this side of Cuba.

The Floridan was notable for two things. One, its walls were so thin, they were nearly transparent. In some places, they actually were. Upon checking in, the veteran players took note of peep holes located in strategic places. Two, the Floridan's lounge was usually filled with handsome women from all over the area, there to mingle with the players. The hotel called its lounge The Sapphire Room, but the regulars knew it as The Sure-Fire Room.

To Lawson, whatever happened to players there—or elsewhere— was merely background. "You have to know what is going on," he said. "You need to know everything that is playing a part in what's happening on the field. But," he always added, "you never report it until it reaches the police blotter. Then it's public, you report it, and you pity the poor bastard who made such a mistake and jeopardized his career. As bad as you might feel about it, you have to write it. That's the job."

Always mindful that he had one of the best seats in the house, Lawson accurately viewed his position as a privilege. He arrived at the ballpark early and stayed late. His hours were driven by the fear that he might miss something. He knew every hot spot in Tampa, Hillsborough County, and the entire Bay Area. He visited them frequently. He knew who was out late and who was early the next day. All this informed his work.

On a routine day, Lawson was everywhere: the dugout, the clubhouse, the manager's office, and the general manager's office. Players saw him when they went out to eat. He was on the bus, on the train. He was omnipresent.

He didn't exactly interview people, he found a way to involve them in conversation, and then he listened. He had a good ear and he liked what he heard from Joe.

They talked about the team, baseball, and pitching. Joe told him about his marriage and the birth of his first child, Phil, born the previous August. He was in San Antonio for a game and couldn't get home in time to be with his wife for the birth. Neighbors took Donzetta to the hospital. Joe felt guilty and Lawson understood. He tried to tell Joe about the sacrifices that came with the game.

Those days and nights in Tampa forged the foundation of a friendship that would last decades and assist Joe in his career more than once. The spring of '52 was the first occasion.

"This was a guy," says Bailey, "that could help you or he could hurt you and he was always there with his two cents' worth, having his say. Hell's fire, this was a guy who could affect your livelihood. I got along with him fine, but his politicking—that really bothered some players."

While Joe did his work on the field, Lawson cultivated the young left-hander's position with the team. He was a subtle lobbyist who, when taking a cause, offered statements around the batting cage or the dugout.

*"Got to like this kid. Gives it everything he's got every day.
I was out here the other day, after the workout, I saw him doing
extra throwing and some extra running. Has the kid got a chance?"*

"I remember him coming by once in a while and saying, 'I'm working it. I'm working it,'" Joe says. "I honestly don't know how much he helped me in '52. But I know he helped me several times during my career."

BENCH STRENGTH—THE NUXHALL CLAN SOAKS UP

SOME FLORIDA SUN DURING SPRING TRAINING IN 1953. THAT'S PHIL

IN JOE'S LAP AND KIM AT RIGHT WITH DONZETTA.

As spring training wore on in '52 and the numbers thinned, Joe's position grew stronger. By Opening Day, the roster had to be cut to thirty. In those days, teams were allowed to carry thirty players for the first month of the season. At that point, five players had to be assigned to the minors.

In the final days of camp in Tampa, Joe dug in. He threw himself into every exercise, no matter how tiresome, and grasped every chance he had on the mound. He had no more taste for Tulsa or Charleston. He couldn't stand the thought of going back home as a minor league ballplayer.

"I remember the day they made the final cuts that spring," he says. "Damn, what a day. I was still there. It was one of the best days of my life. It was a good day for all of us: Donzetta, my family. Phil, my first son, wasn't even a year old. Finally, I had made it back and I could do something for all of them.

"I remembered the strangest things that day. I remembered driving home from Tulsa after the season in '51, Phil just a little bitty baby and how hard that was for him and Donzetta."

Back then it made him mad and determined. He wanted more. His family deserved more. It was hot. The road went on forever. He was tired of old cars and bad apartments. He wanted more for Donzetta. She deserved more than washing his socks by hand in the bathroom sink. The more he thought about it, the madder he became. The very emotion that had hobbled him on the field drove him to go forward.

"It was time," he says. "I had to get back and make my place. I had to do that. Finally I could go back and get that third out, the one I didn't get in 1944. Has to be some kind of a record—eight years before a guy gets three outs in the major leagues."

OPENING DAY FOR THE REDS IN '52 was April 15. Herm Wehmeier, a right-hander and a Cincinnati native, was the starter that day. The Reds lost, 6-5, to the Cubs.

Joe opened the season as a relief pitcher and was used sparingly. He made it through the first month of the season when the roster was cut to 25 players. But things were not going well for Luke Sewell's Reds. By mid-May, they were hovering around .500. Paul was not happy because his boss, Powel Crosley, was not happy and Sewell was increasingly under the gun.

On May 9, the Reds began a ten-game road trip that took them to

EARLY JOE—THE MINOR YEARS HAD TAUGHT HIM SOME THINGS. GIVE 'EM WHAT THEY DON'T EXPECT, HE SAID, AND YOU WERE AHEAD OF THE CURVE.

St. Louis, New York and the Polo Grounds for a two-game series, back to Philadelphia for three games, and finally to Brooklyn for a two-game set.

By the time they reached Ebbets Field, the Reds were 3-5 on the trip and 15-13 overall.

On May 21st, they were murdered in Flatbush. It was a humiliating, historic loss for the Reds. Ewell Blackwell started the game and retired the first hitter he faced. Billy Cox grounded out to start the inning.

After that, the pitcher known as "The Whip," 6-foot-6, 195 pounds and a 22-game winner in '47, had no sting and no snap. The Dodgers scored 15 runs in the first inning. A record 19 consecutive hitters came to the plate and reached first base. Pee Wee Reese walked twice and reached base three times in the first inning. Andy Pafko was thrown out trying to steal third base, and Duke Snider struck out to end the inning. The Dodgers' starting pitcher, Chris Van Cuyk, had two hits in the inning.

Blackwell, who had come to Cincinnati in 1942, was nearing the end with the Reds, as were the pitchers who succeeded him in that fateful first inning.

"It was awful," Joe says. "I will never forget it. Guys were hiding in the dugout. It was like watching a car wreck. You want to look away, but you couldn't."

He began to get a familiar feeling. He calmed his mind, and he watched everything happening on the field. He saw which players were hitting what pitches. He had time enough to see tendencies.

Once again, he was told to warm up. This time he didn't trip on the steps of the dugout. He was about to face Reese, Snider, Jackie Robinson, Pafko, Roy Campanella, Carl Furillo, and Gil Hodges. But after eight years and now—just possibly—at an appropriate age, he took the mound with the tools required to pitch at the major league level.

He was learning that pitching was largely a matter of deception. Give them what they didn't expect, and you were ahead of the curve.

"I threw three shutout innings," Joe says. "I was prepared. I had spent all that time in the minors learning that you have to be ready when your chance comes along. In '44, no way was I ready. That day in Brooklyn, that was my chance."

He had learned that a good arm and his father's teachings were not enough. He didn't know it, but he was dabbling in the alchemy of pitching, whose permutations would hold his attention the rest of his life.

The Reds lost that game, 19-1. Their only run was scored on a homer by reserve catcher Dixie Howell. The next day they lost again. Brooklyn beat the Reds, 8-7. The humbled Reds left New York. Their record was 15-and-15. The train ride back to Cincinnati was quiet. Blackwell said nothing. He was too tall to sleep in the berths and too troubled by his disastrous start against the Dodgers.

"When we got home, I had a message to come see Gabe Paul," Joe says. "Well, damn, you can imagine I was scared to death. I figured—this is it—I'm going back to the minors. I go into his office and he's sitting there. I'm shakin' in my boots and he looks at me real hard.

"He says, 'Joe, my mind was made up. When you came back from this road trip, I was gonna send you back to Tulsa. But after what you did against the Dodgers, I changed my mind. You're stayin'.'"

"I had spent all those years in the minors learning and getting ready. At 15, you think you know so much. You think you got so much. And then you find out—you got nothing. You are nowhere close."

Chapter fourteen

Joe hated New York. It was too big and too busy. There were people everywhere at all hours of the day and night. The noise never stopped and the traffic never moved. Crossing the street was like running the football: cut, move, dodge, and for God's sake, keep up. The cabbies were cranky, the subway was hell and—worst of all—there was no place in Manhattan where you could feel the sun on your shoulders.

The only retreat from his disagreeable Gotham bivouac was the ballpark, but gaining entry to the Polo Grounds in Harlem or Brooklyn's Ebbets Field presented another test. Visiting players had to pass through a gauntlet of unruly fans.

"They would beg you for an autograph in one breath and call you an SOB with the next," Joe says. "I don't know how many guys had suits and shirts ruined by those so-and-so's."

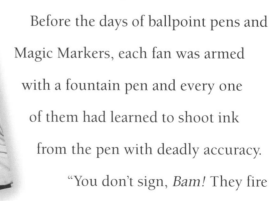

Before the days of ballpoint pens and Magic Markers, each fan was armed with a fountain pen and every one of them had learned to shoot ink from the pen with deadly accuracy.

"You don't sign, *Bam!* They fire

HANGING

DIVE PLAY—JOE TIES SCORE IN 6TH INNING AGAINST PHILLIES ON KLUSZEWSKI'S FLY BALL TO RIGHT IN A 1955 DOUBLE-HEADER. INSET, BOTTOM LEFT, IS GUS BELL, JOE, ROY MCMILLAN, AND TED KLUSZEWSKI.

WITH 'EM

at ya. Like damned squirt guns," Joe says. "Happened all the time. Sumbitches. Ya go out to run before the game or you are out in the bullpen. They are throwin' every word in the book at you and anything they can get their hands on. Pocket change. Beer. You name it. If they could have pulled the seats out, they would have thrown them.

"Then the game's over and they are out there waiting and yelling for your autograph again...."

NEW YORK. NUMBERED STREETS. Numbered avenues. Some ran north and south. Some ran east and west. But which ones went which way? He could never get it straight. There was Midtown and Uptown. There was Lower Manhattan, the East Side, the West Side, but where was Tribeca and what the hell was Soho?

Joe heard about The Village but nothing he saw looked like a village. He heard about Central Park but was told not to go there. Why on earth, he wondered, should you stay away from a park?

It was just too complicated for him. He liked things simple. He hated New York but he did love to eat, and he could usually find his meal of choice—a thick steak, a baked potato, and an ice-cold beer—without straying far from his hotel. He could always find some small place where he could throw back a Manhattan, which was his only affinity with this uninhabitable place.

For Joe, eating was a blessed avocation. For his teammate, Roy McMillan, eating was a grievous obligation, a formal contract to which he was held by his noodle-thin body.

Mac was built like a rope, 5-foot-11 and 170 pounds on his heaviest day. He made the club in 1951 and quickly became one of the finest fielding shortstops of his time. He had a sense for the ball. He knew the hitters and his arm was better than most. But the grind of the season and the position took its toll on his body.

"Wearing those flannels, guys would lose eight, ten pounds in the course of a game, and on Sunday doubleheaders it was more than that," Joe says.

"Roy wore those glasses," says Jim Greengrass, "and as the season went on, he got skinnier and skinnier. He would start shrinking in his suit until he began to look like a professor. But the man was one helluva shortstop. He did things in the field that took your breath away."

"One time he got hit in the first game of a doubleheader," John Murdough says. "The ball knocked some of his front teeth loose. We

KEEPING UP HIS STRENGTH—FROM HIS DAYS IN THE MINORS, JOE KNEW WHERE TO FIND A GOOD MEAL. SAID BERNIE STOWE: "HE WAS A GOOD MAN TO FOLLOW IF YOU WERE HUNGRY."

took him to the dentist and the dentist said the teeth would have to come out and they would make him a plate. Mac said, 'We'll do it tomorrow.' So we went back to the park and played the second game."

IN 1952, THE REDS STAYED at the Biltmore Hotel in New York. One night after a game, Mac and Joe went out late to get something to eat. Joe was working as a relief pitcher, drawing a start here and there.

"I wasn't exactly shining," Joe says, "but I was doing okay. We're walking back from the restaurant and Roy challenged me. We stopped right there on the street and talked. He said, 'Joe, you never pitch inside. You never drive people off the plate.'

"Fact was, I didn't 'cause I never knew where the hell I was gonna throw the ball. I didn't want to kill somebody.

"So Roy says, 'That's not going to work, Joe. You got to own the plate, all of it. You got to get 'em off the inside corner. Otherwise, you will never last at this level.'

"I listened to him because I trusted Roy, and I knew in my heart he was right. Well, right there in New York—the city I loved so much— I changed. I wasn't the same pitcher after that."

Joe stuck with the club the entire season. His record was 1-4. He made five starts, pitched two complete games, and his ERA was a respectable 3.22. He walked only 42 in 92^1/$_3$ innings. But in spite of his Manhattan epiphany, he was still subject to fits of both wildness and temper.

The Reds had three managers that season. Luke Sewell was fired after 98 games when the Reds were 39-59. Earle Brucker was hired on an interim basis for five games, then Gabe Paul hired Hall of Famer Rogers Hornsby.

Hornsby began his big league career with the Cardinals in 1915. Seven times he led the league in hitting and three times he hit over .400. Nine times he led the league in slugging percentage. He was a two-time MVP and led the Cards to their first World Championship in 1926. Besides the Cardinals, he managed Boston and the Cubs. He managed the Browns from '33 through '37, then worked in the minors before returning to the Browns to start the '52 season. His player pedigree was beyond reproach, but few liked him as a manager.

"He was a son-of-a-bitch," says Murdough. "He didn't like anybody who wasn't of his era. He would mutter and cuss. He thought the players were soft. He called Kluszewski and Grady Hatton 'college boys,' and said he had no use for them. If you weren't a 'college boy,' you were a 'no good politician.' He didn't have anything good to say about anyone."

Especially pitchers. Hornsby hated pitchers. He couldn't understand someone who worked only once every four games. Pitchers had been his victims. In the large-format photograph of all those who failed to meet Hornsby's standards, pitchers were in the back, standing on tip-toe. Of the microscopic allotment of respect he reserved for others, pitchers deserved the smallest portion. He wouldn't establish a rotation, and once he changed starting pitchers while his first choice was warming up.

Hornsby didn't allow newspapers in the clubhouse, books, magazines, card games, or radios. Reading, he said, was bad for the eyes. When he was a player, he wouldn't go to movies and it was said he refused to look out of train windows.

He was openly hostile toward black players, but his vulgarity was nonpartisan. After games, while the players showered, Hornsby would walk in, soap up, and urinate on the floor.

Player representative Grady Hatton lodged a formal complaint with Gabe Paul, who tried desperately to stay out of disputes between the players and the manager. Hatton told Paul he understood his normal stance but this was something he had to confront.

"From the look on Gabe's face," Hatton said later, "I didn't know if he was going to laugh or cry."

Paul ordered signs posted: *Please Don't Urinate In The Shower.*

"THE PLAYERS," EARL LAWSON ONCE SAID, "absolutely hated this shower-pissing son-of-a-bitch and why wouldn't they? He treated them like dirt. He was the only bleeping soul in the world who knew anything about the game."

He was belittling and belligerent and loved to talk about what he had done in his career. The team's main draw was Kluszewski, a gray-eyed giant of a man whose intellect and popularity posed a threat to Hornsby.

Yet every time Kluszewski's name came up with Paul, Hornsby would say, "We ought to trade the big lazy Polack." Kluszewski was a graduate of Indiana University. In his idle time, he read books. Hornsby didn't like books.

Shortly after hiring Hornsby, Paul became aware he had made a mistake.

Paul asked him once why he had sold his investment properties in Chicago. Hornsby told him the "kikes" were moving in all over the place. Hornsby had no idea that Paul was Jewish. Paul said nothing, but he began to understand why Browns owner Bill Veeck had fired Hornsby: Every time he opened his mouth, he exposed himself.

"I don't like to sound egotistical," he once said, "but every time I came to the plate with a bat in my hands, I couldn't help but feel sorry for the pitcher."

Asked about golf, Hornsby said, "When I hit a ball, I want someone else to go chase it."

His place was the ballpark. It may have been his only place. On the road, he often ordered the bus to leave hours before its scheduled departure. When players were left behind and objections raised, he glowered and said, "We're on Hornsby time now."

Murdough complained to Paul about the practice and it stopped. But it was one in a long line of incidents that led Hornsby to refer to Murdough as "that fat little stoolie."

Hornsby had not played since 1937 but he continued to hit and play catch nearly every day. In '52, Hornsby was 56 years old. "And he could still rope," Joe says. "I can remember being at the Polo Grounds. He's out there bouncing balls one-hop, two hops off the wall in centerfield. It was 455 feet."

"One day," Bernie Stowe says, "I'm just a kid, a bat boy, and he asked me to play catch. So we go on the field and I'm trying to do the best I can. I'm a little guy, but I'm trying. He just stops. Walks away and says, 'You throw like a c---.' Everybody hated him."

AND YET HORNSBY PLAYED A ROLE in the advancement of Joe's career. While Hornsby didn't like pitchers, he did like players who worked hard and stayed out of his way. He knew Nuxhall from the Texas League. Hornsby had spent some time with Beaumont while Joe was playing for Tulsa. He didn't think much of Nuxhall's control, but he liked the kid's pluck. He pitched like a player, he ran the bases hard, and he wasn't bad with the bat.

Nuxhall was acceptable, although Hornsby would never tell him he was. In the spring of '53, Hornsby was trying to come up with a fourth starting pitcher, but he had few options. Blackwell, at his suggestion, had been traded to the Yankees. He had Harry Perkowski, Ken Raffensberger, tall Bud Podbielan, and then what?

If there was anything Hornsby liked less than pitchers, it was writers. Especially this new breed who strutted into the clubhouse asking why you did this and why you did that? In Cincinnati, he was confronted with a member of the new breed—Earl Lawson.

What bothered Hornsby most about Lawson was that management liked him. They actually listened to what Lawson had to say. They thought he knew something about the game.

As preposterous as it seemed to Hornsby, he was caught in the middle of a relationship between his bosses and this little poodle of a man.

Late in the spring, Lawson continued to push Nuxhall as the fourth member of the rotation. Why not give him a try? he asked. Hornsby said nothing. He wasn't about to let anyone suspect that his judgment could be swayed. His dislike for Lawson was growing. Lawson represented all the changes he abhorred in the game. Other people were trying to tell him what to do. *Him*, Rogers Hornsby, Hall of Famer!

When management suggested Hornsby take a look at Joe as a starter, their relationship worsened. Hornsby complied, however. Lawson was eventually banned from the clubhouse for questioning managerial moves, and Hornsby was fired with eight games left in the season. He would never manage again.

"The guy knew the game inside out," Joe says. "And I was grateful to him for giving me a shot. But as a human being—Christ almighty—you can't go around treating people like that."

"He was an arrogant, self-absorbed ass," Lawson said.

By 1954, "HAMILTON JOE" was gaining popularity with Reds fans. He was on his way to a 12-5 season, and management embraced him as a player to be promoted. "It was about that time we got the idea of having a Hamilton Night for Joe," Murdough says.

"We never dreamt we would get the response we did. My God, if there was anyone left in Hamilton or Butler County I would have been surprised. The traffic was ridiculous. Buses and cars were everywhere; they lined up for blocks, and all the way around the stadium.

"It was then we realized how much this guy was loved. Now don't get me wrong, Joe was a good pitcher, but he was no Warren Spahn. Yet the people loved him—especially in the mid '50s—and that made a hell of an impression on everyone in the front office."

With Donzetta at his side and Phil, his first child, in his arms, Joe was honored in pre-game ceremonies. The crowd cheered and screamed his name over and over again. Each time he spoke, the crowd cheered louder. Adoration filled the air at Crosley, and Phil remembers being scared to death.

"As a child, seeing thousands of people screaming and clapping for your father was really frightening," Phil says.

In the mid-1950s, Joe was part of the one of the most popular teams in Reds' history. They didn't always win, but they were competitive, and their power and personality delighted fans around the league.

George Robert Tebbetts had been hired to replace Rogers Hornsby. He made his name as a serviceable catcher with Detroit and Boston, and was just two years away from his playing career. He was squat and jovial, nicknamed "Birdie," according to the popular accounts, because of his high voice and chirping laugh.

In college, he had given up pre-med when he found that lab work conflicted with baseball practice. Still, he almost graduated *cum laude*. "All I needed were a few percentage points," he said, "and I lost those in a couple of dance halls in Providence."

He was comfortable with the press and popular with the players. He had a cocktail at night, a smile in the morning, and he was a soothing poultice on the wounds inflicted by Hornsby.

He also had a better club than Hornsby. Kluszewski was a fixture at first and in '54 led the league in home runs with 49. Johnny Temple, an exquisite fielder at second, had come up from the minors. With McMillan at short, the Reds had one of the best double play combinations in baseball.

Chuck Harmon, the Reds' first black ballplayer, shared time at third base with Bobby Adams, who was so enthusiastic about being in the big leagues he worked in the Reds' ticket office during the off-season.

Sturdy Jim Greengrass, picked up from the Yankees in the Blackwell trade, was in the outfield, and Gabe Paul had acquired outfielder Gus Bell from the Pirates after the '52 season. He was an All-Star the following year and reminded people of DiMaggio, seemingly effortless with the glove and at the plate.

Wally Post, who began his career as a pitcher, had developed into one of the best power hitters in the organization, and slugged his way into the starting lineup. The skill he had shown as a minor league pitcher helped him become a feared major league defender.

"Everyone always talked about Wally's power, but he had one of the best arms I have ever seen," Joe says. "No one was more accurate.

HAMILTON NIGHT—ORVILLE AND NAOMI (AT LEFT) CELEBRATED WITH JOE AND DONZETTA, ALONG WITH A SOMEWHAT RELUCTANT PHIL.

The infielders seldom had to move the glove. Wally put it right there."

And a new catcher was on board as well, a tough-talking Army veteran and college graduate named Edgar Lonas Bailey, from Strawberry Plains, Tennessee, whose country drawl belied his intelligence and perception.

Of all his players, Tebbetts, a former catcher, rode Bailey the hardest. "Oh, son-of-a-bitch, he never got off me," Bailey says. "But he did it for one reason. He wanted to make me better and he never did it in a demeaning way. Birdie was nothing like Hornsby. With Birdie, it was always about the team."

While the Reds were building a powerful lineup, pitching remained an issue. In '54, they had no one who approached 20 wins. Joe, Art Fowler, and Corky Valentine each won 12 games. Beyond those three, the Reds were largely destitute. The '54 Reds were 74-80. They finished

SPRING BREAK—

THE BABE—ZAHARIS—HOLDS COURT
IN TAMPA, ENCIRCLED BY YOGI BERRA
(AT LEFT) BIRDIE TEBBETTS, CASEY
STENGEL, AND JOE.

in fifth place and went home to watch the Giants sweep Cleveland in the World Series.

From '53 to '54, Reds' attendance had jumped over 155,000. There was a new optimism surrounding the ball club. "We weren't winning that much," Murdough says, "but the people could sense there was something special about this group."

"I played for fourteen years," Bailey says, "and I was never on a team that had better chemistry. When everybody gets along well, it's easy to go about your work, and it shows on the field.

"Hell's fire, we traveled together, played together, and when we were home in Cincinnati and had an off day, we would end up at Joe's or Gus Bell's house grilling steaks, having a few beers, and just talking."

The Reds had power, defense, and the chemistry to become a winner. The only thing they needed was pitching.

IN 1955, EVERY TEAM HAD AN ACE. Robin Roberts won 23 games for the fourth-place Phillies. Milwaukee had Spahn. Brooklyn, the eventual pennant winner, had 20-game winner Don Newcombe.

The Reds' ace was Joe Nuxhall. He won 17 games that season. Only Roberts and Newcombe won more. His five shutouts led the league and he made his first appearance in the All-Star game. He pitched $3^{1}/_{3}$ innings of shutout ball at Milwaukee's County Stadium that day, setting up the Braves' Gene Conley for the victory. Conley struck out the side in the 12th and Stan Musial hit a home run in the bottom of the inning to give the National League a 6-5 win.

Joe established himself in 1955, but it wasn't enough for the Reds. Art Fowler was the only other pitcher who won more than 10 games.

The Reds continued to delight fans with the long ball. Kluszewski hit 47 home runs, Wally Post had 40, Gus Bell hit 27, and Smoky Burgess, who had come over from the Phillies in a trade, had 20. Yet the Reds were still a fifth-place club. Brooklyn ran away with the pennant.

Brooklyn's pitching was notable. Beyond Newcombe, there was Carl Erskine, Johnny Podres, and tireless Clem Labine in the bullpen, all of whom benefited from the lineup Branch Rickey put together.

"They had Pee Wee Reese always getting on base," Joe says. "They had Duke Snider for power—only guy who ever hit a grand slam off me. They had Roy Campanella, one of the best-hitting catchers before Johnny Bench came along; Carl Furillo, another .300 hitter; and, of course, Jackie.

FAMILIAR PICTURE—JOE DEBATES UMPIRE KEN BURKHARDT, WHO FAILS TO BUY JOE'S REASONING AND TOSSES HIM IN THE FIRST INNING OF A GAME WITH THE CUBS.

"Geez, Jack changed everything," he says, "and I'm not just talking about the obvious, breaking the color line. The man changed the game and the way it was played.

"He would get a base hit or a walk, bunt his way on, and there you are on the mound watching him at first base. He's dancing back and forth. He's just begging you to make a mistake. Drove me crazy.

"You throw over and you think you got him. You didn't have him. Never had him. Then some guy hits a weak single or a right-side grounder, and he's gone. He's taking two bases and maybe three and forcing the fielders to make a play. Some times they did. Most times they didn't, because no one before Jack ever did the things he did.

"He elevated the game. He made it faster, made it better, and then guys like Willie Mays came along and took it even further. But Jack, by God, he earned everybody's respect. Maybe they didn't want to admit it, but he did.

"You couldn't watch the man play and know the things he went through and was going through and not respect him. We learned something from him—even the guys who didn't want him around and, believe me, there were a lot of 'em and years after he broke in. Hell, our guys, starting with Chuck Harmon, they went through hell. It wasn't fair. It wasn't right, but what the *bleep* are you gonna do? That was the way it was back then. Thank God it changed 'cause it was wrong."

Joe did not understand segregation. He had never really confronted that division in American society until he was sent to Birmingham in '44. It was foreign and somehow frightening. He didn't like the anger. The jokes made him uncomfortable.

Back home in Hamilton there was separatism, but it ended at Ford's Fields and the basketball court.

IN 1956, JOE WENT TO CAMP EARLY where he was met with extraordinary press reports in which he barely recognized himself.

Birdie Tebbetts was a good manager, but he was a better salesman. When Arthur Daley of the *New York Times* caught up with him in March, the Reds manager spun a giddy tale of transformation and success.

Birdie told Daley how, in 1954, he had talked Nuxhall out of his temper tantrums and pitching coach Tom Ferrick taught him a slider. Birdie sang on. Nuxhall won 12 games, then 17 the next year, earning a spot in the All-Star game and, damn, how he wowed them in Milwaukee: three hits, two walks, and five strikeouts in $3^1/_3$ innings.

GOOD FORM—IN 1955, PITCHING COACH TOM FERRICK TAUGHT JOE

A SLIDER, THEN STOOD BY WHILE JOE PRACTICED IT OFF THE MOUND.

THE ALL-STARS OF '57—

THAT'S JOE AT LEFT, WITH GUS BELL,
BROOKS LAWRENCE, TED KLUSZEWSKI,
BIRDIE TEBBETTS, ED BAILEY, FRANK
ROBINSON, JOHNNY TEMPLE, AND ROY
MCMILLAN. REDS FANS VOTED IN MOST
OF THE STARTING LINEUP.

"I don't know how Joe can miss as a 20-game winner this year," Birdie told Daley. "He has what he needs. He's almost as fast as Newcombe, is an agile fielder despite his 220 pounds, and is a solid hitter. He belted seven homers last year, two of them winning games."

Daley wrote a column praising Nuxhall while referring to Tebbetts as "a con artist supreme," and Tebbetts' prediction was somewhat off. The slider was a valuable asset and Joe did throw hard, but his temper was barely restrained. Joe won 13 games and lost 11. Along the way, he kicked, stomped, and defeated one clubhouse after another. He was also an All-Star for a second straight year.

The fans were wild about the team. The Reds chased Brooklyn and Milwaukee all season, remaining within striking distance of the pennant until the final days. They finished in third place just two games behind Brooklyn and one game behind Milwaukee, and with their 221 home runs, they tied a Major League record.

Rookie Frank Robinson, signed by Bobby Mattick, Joe's coach back in Birmingham, led the team with 38 and was named National League Rookie of the Year. Kluszewski hit 35, Bell had 29, and Bailey 28. But Joe's best friend, Wally Post, was the most prodigious.

Post hit 36 home runs that season and pulled so many over the scoreboard in left field that he was quickly one of the best-dressed men in all of major league baseball.

Post owed his sartorial splendor to the Siebler Tailoring Company, whose management had placed a sign high atop a laundry beyond the left field scoreboard. *Hit the sign; win a suit.* Post dressed in blues, grays, blacks, tans, and olive greens. His ties were smart. His shoes were shined. He was immaculate, and the fans loved him. The folks at Siebler Tailoring liked him most when he was on the road.

"And to think," Donzetta says. "the first time Joe introduced him to me back in Muncie he was wearing these horrible orange shoes."

EVERYBODY HIT HOME RUNS IN 1956. Joe had two. At the end of the season, every player was given a ring. They were simple flat gold, engraved with the number 221. Joe lost his some years later. He thinks it fell down the sink.

"He didn't lose much," Murdough says. "We had a connection with a jeweler in town. I think he made them for $10 apiece. Hell, I lost mine, too. Bernie Stowe said he lost his and I gave him mine to get a copy made. I think the little shit still has it."

SWEET HOME—JOE SLIDES SAFELY ACROSS THE PLATE IN A 1957 GAME WITH MILWAUKEE AS CATCHER DEL RICE WAITS PATIENTLY FOR THE THROW FROM HENRY AARON.

They were young, happy, and popular. Life was moving fast. They bought nice cars and nice homes, and in 1957 they were at the center of the universe. They were also at the center of a controversy.

The Cincinnati fans believed there was no one better than their boys. In All-Star voting that year, they voted again and again. When the balloting was done, a Reds player had been elected to seven of eight starting positions. Only Stan Musial withstood the fervor of Reds fans.

Commissioner Ford Frick stepped in and kicked Post and Bell off the team in order to make room for Willie Mays and Hank Aaron. In the interest of the game, Frick took All-Star voting away from the fans and handed it back to the players, managers, and coaches. The fans would not have a part in All-Star voting again until 1970.

By that time Joe's career was in decline. Joe won 31 games and lost 30 from 1957 through 1959, and while he began to fall from favor with the fans, his reputation in the game was never in question.

"This was a guy who came at you hard every time he had the ball," says Hall of Famer Billy Williams, who came up with the Cubs. "When I broke in, Joe was straight at you. Over-the-top fastball. Hard curve. Hard slider. You knew what you were going to get and you best be ready. He never let up when, in fact, he would have been better served had he mixed things up."

Bill Giles, now chairman of the Philadelphia Phillies, was then the GM's kid in the Reds' front office, stuffing envelopes and running errands for his father.

"Joe had great stuff," Giles says. "But he was a perplexing sort. No one worked harder, and you couldn't find a nicer guy. But he never won as many games as we all thought he would. He was such a competitor and he was so driven, yet those same qualities were also a detriment to his career. He would get so angry with himself."

Willie Lee McCovey was a big, easy-going first baseman from Mobile, Alabama. He was 6-foot-4, weighed over 200 pounds, and whipped the bat around like a broomstick. He was an imposing figure who spent his career lashing home runs and line drives against the best pitchers in baseball. He hit 521 home runs in his career and was elected to the Hall of Fame in 1986.

"The first time I saw Joe I was scared to death," McCovey says. "He was a big man and he had this way of looking at you when he was out on the mound. He used to just stare at Willie Mays. Stand there and hold the ball for the longest time.

"Willie would step out of the box and say, 'Joe what you looking at? Come on and throw the ball.' Well, I knew nothing about the guy. I was a rookie and we had Willie Kirkland and Leon Wagner on our team. They were both left-handed hitters like me so I go ask 'em about Joe.

"They said he was one of the meanest, nastiest guys around. Said he hated left-handed hitters and hated it when he gave up a hit to a left-hander.

"I took that to heart and for the longest time I didn't do any good at all against him. Finally, we're at Candlestick, playing the Reds, and he's pitching. He comes in with the fastball and I get him. Hit a home run.

"So I'm headed to first base but the whole time I'm wanting to look over my shoulder 'cause I was sure that he was gonna come off that mound after me. Looking back, it's kinda funny 'cause I later found out Joe was one of the nicest guys in the world—until the game started. Man hated to lose as much as anybody I ever saw."

IN 1960, JOE HAD A DREADFUL SEASON. He appeared in 38 games. He won one. He lost eight. His earned run average was 4.42 and he was booed relentlessly.

"Oh, they let me have it but good," Joe says. "I couldn't stick my head out of the dugout without being booed. Hitler would have gotten a better reception at Crosley Field than I did. But they had a right. I was horseshit. No question about it."

"The fans were unmerciful," says Bailey. "I'd never seen anything like it. Seemed like the Cincinnati fans were harder on their own—guys from that area—than they were on any of the rest of us.

"It was the same way with Herm Wehmeier. The guy was a helluva pitcher and they booed him right out of town. Drove him crazy. I often thought that if he and Joe had played in another city, things might have been completely different."

Joe had been booed before and heartily. In Columbia, fans booed when he came out to warm up. But in 1960, it was different. Much of it was mean-spirited. Donzetta stopped attending games when Joe was scheduled to pitch.

"I'm as stout-hearted as anyone," he said at the time. "But when you keep hearing them, it's going to get to you. Anyone who says it doesn't is just kidding himself.

"At first, you don't mind it much. It's their right to boo if they want to, you say. Then it keeps getting louder and louder. It hurts when you know you're doing your best. You begin trying too hard. And when you do that, it's just as bad as not trying at all."

Joe's treatment by the fans did not go unnoticed in the Reds' front office, where team owner Powel Crosley never interfered with management.

"He was too busy with all his other businesses, the radio station, all those things," Murdough says. "He didn't know the ballplayers and he didn't want to get to know them. Well, even *he* gets involved. I don't know if he was at a game or read something. Anyway, he calls Gabe Paul one day and says, 'I don't know anything about Nuxhall other than he is supposed to be a great guy. But you have to do something. This is not good for him or his family and it's not good for the ballclub.' Mr. Crosley getting involved was completely out of character.

"That kind of pushed things. Hell, we all felt the same way. Everybody liked Joe and it was awful seeing him go through something like this. He kept his head up, didn't say anything, but we knew it was getting to him."

ON JULY 26, NATIONAL LEAGUE President Warren Giles fined Nuxhall $250 and suspended him five days for an altercation with umpire Ed Vargo. Joe was pitching against the Cubs at Wrigley Field. George Altman hit a ground ball to Gordy Coleman at first. Joe raced off the mound to cover the bag. When Vargo called Altman safe, an enraged Joe barreled into the umpire. Manager Fred Hutchinson ran from the dugout to the field to restrain his pitcher. He did so but only with help from Coleman and second baseman Billy Martin.

"When the umpire made no sign," Joe said, "I went toward Altman to tag him. The fact he tried to elude me seems to indicate he thought he missed the base. But when the umpire ruled him safe, I blew my cork."

Everyone knew about Joe's temper, but this seemed extreme. Paul began attempts to trade Joe.

After the 1960 season, Bill DeWitt, Sr., former owner of the Browns, succeeded Paul as general manager. Paul left the organization to lay the groundwork for the expansion Houston Colt .45's. DeWitt continued the efforts to trade Nuxhall, but there was little interest. In the meantime, Murdough, as business manager, started contract negotiations with Joe. In January, Murdough and Nuxhall concluded a deal for the 1961 season.

"It was one of the worst days of my life," Murdough says. "I had just done the deal with Joe, but I didn't have a chance to tell Bill about it. He walks in the office and it's early. I tell him I got the contract from Joe. He says, 'Oh, no. I traded him to Kansas City last night.'

"So I got to call Joe. I get Donzetta on the phone and tell her what's going on. She says, 'Joe is not gonna be happy about this.'

"Joe takes the phone and, my God, he goes off. He calls me every name in the book. I've never been cussed out like that in my life.

"We were doing it for his own good, but he had a right to be mad. In those days, you never signed a guy before you traded him. They went to the other club, worked out a new contract, and usually got a nice bonus. Joe didn't have that opportunity. But that's not why he was mad. He didn't want to leave. This was home. He had a family, two young sons.

"I didn't see Joe for about a year after that. I didn't want to. I was afraid of what he might do or say. God, he was mad at me. I think he finally got over it, though. I hope he did, anyway. Worst thing about it was—we win the pennant the very next year. That killed him."

"It was the best damn thing for him," Bailey says. "Go somewhere and get a fresh start. Clear his head. Ol' Knucklehead. I told him that at the time. Wouldn't listen. But it ended up turning his career around."

The transformation, however, was not immediate. Joe spent a lackluster season with Charlie Finley's Athletics, winning five games and losing eight. Kansas City lost 100 games that season and finished the season tied for last with Washington. Joe spent an inordinate amount of time looking at the Reds' box scores.

HE HAD TO ADMIT THE REDS had good young pitchers: Jim O'Toole, Joey Jay, Bob Purkey, and Jim Maloney coming along; Bill Henry and Jim Brosnan in the bullpen. The Reds had a fine club. The Athletics were awful.

They committed 175 errors that season and gave up 629 bases on balls. The team batting average was .247, which ranked eighth in the American League and—worst of all—the Athletics managed to hit just 90 home runs all season, 27 fewer than the Senators, 150 fewer than the pennant-winning Yankees.

"No power. None," Joe says. "It seemed like weeks would go by and no one would hit a home run. It was bad."

This lack of power truly bothered Finley. He didn't like losing, and he didn't like the fact that his fireworks were being wasted.

"He had these big fireworks set up out beyond center field and they fired 'em off every time somebody hit a home run," Joe says. "These things were huge. I mean cannons.

"There was this grassy hill out in center field. There were no seats there because it was right behind the mound, you know, in the hitter's line of sight. It was so steep they had trouble mowing it. So, Finley brings in these sheep. He just lets 'em loose and they are grazing out there.

"They were kinda pretty to look at. They were all dyed different colors. Anyway, we go days and nobody hits one out. Then we go on a long road trip. Now we're back and the first night somebody hits a home run.

"*Boom! Boom!* The fireworks start going off. One after another. Well, we look and the sheep are scattering. They're running here and there, but one is just rolling down the hill. Damn thing died of a heart attack."

The unfortunate case of the fallen sheep stands as Joe's lasting memory of his days with Kansas City. At the end of the season, Finley gave Joe a wristwatch and a raise. That Christmas he gave him his release.

JOE WASN'T WITHOUT WORK LONG. Baltimore invited him to spring training. He didn't make it through camp with the Orioles, but it may have been the most fortuitous stop of his career. Before the Orioles told him they had no place for him, he learned to throw a change-up.

Harry "The Cat" Brecheen, the former Cardinal pitcher, was working for the Orioles as a coach. He instructed Joe on the fine points of the pitch and praised its benefits.

"He told me it could add years to my career," Joe says. "It took strain off the arm and gave you another tool against the hitters."

Released by the Orioles, Joe's contract was picked up by the Los Angeles Angels. He lasted five games before they cut him. Joe went home to consider his future.

He didn't know that his name was being bandied about in the Reds' front offices. When his name hit the waiver wire a second time in a matter of weeks, DeWitt suggested they give Joe another try.

"Our focus was on winning the pennant again," Murdough says, "and with pitchers, you never know. The thinking was let's bring him back and see if he can help us. Phil Seghi called him that day."

A PAIR OF VOICES—JOE APPROACHED HIS SECOND TOUR OF DUTY AT CROSLEY FIELD WITH TREPIDATION. BUT WAITE HOYT PREPARED HIS WAY. JOE WOULD ALWAYS BE GRATEFUL..

The offer was conditional. Joe would start the season with San Diego in the Pacific Coast League. If he performed well, he would be promoted to the big league roster. Joe accepted the offer but with one provision. He would only go to the PCL as a starting pitcher. Seghi agreed and Joe was moving for the third time that spring.

At age 33, Joe was back in the minors and this time, he was dominant. His record was 9-2. He was not only winning games, he was demonstrating new talents. His control was improved, and his anger was in check.

"A lot of fellows who have been major leaguers figure they don't have to do any work at all when they drop down to the minors," said Don Heffner, Joe's manager in San Diego. "Not Nuxhall. He was the hardest worker I had. He was good for the club, too. Youngsters on the team had to be ashamed of themselves if they didn't put out just as much."

By mid-season the Reds wanted him back.

"I HAD NO IDEA WHAT TO EXPECT," Joe says. "My last days at Crosley weren't, ya know, filled with fond memories. First day back, I'm getting dressed and I am actually nervous. I don't know how the fans are going to react. Time comes to take the field and the reception really surprised me. Everybody was cheering.

"Come to find out Waite Hoyt kinda smoothed the way for me. Guys told me he had been talking about me coming back on the radio for several days. I was always grateful."

"When Joe came back," says Billy Williams, "he was completely different. He was a *pitcher*. He was working it in and out. Changing speeds, mixin' it up, and not giving you much."

"He had either lost a little bit off his fastball or had learned how to take something off," says Willie McCovey. "All of a sudden, he's not the same Joe. He's different and he's giving you problems."

"I got so I could even hit spots," Joe says. "Didn't take long—just 18 years."

Joe finished the season 5-0. His ERA as a starter was 2.45, 3.03 overall, and—strangely enough—he was a self-proclaimed control pitcher.

"I have some reasons for the improved control," Nuxhall told Lawson. "I'm not working as fast as I used to. I'm thinking ahead all the time, trying to set up the batter for a certain pitch. And if I miss on a pitch, I'm not getting mad at myself. That's what I used to do. I'd always wind up trying to fog the ball past a hitter."

THE FOLLOWING SPRING, a crew cut kid was trying to make it with the Reds. He didn't think, as he put it, "that I had a chance in hell."

The position he played was already taken. He wasn't fast and he didn't have much of an arm. But he could hit from both sides of the plate. His sheer enthusiasm for the game made everyone take notice.

Yet Pete Rose found it rough going in the clubhouse.

"No one would talk to me," Rose said. "Here I was, this punk kid, and I'm trying to take Don Blasingame's job. He was one of the most popular guys on the team. The only guys that would talk to me at first were the black guys, Frank Robinson and Vada Pinson.

"But Joe was good to me. He took me aside and told me how things were. He helped me through. Maybe he did it because he came up so young and it was so hard. I don't know.

"But I'll tell ya what, he was the most competitive SOB I ever played with. I know ya hear that a lot. But I'm telling you. I played with some great players: Johnny Bench, Joe Morgan, Tony Perez, Mike Schmidt, Steve Carlton—all Hall of Famers—and Joe was by far the most competitive of all of 'em. He would fight you to the bitter end every day.

"He did it on the mound. Did it at the plate. Hell, he did it on the bases. People talk about *me* sliding in head-first. In 1963, Joe's out there sliding head-first into first, trying to beat out a ground ball. I'm not talking about once. I'm talking all the time.

"C'mon, he's a 34-year-old pitcher for Christ's sake. Now you want to talk about making an impression—that made a *bleeping* impression. You see a guy out there doing stuff like that, you better believe every guy on the team is busting his ass to do the same thing. That's the kind of effect Joe had on the team."

In his first full season back with the Reds, Joe won 15 games and lost eight. His earned run average was 2.61. It was, as Rose says, an incredible comeback.

But to Rose and everybody else on the team, Joe was always a contradiction—strong and controlled one moment, emotional the next.

In 1963, the great Stan Musial, having announced his retirement, was making his final tour through the league. At the time, he held or shared twenty-nine National League records—seventeen Major League marks. He was a seven-time batting champion who held nine All-Star records, including six home runs.

He was honored at every ball park in the league. During pre-game ceremonies at Crosley, Joe sat quietly in the dugout. Then the other players noticed he was crying.

They asked him what was wrong. "I can't believe he is quitting," he said, wiping away his tears. "This is one of the greatest players we will ever see."

Joe pitched that day. It was September 22. Joe struck Musial out in the first inning and, on a fly ball to right, retired him in his next at bat. Musial went to the bench after that. Joe seemed to take no joy in his 5-2 win over the Cardinals, and none in his final success against Musial.

After the game, reporters asked Joe how he had dealt with Musial. Fastballs, he said. They asked him about the first time he had faced The Man, in '44. The writers wanted to hear a note of retribution. But they didn't get it. When Joe drove home that night, he was quiet and sad.

"That was the thing about Joe," Rose says. "He was real. He didn't know how to be phoney. He didn't even know what it meant.

"In '64, we're playing Houston," Rose says. "Ken Johnson starts for them and Joe's pitching for us. Johnson is throwing a no-hitter. But we score in the ninth. I get on with a walk. They make two errors and I score. We win 1-0. Joe gets the win on a four-hit shutout. Johnson loses a frickin' no-hitter.

"We're getting ready to get on the bus and they call over and say Johnson wants the ball 'cause he pitched a no-hitter. Joe stands up and says, 'Screw him! I got the shutout and I got the win. I'm keeping the damn ball.'

"That was Joe. You think you are gonna beat him. The hell you are! And he was like that until the very day he took off the uniform."

BILL DeWITT WAS A MAN OF DETAIL. His approach was to take care of the small things and larger matters would fall in place. One day, he noticed an area in the outfield grass. The more he studied it, the more it resembled a path. Everything around it was green, but this area was turning brown.

He called the grounds crew, but they had no answer. He asked around the front office. Everyone seemed to evade the question.

"Finally, someone told him," Murdough says. "It was Joe. He ran the same path every day. From the left field line to the fence in right-

THREE OF A KIND—JOE SHARES A DUGOUT IN SAN DIEGO
IN 1963 WITH JIM MALONEY AND KEN WALTERS. MALONEY WAS 23-7 THAT
YEAR WITH 265 STRIKEOUTS IN 250 INNINGS.

center, and then back again. He did it over and over every day. He was killing the damn grass."

"Until the day he quit," says Sammy Ellis, who came up with the Reds in '62, "he ran more than any of us. He threw more than any of us. In his late 30's, he was probably in better physical shape than most of us."

"Joe loved the good life," Rose says. "He loved to eat and he loved to have a drink or two, maybe three. I remember one time in Chicago we're coming down Rush Street and there's Joe and Deron Johnson coming out of this bar. Well, Deron's so drunk he couldn't have shit in a ten-acre field, and Joe is not far behind him.

"But here's Joe, trying to fold Deron into this cab. Deron's flopping all over the place. Joe finally just flings him in the back seat and they are gone.

"Next day, Joe is out there early, running at the ballpark and wearing that damn rubber jacket he always wore to sweat off the pounds.

"There were two times you didn't want to be around Joe," Rose continues, "when he was mad—'cause he would clean out the clubhouse—and when he took off that damn rubber jacket. He would take it off and wring it out, and it smelled like a *bleeping* Black Russian. He wrings it out, you got a Long Island Iced Tea right there on the floor. But tell ya what. He was always ready. Living that good life never got in Joe's way like it did with other players. But, my God, did he love to eat. By the time I came up, Joe dealt with his anger in two ways. He would tear up the clubhouse or he would eat.

"Norm Gerdeman was the clubhouse guy in Houston and he had the best spread in the league. He had chicken and steak and fish on Fridays. He always had these great deviled eggs. Hutch looked forward to going to Houston 'cause he loved those eggs."

Gerdeman knew about Hutchinson's appetite for his deviled eggs so he always made more when the Reds came to town. He made *dozens*.

"Joe starts our first day in and he gets knocked out of the game," Rose says. "So he is pissed. He goes to the clubhouse, sits down, and eats all the eggs. Must have been three dozen, maybe four. Joe's in there pounding down eggs like Cool Hand Luke. After the game, Hutch comes in and there are no deviled eggs. He is more pissed at Joe for eating all the eggs than he is about us losing the game. He is raising all kinds of hell. Joe is just sitting there with this sheepish look on his face—belching."

In 1964, the Reds were locked in a tight race with the Phillies and Cardinals. Joe started out strong. He won six games, four of them shutouts, before he jammed his shoulder trying to make a diving tag on San Francisco's Jose Pagan at first base. He didn't help much after that, and the Reds lost the pennant to the Cardinals by one game—on the last day of the season.

That fall, writers and players all wondered if things would have been different had Joe been healthy. But time was beginning to catch up with him. He won 11 games in '65 and six in '66.

In the spring of '67, everybody's favorite teammate was on the bubble. Camp was filled with young left-handed pitchers: Billy McCool, Gerry Arrigo, Teddy Davidson. The club had been sold and Bob Howsam, who had trained under Branch Rickey, was the new general manager. His first official business in his new capacity was showing a fan where the men's room was.

Howsam was a man with foresight and an eye for talent, a congenial man but like his mentor, Rickey, steadfast to the facts. Emotion could never be an obstacle. The players were parts, tools—each a means to a greater end. It was no small irony that his greatest teams were known as The Big Red Machine.

He remembered one Rickey story very well. While Rickey was with the Pirates, he was involved in contract negotiations with Ralph Kiner, who was demanding a raise.

"Why do you think you deserve a raise?" Rickey asked.

"Because I led the league in home runs," Kiner replied.

"And where did we finish?" Rickey said.

"We finished last," Kiner said.

"We can finish last without your home runs," Rickey said.

Howsam wasn't a hard man, but he was a realistic one. His first question—was this a player who could help his team? In mid-April 1967, he asked Joe to come to his office.

"That," Rose said, "was a bad day for everybody."

Chapter fifteen

Teddy Davidson was tall and trim, a good-looking kid on the edge of promise, although in March, there was so much promise in Tampa the ground crew had to sweep it off the infield.

Teddy had more than promise: He had a great fastball, a nasty curveball, and he cheerfully admitted to the occasional use of a spitball. He was considered a classic left-hander, one of that small but irrepressible tribe of hurlers who could provide headline performances, although not always on the field. The geographic fact that he was from Las Vegas made some think that he had been genetically influenced by the city's glitz and sense of abandon.

But whatever any of them thought about Teddy— teammates, coaches, management—they watched him throw sidearm to left-handed hitters and all of them thought he was a fixture in the major leagues.

And so it was spring, the air filled with the smell of citrus trees, salt spray, and hope. Teddy was coming out of a bar on Kennedy Boulevard in Tampa, on his way to the parking lot when his estranged wife, Mary, confronted him.

TALK OF THE TOWN—ALL JOE HAD EVER WANTED

WAS TO PITCH. NOW HE WAS THROWING WORDS WITH JOHNNY BENCH.

SOON, HE LEARNED THAT HE STILL NEEDED CONTROL.

BOOTH

They argued. They shouted. Then she shot him twice with a .25 caliber pistol. The bullets struck his abdomen, his shoulder, and lodged in his rosy future.

"It was touch and go there for awhile," said Tommy Helms, the Reds' Rookie of the Year in '64. "You expect certain things to happen in spring training. You expect guys to blow out a hamstring. You don't expect a guy to get *bleeping* shot."

Davidson was in intensive care for several days. When his condition improved, Reds manager Dave Bristol and Jimmy Bragan, one of his coaches, visited him in the hospital. Tubes ran from Davidson's chest and stomach. The fluids coursing through the tubes were red and pink. The machines bleeped and blinked and mixed with the sound of Teddy's labored breath. The prognosis was good but Teddy looked bad.

Bristol, a tough horseman from North Carolina, didn't stay long. He told Teddy he was thinking about him and left the room. When Bragan walked into the hall, he found Bristol passed out on a crash-cart. Bristol was a blood-and-guts baseball manager, but he had no stomach for bullet wounds.

"Before Teddy was shot," said pitcher Jim O'Toole, "it looked rough for Joe. We had a lot of good young pitchers. Gary Nolan was coming along and Joe was getting older. But after the incident with Teddy, we all thought Joe was a lock to make the team."

They couldn't imagine the team without him. To them, he represented both the historic past and the immediate future, which was the next day's game. In their young lives, he was *context*, although most of them wouldn't have recognized it at the time. He was also their senior statesman, instructing and pushing them.

"He was always riding us," O'Toole said. "'If you can't push yourself for two and a half hours, what good are you?' God, that echoes in my head. If he saw you loafing on the bases, he'd say, 'What, you can't run freakin' ninety feet?'"

"Damn, Joe knew the '40s and the '50s and the '60s," said Helms. "He had seen ballplayers we had only heard about. He was history walking, but it was a bad damn walk. I never understood how he walked on them damned knocked knees, much less pitch or run."

"We were all hanging out in the clubhouse one day and we hear that Joe had been called in to meet with Bob Howsam, the new general manager," O'Toole said.

"We just figured Mr. Howsam was calling him in to tell him he had made the team," Sammy Ellis said. "Nobody thought anything about it."

Joe was gone a long time. When he came back, he sat down in front of his locker. He didn't say anything.

"Finally, I walked over to him," said Helms. He was sitting there with his head in those big ol' hands. I asked him if something was wrong.

"When he looked up at me, tears were running down his cheeks. 'I'm done,' he said. 'They told me I'm through.'"

"He had spent his whole life in baseball," said Pete Rose. "Twenty-three years and it's done. Just like that. Baseball was everything to Joe. What do you say in a situation like that?"

In the end, they left him alone. Baseball players don't like it when a teammate is finished. It forces them to face the fact that their careers will come to an end, too, that youth and success will not always be at their side.

Some are compassionate. Some avoid the retiring ballplayer as if retirement is contagious.

"But you never really understand it," Rose says. "Until it happens to you. But we felt for Joe. We all loved Joe."

THE FRANCHISE HAD BEEN SOLD after the '66 season, and team president Frank Dale, who was also publisher of the *Cincinnati Enquirer*, had chosen Howsam as his new general manager. Howsam had worked for the Cardinals and schooled under Branch Rickey. He was direct and dispassionate, and he liked his ballplayers young, talented, and cheap.

"Joe was getting on in years," Howsam said, "and we just didn't think he could help the club."

Joe argued that he still felt he could pitch and help the ball club.

"I told him if he felt that way, I would call other clubs and see if they had a place for him," Howsam said. "There were a few teams in the American League that I thought were interested. But I made it clear we couldn't use him.

"When you run a club, you have to do things that are very difficult," he says. "You lose sleep and you worry. 'Did I do the right thing?' I faced that many times.

"The fans often think we are hard and unfeeling. Nothing is further from the truth, but you are entrusted to do what is best for the club. Then you live with your decisions."

Sometimes they are right. Sometimes they are wrong. In Nuxhall's case, Howsam was sure he was right. Howsam did have a proposal for Joe, one that had been brewing for years.

"I told Joe that I would like him to become part of our radio broadcast team," Howsam said. "I told him that I thought he had great promise as a broadcaster. He laughed at first. He was not pleased with me. I knew that. Joe was never good at hiding his emotions."

"Joe went back to the clubhouse, changed into street clothes, and went to the broadcast booth that day," says Murdough.

HE HAD NO TRAINING AND LITTLE PREPARATION. He had done basketball games for Miami University on its flagship station, Hamilton's WMOH. He teamed with Ray Motley, a drawling Texan, who had called Joe's high school football games.

There is Nuxhall back to punt and as you know, he kicks them as he throws them, left-handed.

Perhaps Motley's influence made an impression. During his time with Miami, Joe was noted for his ardor. Frequently, he lapsed from his role as analyst into that of cheerleader and coach, standing courtside, screaming, "Shoot!" and blasting officials for what he viewed as questionable calls. He cheered Miami. He was a "homer" and he offered no apologies for being one.

Joe went to the Reds' broadcast booth, sat down between Claude Sullivan and Jim McIntyre, and began his new career. He didn't know what to do. He didn't know if his new job would last. Once again, he had been handed the ball and ushered into a new game.

"So many times I was given opportunities" he says. "I wanted to play. I felt that I could still pitch. But this was, well, reality. Maybe they were right. So you run with it.

"That first day, I muttered and stuttered and I'm sure anyone who has ever listened to me isn't surprised by that. I was worse then than I am today and that's bad enough. I felt like I had to comment on every pitch and every move. I talked all the time and I screwed up all the time.

"That whole left-center, right-center thing. That started back in the '60s. I say today I hope I live long enough to get right and left center field straightened out. I got so excited when someone hit one in the gap, I didn't know what I was saying. Hell, maybe I am, what do you call it?

SHOE ON THE OTHER FOOT—THAT WAS THE HEADLINE ON THIS PHOTO OF JOE A WEEK INTO HIS NEW CAREER AS HE INTERVIEWED JIM MALONEY (LEFT) AND DERON JOHNSON IN TAMPA.

Dyslexic? Sometimes I asked myself why the hell they kept me.

"We had to do all the commercials live for the brewery. There was one word I could never get right."

He doesn't remember the exact word; perhaps it was "pasteurized," or "homogenized." He doesn't know. "It got to the point when I had to read that word, I just stopped and Jim McIntyre said it for me."

In his radio career, Joe always seemed to need an assist.

IN THE EARLY DAYS, he muddled on. At night, he thought about Dick Bray and Waite Hoyt. He thought about how they did it. He turned off the lights and tried to sleep, wondering what to do next.

All he had wanted to do was pitch for the Reds. Now he *spoke* for the Reds. He had no idea how he had come to such a place.

IN 1965, THE REDS SUFFERED A LOSS. Burger Beer, their longtime sponsor, was facing difficult times and backed away. Wiedemann jumped in, but the change in sponsorship cost the ball club a valuable commodity.

Waite Hoyt, a Cincinnati tradition, retired. Hoyt told Reds management he simply could not sell another beer after backing Burger for so long. He said it would be hypocritical.

Hoyt's voice was deep and strong and carried an Eastern edge. He was elegant in speech and dress. And he was honorable—not given to the shifting commercialism that was changing the game on many fronts. Hoyt and announcers like him—Red Barber, Ernie Harwell, and Harry Caray—were expanding baseball's reach, extending its ability to make money beyond the turnstiles.

Hoyt was handsome and charming, and he had quickly become a Cincinnati icon. His hair was silver. His face was tanned. He smelled good. He looked good. He had made money, lost money, then made some more. He had succumbed to drink but eventually he had been able to quit. He had traversed many turns on his particular highway, and the fullness of that journey seemed to come across on radio.

Hoyt grew up in Brooklyn and pitched with the Yankees from 1918 until 1930. He played for eight more years with Detroit, Brooklyn, and Pittsburgh. He seemed to know everyone in baseball and something about each of them.

When rain stopped a game, he told stories about Ruth, Gehrig, and Foxx. He knew Ty Cobb and Tris Speaker, and he was such a talker that fans often hoped for a downpour.

On a particularly hot day during a series in Brooklyn, the Dodgers' public address announcer asked Hoyt to stand and take a bow before the Ebbets Field crowd.

Hoyt didn't move. The crowd cheered and the P.A. announcer again asked Hoyt to acknowledge his fans. Hoyt stood briefly, waved to the crowd, and the television cameras caught a brief shot of Hoyt wearing nothing but his boxer shorts.

He was, of course, merely following a practice of the time. In the

MAN IN THE GLASS BOOTH—HISTORICALLY, THE REDS

HAD GREAT ANNOUNCERS, BEGINNING WITH RED BARBER IN THE 1930s.

THEREFORE, THE BOOTH WAS AS DAUNTING AS THE PITCHER'S MOUND.

men's world of the press box, writers and broadcasters often fought the heat by stripping down to their underwear.

Soon a wire arrived in the broadcast booth. It was from Hoyt's wife.

"Put your pants on and come home," it said.

Hoyt dictated an answer to the Western Union operator.

"Take yours off," Hoyt replied, "and I'll be right there."

HOYT TILLED THE GROUND THAT CAME to be known as Reds Country, an expansive radio market that reached into seven states and was rivaled only by St. Louis. He was loved by fans and treasured by management, and when he left the booth, it took two men to replace him: Claude Sullivan, the play-by-play man for Adolph Rupp's University of Kentucky basketball teams, and Jim McIntyre, who announced the UK games on television.

Sullivan and McIntyre were smooth and professional. The broadcasts were clean and without error. But something was lacking. Reds management had a voice when what it wanted was a presence. Management wanted someone like Hoyt, and so did Wiedemann.

It was Gabe Paul who first thought about putting Joe in the broadcast booth. He liked the idea but, as with most things, he sought other opinions.

"We all thought Joe would be great on the radio," Murdough said. "He loved to talk and tell stories. He sure as hell knew the game."

Paul loved Dizzy Dean, the former Cardinal pitcher and ringleader of the Gashouse Gang. Dean had been discovered on a Texas sandlot. From 1932 through 1936, he won 120 games, an engaging and natural phenomenon who played to the crowds with his tongue as well as his arm.

He baited pitchers and boisterously entered into the lexicon of baseball the phrase, "It ain't braggin' if you can do it." In the 1934 World Series, he was hit in the head and afterward, when a reporter asked him how he felt, he said he was fine.

"The doctors X-rayed my head," he said, "and found nothing."

In 1941, he left his playing career behind and went to work calling Cardinal and Browns games on radio in St. Louis. His language was colorfully original, filled with malaprops and constructs in which players "slud" into bases. He explained that "slud" was quite different from "slid." It meant, he said, "sliding with great effort."

On one occasion, he admitted that the locations of filling stations puzzled him. "Just how did they know gas and oil was under there?" he asked. As always with Dean, it was difficult to know where literacy left off and showmanship began, a distinction never made by his large and appreciative audiences. The more educators complained, the higher his ratings climbed.

"Gabe thought Joe could be the next Dean," Murdough says, "and DeWitt felt the same way. When the contract changed from Burger to Wiedemann, DeWitt and I started pushing Joe. I don't know how many times we met with Roy Warner at the brewery.

"But they had some concerns about the way Joe talked. Finally Dewitt says, 'Have you heard Dizzy Dean on *The Game of the Week*? It's hardly English! Joe might not sing *The Wabash Cannonball* like Dizzy but he's just like him.'

"DeWitt sold them that day," Murdough says.

Once sold on Joe, Warner and Wiedemann never gave up. When Joe's playing days were done, they wanted him in the broadcast booth.

NUXHALL LEFT THE CLUBHOUSE in the spring of 1967 for the broadcast booth with 135 career wins and 117 loses. He appeared in 484 games with the Reds and pitched 2,169 innings. He had 1,289 strikeouts, giving him a place in the Reds' all-time top five.

He didn't want to quit. And he didn't want to leave the Reds. So he took his place in the broadcast booth not knowing if he could do the job or how long it would last. He had one thought and he leaned on one memory: Bill McKechnie handing him the ball in 1944.

"Just do the best you can, son," McKechnie said.

"In the beginning, Joe was very rough," says Howsam. "Oh, my goodness. I tried to get him to listen to tapes. I thought it would help him. He wouldn't do it. Joe was stubborn that way."

"I didn't do it because I didn't want to be like anybody else," Joe says. "I knew I couldn't be anybody else and I knew if I tried I would come across as phony.

"I just wanted to be who I was and I wanted the fans to know I was being honest with them. I didn't want to be no damned showman."

The Reds were on a train leaving Milwaukee, bound for St. Louis and a series with the Cardinals. Several of the players had gathered in the club car where they listened on the radio to the Cardinals playing the Dodgers.

"Harry Caray and Gabby Street were doing the game," Joe says. "Well, Bobby Del Greco was having a helluva game. He makes a diving catch. And later he runs back to the wall and makes another great catch. We're all looking at one another saying, 'Damn, The Greek is going good.'

"Later that night, we're all out getting something to eat and we run into Bobby. Somebody said, 'Nice game.' And he just kinda looks at us. We tell him we heard about him making two great catches on the radio.

"The Greek just laughed. 'Routine,' he says. 'Nothing special about 'em.'

"That kind of embellishing happened frequently. But I wasn't about to do it. I wanted people to always know I was tellin' them the truth. If a guy hits a line drive, just say it. Same thing with a routine ground ball. 'Course, those 'tweeners,' the shots that look like they may go out of the park and then stay in, them damn things get me every time."

BOB HOWSAM IS A BIG MAN. When he laughs his eyes seem to disappear and his entire torso shakes up and down. It is a good, infectious laugh.

"My goodness," he says, his laughter subsiding, "we had our times. Joe had his problems with the language and, shall we say, some unfortunate things that made the air and caused some irritation."

Howsam is referring, of course, to a legendary story involving Joe and a ten-letter word not customarily found in the vocabulary of most Midwestern Methodists. The word inadvertently found its way onto the airwaves. The basic story, which has many versions over time, involves Phil Gagliano tossing pebbles at Joe while he was attempting to tape his pre-game show, and Joe responding with what would become an historical broadcasting rejoinder.

On more than one occasion, Joe's banter with the players distracted him in the use of his tape recorder and words best left in the clubhouse made their way into all corners of the Reds' growing network.

The players found each *faux pas* hilarious. Management, stung by the complaints of fans and advertisers, did not.

"We did have to call Joe in a couple of times and have a chat," Howsam recalls. "After one particular incident, he was sure we were going to fire him. We weren't. As offended as some were by the blue language, they were honest mistakes. No one was truly injured. And for every call we ever got complaining about Joe, we received fifty to a hundred telling us how much he was loved."

"Of course, Joe had some marvelous partners. Jim McIntyre and Claude Sullivan in the beginning and later the great Al Michaels, who went on to achieve such wonderful things, and, of course, Marty Brennaman.

"But through all those years Joe was the consistency and he was critical in our club, building the radio network into the success it became. At one time, we had 114 affiliates in seven states, from small towns to large cities.

"I have always believed Joe was essential to that achievement. He was just a good, old-fashioned boy who loved baseball and enjoyed talking about the game and telling stories. But there was something else that set him apart. With certain people you get a genuine sense of their character just by listening to them speak.

"Joe was one of those people. You immediately knew he was sincere, that he was a good person who loved the game and loved people. That came through and it endeared Joe to so many.

"There were times when I know Joe was just as popular, if not more so, than some of our great ballplayers. And to think—when I first asked him about becoming a broadcaster, he didn't want to do it. He was mad at me. I think it all worked out pretty well."

"Hell, he was one of us," Pete Rose says. "He knew us all, knew everything about us. After he went to radio, he is out there throwing batting practice every day and doing it for forty-five minutes off the mound and doing a damn good job. He's still wearing that damned red rubber jacket. He is throwing in, down, and away. He's making you actually work.

"Geez, today guys throw fifteen minutes of BP from forty-five feet and they are done. He would do that, shower, and go to the radio booth.

"He wasn't the best. He knew that. But he was so damn human you couldn't help but love him.

"I remember one night, it was '75 or '76, one of the World Series years. Davey Concepcion and Joe Morgan turn one helluva double play. And Joe says on the radio, 'If you are scoring in bed at home, that's 6 to 4 to 3.'

"What? 'If you are scoring in bed...' After the game, he's sitting there having his beer, and we just gave him hell. But that was the thing about him. Even his mistakes make him more likeable. How could you *not* love the bleeping guy?"

Names.

Joe had trouble with names.

For the longest time, Brennaman and Dave "Yiddie" Armbruster, the long-time producer and engineer for Reds' radio broadcasts, kept a file of names Joe botched on the air.

"Remember Cecil Espy, played for the Pirates," Armbruster says. "Joe always called him Epsy.

"The Pirates are in town and all night Joe is calling him Cecil Epsy. There weren't many people at the ballpark that night and all of sudden some guy yells from the green seats at Riverfront just below our booth.

"He's yelling at the top of his lungs, 'God love ya, Joe, but it's Espy, E-s-p-y. *Espy!*'

"Marty and I are howling. Joe says real slow, 'Cecil *Essspy* at the plate.'

"Now he is laughing and I have no idea how we got through the inning. My God, he made it fun."

"Ah, hell, you got to laugh," Joe says. "Not long ago, I'm doing this spot, and it had the word d-e-b-r-i-s in it. I musta read that thing fifteen times and I kept saying *derbis*. What the hell is *derbis*? They finally had to change the copy."

Joe never changed from who he was or how he felt about his work, but he did learn.

McIntyre and Sullivan taught him the importance of silence. "They taught me to shut up," Joe says. "That I didn't have to comment on every damn thing that happened on the field."

He learned that the sounds of the game and the ballpark passed through the microphone and gave people a sense of presence.

Michaels taught him the importance of the rhythm between the play-by-play announcer and the color man, and that it was okay to joke around during the broadcast.

Michaels and Nuxhall did the games and jousted throughout. Joe teased Michaels about his West Coast roots. Michaels said Joe was the only broadcaster who kept his job because of his arm.

"Al and I kidded around a lot," Joe says, "but not like me and Marty. That was a whole different thing."

ALWAYS PITCHING—IT WAS HARD FOR JOE TO STAY

OFF THE FIELD. FOR THEIR MONEY, THE REDS STILL HAD A PITCHER.

HE THREW BATTING PRACTICE, THEN HEADED TO THE BOOTH.

Chapter sixteen

Marty Brennaman paces outside the Reds' offices in Sarasota, occasionally glancing at his wristwatch. His briefcase sits on the ground beside a neatly folded plastic bag filled with newspapers. During spring training he reads seven papers every morning and more on-line at night.

Newspapers have always been the foundation for each of his working days. He goes to the broadcast booth bursting with news and information, not only about the Reds but every team in the league.

Joe, meanwhile, leans casually against a picnic table. His hands are free except for a cigarette he has snagged from someone on the grounds.

"Where the hell is he?" Marty complains.

"Probably running some damn marathon or something," Joe says.

They are waiting for Dave "Yiddie" Armbruster, their spring training wheelman and long-time producer, who will drive them to Clearwater for that day's game against the Phillies. But he is tardy, which causes Marty to grow more impatient with each passing moment. The team bus idles nearby,

THE ODD COUPLE—THEY EAT BREAKFAST TOGETHER. THEY PLAY GOLF TOGETHER. THEY GO TO THE BALLPARK TOGETHER. AND IF SOMEBODY SEES ONE OF THEM ALONE, THE QUESTION IS ALWAYS, "WHERE'S MARTY?" OR, "WHERE'S JOE?"

H MARTY

waiting for the players, although most are still dressing in the clubhouse.

While Joe has a pace all his own, Marty is supremely punctual.

"What time did you tell him to be here?" Marty snaps.

"Uh, he said he would be here at 9 or 9:15," Joe says, shrugging. "What time is it anyway?"

"After nine," Marty says.

Rick Stowe, the Reds' equipment manager, is standing nearby.

"Look at them," he says. "They're like an old married couple."

Stowe began his Reds' career as a batboy in 1981, working around the clubhouse with his father, Bernie, and older brother, Mark.

The conversation between Marty and Joe has turned to a pitcher scheduled to work that day against the Blue Jays.

"They even finish sentences for one another, " Rick says.

As if on cue, Marty and Joe flow into a conjoined conversation.

"The way he finished last year…," Joe says.

"He better make a statement and fast, like today," Marty chirps.

"Thank you very much," Joe says.

"If he doesn't…," Marty says.

"Gone!" Joe says.

"In a New York minute," Marty concludes.

Stowe erupts in laughter, slapping his thighs.

"What?" Joe says, smiling. "It's true, isn't it?"

"What's so damn funny?" Marty says. "Where the hell is Yid?"

"Oh, he'll be along," Joe says. He never looks at his wristwatch. Marty constantly looks at his.

Stowe walks away, grinning with delight. "Now watch," he says. "When Yid *does* pull up, Joe will get in the front seat. Marty will get in the back and tell Yid to turn down the radio 'cause he wants to read."

There is a flurry of activity when Armbruster arrives. Doors open and close on the car. Marty gripes. Joe jibes. Armbruster, tall and weathered, smiles as if he is picking up his elderly parents.

"See ya over there," Joe calls, waving out the window.

"Turn the damned radio down," Brennaman barks.

FOLLOWING THE 1973 SEASON, Al Michaels resigned to join the Giants' broadcast team. He knew he was leaving an enviable position, but he wanted to be closer to his home in the Bay Area.

The Reds were rapidly approaching the highest point in franchise history. They won the National League pennant in 1970, only to fall to the Orioles in the World Series. They took the league title again in '72 but lost in seven games to Oakland. The following year, they lost to the Mets in the playoffs.

There were over 200 applicants for Michaels' job. The Reds' choice was Marty Brennaman, a graduate of the University of North Carolina, class of '65.

He was young and smart and his voice carried just a touch of a southern accent. There was something in Brennaman that kindled thoughts of Mel Allen and Red Barber. He was inexperienced at the big league level, but he was promising.

"I was also very cheap," Brennaman says.

Bob Howsam, forever steeped in the higher economics of baseball, felt Marty was perfect for the job.

Brennaman's first public appearance as the Reds' new play-by-play man was February 1, 1974. The annual Winter Caravan started with a luncheon in Cincinnati. The first stop on the road was Suttmillers Restaurant in Dayton.

"Before that stop at Suttmiller's, we were asked to go to a studio in Dayton for some publicity shots," Marty says. "That's where Joe and I met for the first time. I remember the exact words I said to him that day. I said, 'I have your baseball card.' I think he had heard that before and I know he has heard it a million times since. He just smiled."

Weeks later, they were in spring training. Marty was a stranger, marveling at his partner's popularity. Everyone knew Joe, and Marty had never broadcast a big league game in his life. He had never been in a big league camp. These were the Reds, quickly becoming the most respected—and most hated—team in the country.

Outside Reds Country, the Reds were viewed as a cocky over-achieving bunch led by floppy-haired Pete Rose and Johnny Bench, the kid from Oklahoma who showed up on the *Bobby Goldsboro Show* and sang with country music star Charlie Pride.

"I was thrown into this," Marty says. "And I thought, *This is just the way it's supposed to be.* I wasn't prepared for the adulation that surrounded this team."

Joe was Marty's entree into a world closed to most. "The players all told me that if there was anything they could do to help me, just ask," Marty says. "I don't think that would have happened without Joe. He was one of them. He ushered me into their world.

"That spring, I hooked myself to his belt loop and just followed him around. Ninety percent of everything I learned initially, I learned from him. We hit it off from the very first day, but my monumental screwup in the second spring game seemed to solidify a relationship that has stood us in good stead for thirty *freaking* years."

When Brennaman was hired, he knew nothing about Al Michaels. But he soon learned that his predecessor was popular with the players.

"Everywhere I went all I heard was, 'You got big shoes to fill,'" Marty says. "'Al was great. Michaels this and Michaels that.' He was only there for three years, but it didn't matter. It could have been three months. He was that good.

"I started wondering if I had made the right decision in coming here. Hell, in Virginia I was a big fish in a small pond. I was Sportscaster of the Year four years running."

By the time the Reds' broadcasts began in the spring of '74, Marty was tired of hearing about Michaels and, admittedly, somewhat intimidated.

"So it's the second game of the spring," Brennaman says. "The format is, 'Welcome everybody. It's the Reds against the White Sox at Al Lopez Field. We'll be back with the starting lineups and the play-by-play after this commercial break.'

"And what happens? I say, 'Hi, everybody. It's the Reds and White Sox at Al *Michaels* Field. We'll be back with the starting lineups and the play-by-play after this commercial break.'

"As soon as it was out of my mouth I knew what I had said. I was mortified, I mean *devastated*.

"Well, Joe's sitting there and he's rolling. He's laughing. He looks at me and says, 'I cannot believe it. We have not played a regular season game and I already have material for the banquet circuit.'

"That was the beginning," Brennaman says, smiling. "That formed the foundation of what has been a very unique relationship."

"From the very beginning, you could tell they liked one another," says Bob Howsam. "They were a perfect fit."

The only thing they had in common was a mutual love for baseball and being left-handed. "Which made us," Brennaman says, "inherently different."

When Joe was in high school, he made his major league debut. When Marty was in high school, there was nothing he loved more than the theater, although his baseball card collection ran a close second.

SINGING TELEGRAM—THE BOYS IN THE BOOTH, BOTH JOE AND MARTY, HAVE BIRTHDAYS ONLY TWO DAYS APART IN JULY. THE OCCASION IS USUALLY OBSERVED BY SOME KIND OF NONSENSE OR ANOTHER.

In the summer, he traveled from his home in Virginia to Chapel Hill, North Carolina, where he participated in the university's theater workshops. He immersed himself. He worked as a stagehand, and in summer stock he won the part of Petruchio, the male lead in Shakespeare's *Taming of The Shrew*.

"I was scared to death and I don't think I was very good," he says. "But, God, did I love it."

He spent his days in the library. He spent his nights trying to find his place on the stage. After his senior year in high school, he was determined to leave Virginia for New York.

"I fought with my mom and dad about it for weeks," Marty says.

"Finally—and I swear to this day they set this up—they introduced me to two friends of theirs. These guys convinced me they were starving to death trying to make a living in theater in New York, that it was nearly impossible."

MARTY ABANDONED HIS DREAM of a career in theater and began the pursuit of another. He studied history and communications at Chapel Hill. He had a new goal—to be one of the best play-by-play men in the country. He did minor league baseball games in Tidewater, Virginia, and Virginia Squires' games in the progressive American Basketball Association where he had the difficult task of describing the indescribable moves of Julius Irving, "Doctor J," who eventually transformed the topography of professional basketball.

Brennaman was a precocious announcer with a tight, clear voice. "I sounded," he says, "like somebody had me by the you-know-what. My voice was somewhat high."

He came to Cincinnati with little more than a briefcase—startingly similar to the one he carries today—and bravado.

"Let's just see what I have in here," he says, sitting in his room at Le Centre Sheraton in Montreal, during a Reds' series against the Expos. "Hmm, nineteen Number One pencils because I like dark lead.

"I keep them," he says, his voice taking on a slow, secretive tone, "in a little plastic pack like kids take to grade school. They are all sharp, all the time, and I don't like anybody screwin' with my pencils. I'm queer for my pencils—if you know what I mean.

"I have White Out. White Out is key, because, I do not like mistakes. Not in my scorebook, not in the books on the players. I keep a book on every player and pitcher and what they do in every game. Not just stats, but observations and tendencies. I have for years.

"And," he says, "they must, *must,* be neat."

Joe has a briefcase, too. "He keeps two things in it," Marty says. "His scorebook and a pen. He keeps score in ink. *In ink!* How the hell can you keep score in ink? It drives me crazy."

Marty insists Joe bought his briefcase when the club outlawed cocktails on commercial flights. Suddenly, most in the traveling party added a briefcase to their carry-on luggage and virtually all contained a bottle or two. Stewardesses served mixers with a wink and a nod, and a rough flight sounded like a dishwasher on the fritz, every air pocket accompanied by the clinking of glass.

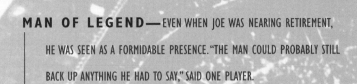

MAN OF LEGEND—EVEN WHEN JOE WAS NEARING RETIREMENT, HE WAS SEEN AS A FORMIDABLE PRESENCE. "THE MAN COULD PROBABLY STILL BACK UP ANYTHING HE HAD TO SAY," SAID ONE PLAYER.

"For God's sake," Davey Concepcion would say, "find some good air or we're all gonna be fined."

"Shut up," Tony Perez would say. "You're gonna give us all away."

The writers sat in the back of the plane, free from team rules, openly toasting the players.

"Sons-a-bitches!" said Tommy Helms, a coach with the team. "I can't believe you guys would torment us like this."

TO BE A PART OF THE REDS' ENTOURAGE was a privilege, and no one was more privileged than Joe. He sat with the managers and coaches, dissecting the latest game. He was invited to play poker with the players, but rarely did because the pots were too large, baffling amounts of cash rising upon the tray tables.

"Too rich for my blood," he said.

He visited with the writers, commenting on one story or another. He told them what he liked. He told them when he thought unfair liberties had been taken. He was a like a politician, but he was never running for anything. He did, however, stay in touch with everything. He was immersed in every aspect of daily life with the Reds. Marty stuck to business and did so on purpose. He had learned that although he walked in the players' world, he did not share citizenship with them.

"Early on, I was talking to Jack Billingham, a pitcher," Brennaman says. "In the course of the conversation, I used the word 'we.'"

"He looked at me and said, 'We? *We*? How many hits did *you* get?' I learned then that I had no inherent part in what happened on the field. I was just there to describe it. Joe could say 'we' anytime he wanted to and that was okay. I couldn't and haven't done so since.

"At first," he says, "I was an unabashed cheerleader—a complete 'homer.' It was shameful. But at the time, I thought that was the way it was supposed to be. I lived and died with every win and every loss.

"Sometimes, after a tough loss, I couldn't sleep. Sparky Anderson gets a hold of me. We sit down in his office and he says, 'It's my job to take responsibility for the games, not yours. Your job is simple—just describe what we do on the field. Besides that, no matter what happens, the sun will come up the next day.'"

That conversation marked the maturation of his career. He lived and traveled with the team, but he buried himself in literature and history and kept his distance. He chastised Johnny Bench for failing to play day games after night games. The year after Pete Rose had passed Ty Cobb as baseball's all-time hits leader, he suggested Pete retire. Rose's bat had slowed down, Brennaman said. Rose may have been a baseball legend, but he wasn't helping the team any longer.

Brennaman said what others were thinking but were hesitant to say or write. And he faced the responsibility of his position. Each day before every game, Brennaman walked through the Reds' clubhouse. "I wanted to make sure that anyone who took exception to what I had said the night before had the opportunity to do so," he says.

He loved his position and his paycheck, but there was an aspect of his profession he held in the highest regard.

"I've said this before, when I die—when all this is over—I want people to say, 'He was one of the most credible guys in the business.'"

JOE, MEANWHILE, DID WHAT HE HAD ALWAYS DONE. He talked and traded stories. He comforted those who failed and was the first to praise anyone who succeeded. Joe was a back-slapper and a hand-shaker. Joe threw batting practice; Marty threw barbs.

"Joe is one of them and always will be," Marty says. "He wore the uniform when he was 15 years old. But that is not to say, as an announcer, he gave every player carte blanche."

"Oh, he wasn't afraid to speak his mind," says Ron Oester. "But he picked his spots. He would sit there at his locker after the game, having a Bud, smoking, someone would come along that he thought wasn't giving it their best and Joe would let loose."

"Thing was, even when he got older," says Chris Sabo, "nobody came back at Nuxie. We all respected him. Besides that—he was still strong. Didn't matter how he looked, the man could probably still back up anything he had to say."

In the spring of 2004, he praised utility man Ryan Freel, a player viewed by most as a minor-league lifer.

"He will make his way," Joe said. "He always works hard. He takes nothing for granted. It's like I always try to tell people. This game is about effort.

"Take Pete Rose. Was he the most talented player in the world? Absolutely not. But who has more hits than Pete and who played in more winning games? No one! He was always pushin' and goin' for more. Christ, I don't know how many doubles he had in his life, but I know he stole more than half of them just by going all out from the time he hit the ball."

Joe always had a place in his heart for the blue-collared, lunch-bucket ballplayer because he was that kind of player himself, and he came from that kind of town.

He appreciated the talents of Deion Sanders and Tom Seaver, but he was more comfortable with Tracy Jones and Lloyd McClendon. He liked the players who had flaws and fought to defeat them.

"You know," he says, "guys who worked their butts off."

Every year, there was Marty, quick and concise in cadence and always correct. And beside him was Joe—slow and meandering, like the game itself. The man who began his radio career trying to say something in every breath became the man who said nothing for so long that everyone wondered if the game was still going on.

"The game is going on and he hasn't said anything for the longest time," Yid Ambruster says. "You start thinking he is asleep.

"Then all of a sudden, he sees something and starts talking about it and it turns out to be essential to the game. I swear to God, you or I could go back and look at the tape a hundred times and would never see what he saw at first glance."

It was a hard-learned lesson with roots that stretched back to 1944 and a day when he didn't pay attention and failed. He had failed, he always thought, because he didn't watch closely enough and therefore wasn't prepared.

THERE IS NO DOUBT THAT THE PHENOMENON of Marty and Joe was buoyed by the success of the Reds in the mid-'70s. In 1974, the Reds won 98 games. They finished second to Los Angeles in the Western Division and failed to make the playoffs for the first time in three years.

Then came the back-to-back World Championships in '75 and '76. The Reds won 108 games in '75, 102 in '76. It was hard to get a ticket for a game, but Marty and Joe always had an inexpensive seat for one and all. All anyone needed was a chair beside a radio.

Hello everyone and welcome to Reds baseball...

"What a time," Marty says. "Every game was an event. Every night there were 35,000, 40,000 people in the ballpark. I don't think Joe or I ever realized it at the time, but we were covering what proved to be one of the greatest teams of all time.

"It was hard not to get caught up in the excitement that surrounded those teams and I hope that excitement came across in our broadcasts."

Marty and Joe became the fans' constant connection to a team that occupied the very center of its city's image. The average citizen might not be able to explain the complicated and antiquated process of its mayoral election in Cincinnati, but they could tell you all about Tony Perez, the Mayor of Riverfront. Marty and Joe made sure of that.

"We covered some great teams," Marty says.

"We covered some stinkers, too," Joe says.

"And that is when we became dangerous," Marty adds.

Any time the game was a blowout, one way or another, during those seasons when the glory of the past was nothing more than a memory, Marty and Joe never feared the side roads. They took their broadcasts places no one else in their position dared to go.

Marty talked about his tomatoes. Joe talked about his golf game. They talked about their children and grandchildren. They laughed and joked and sometimes poked fun at what happened on the field.

"You got to have some yuks along the way," Marty says.

"Sometimes it was so bad out there," says Joe, "what are you gonna do? You couldn't just sit there and talk about how bad they were. Well, I guess we could have done that but it wouldn't have been any fun for anyone."

Instead, they transformed their broadcast into a show, a welcome distraction from the painful performances that sometimes took place on the field.

ONE NIGHT IN THE MIDST OF A BORING GAME, Joe and Marty began to discuss their mutual admiration for the dearly departed "King," Elvis Presley. They praised him as a singer and as a performer. He was, they proclaimed, an American icon. Today, they don't even know what led to this homage.

Within days of their extemporaneous tribute, fans started sending Elvis memorabilia to Marty and Joe. Within weeks, their booth became a shrine to the King of Rock, replete with a life-size bust they displayed squarely between them.

Each day's mail brought more Elvis: velvet paintings and pictures spanning his career from the slender days of "Blue Suede Shoes" to the plump times of Las Vegas and "In the Ghetto."

Every item was promptly displayed and its benefactor acknowledged on the air. Each night, Elvis was a topic of conversation. Television crews panned their cameras over the broadcast booth every night, and Graceland North received so much attention that a group of players complained to management.

They said it drew attention away from the game.

The tribute to Elvis was dismantled.

"That was horse shit," Marty said.

"I didn't understand," Joe said.

"What difference did it make to them?" Marty said.

"Seems to me," said Joe, "their attention should have been, you know, on the game and what they were doing—which wasn't much, as I recall, instead of what was going on in the booth."

By that time, the booth had taken on a life all its own. Regardless of how the team fared, it was the haunt of celebrities from around the country and all walks of life—from professional wrestler Randy "Macho Man" Savage to Dick Cheney, vice-president of the United States.

Savage, a one time Reds' farmhand, preened and posed for the crowd. He growled into the microphone and leaned out of the booth, popping his massive biceps to the delight of everyone within sight. If a turnbuckle had been handy, he would have launched himself into the crowd.

Cheney threw out the ceremonial first pitch on Opening Day of 2004. Later, he came to the booth. Security had strangled the stadium and well into the first inning, writers and other members of the press had been left outside.

When Cheney came to the booth, Joe conducted the interview. He allowed that these must be busy times for the vice-president. Cheney said, yes they were and then said, "I have your baseball card."

Joe laughed. "You're killin' me," he said.

Marty and Joe can't recount the number of celebrity guests they have entertained in the broadcast booth. But the Savage visit was a hallmark.

Principal owner Marge Schott was furious with Brennaman and Nuxhall. She thought the wrestler's act was tasteless and distracting. She told her nephew, Stephen Schott, to order Savage from the booth.

Stephen was a somewhat rotund young man in his 30's. He appeared in the booth but maintained a safe distance from Savage, Brennaman, and Nuxhall. He relayed Mrs. Schott's message. When he was ignored, he bristled and his face reddened. Savage was dressed in purple tights, a feather-boa, a cowboy hat, and large, be-jeweled sunglasses. Stephen Schott was dressed in blue serge suit. He gestured and pointed and eventually stormed out of the booth.

The next day, Marty and Joe were called to a meeting in Mrs. Schott's office. Stephen was there, along with Jim Ferguson, the Reds' director of media relations.

Mrs. Schott offered her view of what had taken place.

Marty and Joe said nothing.

Neither did Ferguson.

As she concluded, Stephen Schott described his treatment in the booth and his confrontation with Savage.

"I thought I was going to have to get physical with him," he said.

The room was silent, then from behind the smoke of a freshly lit Carlton, a smile spread across Marge Schott's face.

"He would have pinched your head off," Marty said.

Mrs. Schott agreed that perhaps she had over-reacted, and one thing was clear as they disbanded: Marty and Joe had reached a status that made them virtually immune to the whims of management.

Marty and Joe were employees of the Cincinnati Reds, but their longevity and their popularity with the fans gave them an extraordinary independence. They operated at the end of a long leash.

By the mid-'90s, Marty and Joe were asked to address team issues more than any member of management. While players often hid in the weight-room and management avoided the press, Marty and Joe were always available. They were forthright and candid, and their esteem continued to grow.

Marty and Joe's place was with their audience. They were urged to tame their criticism, but they continued on their own course, the one they would follow for three decades and more.

"Nothing we ever did was contrived," Marty says. "We never sat down and said, 'This is what we're gonna do.' We never designed anything to enhance our celebrity. It never entered our minds."

"Everything we did," Joe says, "kinda came naturally. We just talked about the team and what we saw and what was going on. There was never anything phony about what we did and I believe the people out there listening—I think they knew that."

"I don't know that what we have done over these past thirty-one years would have worked anywhere else in the country," Marty says. "Me talking about my tomatoes and my daughter, Ashley. Joe screwin' up here and there and talking about his golf game.

"I don't know if that would have flown in, let's say, Los Angeles. But it seems to have worked pretty well here. You know, I was out someplace the other day and I ran into a couple I had never met before.

"They ask me how Ashley was and then they said, 'We have never met her but we have watched her grow up—from swim lessons to dance lessons and being the captain of the cheerleading squad.' They talked about her graduation from Ohio University.

"It hit me then. Joe and I had made our broadcasts very human. By just being ourselves and not trying to be anything else we had been able to reach people."

MARTY BRENNAMAN IS A TOUGH, BANTY-ROOSTER of a man but when it comes to Joe—his demonstrative voice softens. "Each day," he says, "I have looked forward to going to work and it's always been because of him. Joe has always made it fun. I've had the pleasure of working with someone I truly respect and genuinely love as a human being."

He is quiet for the longest time.

"I am not good at sentimentality," he says.

In this case, it was understandable. Joe had been with the organization since 1944. He had broadcast games for thirty-seven years, the last thirty-one with Brennaman. They had long since become the longest-running broadcast team in baseball, surpassing Jack Buck and Mike Shannon in St. Louis.

But in 2002, after Joe had suffered a heart attack during the off-season, Reds management offered him a one-year contract. Reuven Katz, his representative, asked for more. Carl Lindner, who had succeeded Marge Schott as principal owner, agreed to one year and a partial season in 2004.

Management agreed to sixty games in 2004. Joe asked for more and John Allen, Reds' chief operating officer, agreed to eighteen more games.

Management wanted someone new. Was it that Joe was too slow? That he made mistakes? That he had been caught on camera sleeping in the booth? "That was the thing they always brought up, me falling asleep in the booth," Joe says. "I admit, that was wrong. I never should have done that. But it took me awhile to get my strength back after the heart attack."

Maybe it was an excuse. Maybe Joe *had* stayed too long. Possibly,

THE EARLY YEARS—THE EQUIPMENT MANAGER ONCE SAID THAT JOE AND MARTY SPENT MORE TIME WITH EACH OTHER THAN WITH THEIR WIVES. WITH THEM ARE REDS EXECUTIVES WOODY WOODWARD AND KEN COLEMAN.

the job had become too routine. There were times when even Marty wondered if his partner was taking things for granted.

"We have no secrets," Marty says. "I told him, 'You are cutting your own throat.'

"Now," he adds, "I think he has realized just how important this job is to him. Unfortunately, it will go away after this season. He has had a wonderful career, thirty-seven years as a broadcaster, twenty-three as a player and all but one with the Reds. This has been his life. Since he was 15 years old.

"Joe is not like the rest of us. Hell, when I retire, I am gonna walk away clean. That's it. Done! It is not gonna be easy for Joe. It is not easy now."

Steve Stewart was hired to share games with Joe during the 2004 season. He came from Baltimore, a kind man faced with replacing a Cincinnati icon. It will not be an easy job. Joe is like the Ohio, which flows languidly past Great American Ball Park, both a part of the natural landscape.

Joe estimates that he has missed maybe seven or eight games since his career began in the broadcast booth. He missed three when his father died in 1968. "I went home to take care of Mom," he says.

He missed a game when Marty was inducted into the Hall of Fame. He doesn't remember the circumstances surrounding the other games he missed. "I do know," he says, "you could count them on one hand."

He never wanted a day off. That was the irony in his signature sign-off: "This is the Old Left-hander, rounding third and heading for home."

For Joe, "home" was the ballpark. There was no place he felt more at ease. He laughs when he considers that notion. "Well," he says, "sixty years—that's a long time."

OPENING DAY IN CINCINNATI IS A FESTIVE OCCASION. People in Cincinnati, home of the oldest professional team in baseball, refer to it as an unofficial holiday. Kids skip school and executives flee their offices on Fourth Street, AWOL for the afternoon to greet the beginning of a new season.

On April 5, 2004, the stadium was filled to capacity. In pre-game ceremonies, no one received a warmer reception than Joe. The crowd stood and cheered. Joe smiled and waved. In the weeks leading up to the opener, the Reds' publicity and marketing departments began a new campaign. This was "The Summer of Joe."

All winter, Joe fought health problems. In the fall, he was diagnosed with lymphomic cancer. He underwent twelve chemotherapy treatments. They made him tired and he lost weight. That was followed by a bout with bronchitis. Through it all, he missed one public appearance. His biggest complaint was that medicine prescribed by doctors made him "sleepy and goofy."

But on Opening Day, Joe took his place in the booth. As the third inning began, Marty introduced him as "The Old Part-timer."

Joe laughed.

"I have a new credential," he replied. "It says, 'Seasonal.'"

There was more laughter. It was the chorus that has accompanied their work from their first broadcast—two men thoroughly at ease with one another.

Joe's voice was full and clear and he was more optimistic than most about a team *The Sporting News* had referred to as the worst in the game. Joe liked the pitching. He said the offense was better than most people thought it would be.

The following day—an off day for the team—Marty did an interview with WLW's Gary Burbank. Burbank wondered what the day had been like.

"It was your last Opening Day together," he said.

"Oh," Marty said, "we don't talk about things like that. There's plenty of time. I was talking with Rick Stowe about that very thing. He said, 'You know what you are gonna do when that last day does roll around?' I said, 'Hell, yes. I'm probably gonna cry. Two of the last three times I have cried, it has been because of him.'"

Brennaman is not a man given to tears. The only other time he cried was May 13, 2003, when his 85-year-old mother, Lillian, died after spending her last months in the maze of Alzheimer's disease.

During the first series of the season, Joe seemed to have found new energy. Even Marty noticed. "I think he was trying to prove something to someone," he said. "But the fact of the matter is—it didn't matter. This was gonna be his last season in the booth."

On April 7, the Reds had taken a 5-0 lead on Chicago when rain came, and Marty and Joe went to the phones, taking calls from the listening audience. Most callers said the same thing. They would miss Joe. They were sorry this was his last season.

But before it could become a long goodbye, Joe deftly interrupted a caller and said, "I'll be all right. Times change."

And he quickly steered the conversation back to the team. When the topic changed, everyone sensed the relief.

BUT JOE WAS NOT ALL RIGHT. The Pirates followed the Cubs into town. Joe stepped aside and Stewart joined Marty in the booth. That night, Joe was at the ballpark, but he did not go upstairs. He did not want to do anything that might make Stewart feel uncomfortable. He went to Stowe's office in Reds clubhouse, where the radio was tuned to the game.

"He sat there for the longest time and didn't say a word," Stowe says. "Finally, I guess it was about the fourth inning, he looked at me and said, 'It doesn't seem right.'

"I said, 'No, Joe. It doesn't seem right.' He got up and went home."

The next night he didn't go to the park. Instead, he went to dinner with Donzetta; his son, Kim; and daughter in-law, Bonnie. They were all concerned about his state of mind, "this retirement thing," as Donzetta puts it. But they didn't talk about it. The Nuxhalls are not a family that dwells on the unpleasant.

On Easter Sunday, April 11, Joe was back at the ballpark and ready for the upcoming road trip. He watched the Reds-Pirates game from the press box with writers and friends. He didn't say much at first, but then the Reds mounted a rally and Adam Dunn hit a line drive to left.

Joe rose from his seat and yelled, "Get down. Get down!"

When the ball skipped into the gap, Joe lapsed into a broadcast mode, "Here we go," he said. "We got something going now."

Paul Meyer was seated nearby. Meyer covered the Pirates for the Pittsburgh *Post-Gazette*, a crusty, old school baseball writer in his mid-50's.

He turned and scowled at Joe.

"If you're gonna do play-by-play, go back to the booth," he said.

Joe laughed, along with most in the press box. Meyer laughed hardest of all, especially after Joe suggested he go to hell and perform a few unimaginable acts along the way.

"Feelin' pretty good, aren't ya?" Meyer said.

"Now that you mention it, I am," Joe said.

Joe did the next ten games, seven on the road and a three-game home stand against Atlanta. The final game against the Braves was a rain-shortened 5-3 win for the Reds. That afternoon, the team prepared for a three-city, ten-game road trip.

Joe's sign-off that night was more deliberate than most.

"This is the Old Left-hander," he said, "rounding third..."

A long pause followed. "And," he finally said, "hmm, heading for home."

His mother, Naomi, worries about him. She wonders what he will do with himself. He is, she says, "a man of routine. This will be an awfully big change for him."

His wife and his sons shared that concern, as did his friends. Joe wouldn't talk about it. He said the same thing he said on the air when he got confused about the score, or the direction of a line drive.

"I'll be all right," he said. "I'll be all right."

Because he had always told them the truth, his fans trusted that he would be.

While the team was away, Joe played golf and mowed the grass. "He's actually doing some work around the house," Donzetta said.

He returned to the booth in early May, at home against Milwaukee. It was a clear, cool night. As Marty turned the microphone over to Joe at the top of the third inning, the Delta Queen was steaming upriver, on its way back from Louisville and the Kentucky Derby, its calliope piping and singing.

"Now," Marty said, "here's Joe Nuxhall with the play-by-play."

"Thanks, Marty. That's nice to hear," Joe said.

"Yes," Marty said, "it is...."

In the distant background, the calliope was a perfect counterpoint to Joe. Each was a long-standing Cincinnati tradition, and the sound of each transported the listener out of an ordinary existence. The sound of the calliope represented the history of the river from the time of the first boat. Joe's voice represented the history of the Reds from the time of the first pitch.

Joe was to baseball what the calliope was to music: plain, rough, and uneven. The calliope was the only musical instrument said to be tuned with a pipe wrench. It was Joe's kind of instrument.

And his own voice, for over half a century, had given Cincinnati its own distinctive, evocative music.

Joe said Denny's—about a mile or so down the hill from his house—was a good place to talk. Near the front door, a woman stopped and waved.

"Oh, my," she said. "We have a celebrity in our midst."

"We sure do," Joe said. "My partner here is a big man hereabouts."

She laughed, cheered by his humor and humility. "See ya, Joe," she said.

Joe hates the word "celebrity."

"Don't like anything about it," he says. "Don't like what it means or what it stands for."

We took a corner booth away from the traffic, but the traffic found us. A young hostess smiled and asked for an autograph. Joe quickly obliged. The cooks peered through a small window in the kitchen door. They smiled and waved. The waiter was a recent graduate from Fairfield High School. As he poured coffee, his hand shook the least little bit.

"Will that be all, Mr. Nuxhall?"

"You can call me Joe," he said. "Yes, that's all. But don't go far and keep it comin'. We are gonna be here for awhile."

THE LEFTHANDED VIEW—HE HAD OCCUPIED

THE BROADCAST BOOTH SO LONG SOME CLAIMED IT WAS HIS

BY SQUATTER'S RIGHTS.

at DENNY'S

The young man lingered, as if he had not heard. "My grandfather knows you," he said. "He played football with you at Hamilton."

"Yeah," Joe said. "What's his name? What did he tell you about me?"

"He said you were a pretty good player—a fine fullback. He said you were probably better at football than you were at baseball."

"Is that right?" Joe said. "Might be he is right. What's his name again? Hmm. Can't place him. Could be he was behind me a couple of years. Tell him I said hello."

The young man smiled broadly. He wondered if he might get an autograph for his grandfather before Joe left the restaurant. "It would mean a lot," he said.

Joe signed. The waiter thanked Joe and then apologized. "I'm sorry to bother you so long. I better go. I have other tables."

"Don't let us hold you up," Joe said. "Go on with it. You are probably just about the best man they got around here, hunh?"

Joe saw a group of young waitresses huddled around a nearby counter. They were watching and listening to the conversation.

"Except for all those young ladies, of course," he said. "Can't hold a candle to them can you? Hi, ladies," he said. "How are we doing today?"

They were young, not one on the other side of 25. They tittered and laughed like they were in the presence of a rock star. Headed toward his 76th birthday, Joe Nuxhall is a charmer. No matter where he goes, he makes people feel good.

"Now," he says, "where were we?"

HE DID NOT FEEL GREAT THAT DAY. He was in the midst of chemotherapy treatments, fighting cancer for the second time in his life and convinced he would emerge as a victor. He had beaten prostate cancer, now he fought lymphoma and spots on his lungs.

He didn't like to talk about it. He liked to talk about the great players he had faced in his playing career: Mantle, who took him deep; Andy Pafko, who drove him nuts; and Roberto Clemente.

"Clemente," he said. "Great arm. Great bad ball hitter, but Mantle —gawd, could he play the game. Probably the most talented guy I ever played against. Great guy, too. You wonder how good he could have been if he didn't have, you know, the problem."

That's the closest Joe ever comes to betraying the trust that comes with the uniform. Though Mantle's battle with alcohol became nationwide news in the months leading up to his death from liver and lung cancer, it is not something Joe addresses.

That was Mantle's life and death—a result of his decisions. There are certain things that are better left unsaid and who is he, he says, to comment on another man's life.

Initially, Joe did not want to take part in a book on his life. He said he did not want to be a party to any "kinda tell-all thing. There is no good purpose in that," he said.

Beyond that, he didn't view his life as all that interesting.

"Who'd want to read about me?" he said with a laugh.

During a meeting with his attorney, Reuven Katz, he was told he had become a Cincinnati icon. Joe looked around the room and laughed. "I'm not sure what an icon is," he said.

A STATUE OF JOE STANDS ON CROSLEY TERRACE outside Great American Ball Park. His signature phrase—"Rounding third…"—graces the north face of the stadium. The artist, Thomas Tsuchiya, depicted Joe delivering a fastball. When the statue was unveiled, someone asked him if he could still get in that position, "I could get into it," Joe said, "but it would take a crane to get me out."

He and Marty receive mail simply addressed: Marty and Joe, Cincinnati, Ohio. He was nominated for induction into the broadcasters' wing of the Hall of Fame, but failed to receive enough votes for election.

"It's an honor," he said, "just to be considered."

In November of 2003, over 800 people filled a room in Fairfield to honor Joe, his career, and the initiation of the Joe Nuxhall Character Education Fund. It was a three-hour ovation.

Joe takes none of this for granted. He is proud but not prideful.

That afternoon at Denny's, one person after another approached him for a word or an autograph. No one went away disappointed.

We were supposed to talk about his playing career that day. I asked him about the disappointment of being traded to Kansas City in 1961, and he said it hurt. Then he talked about the privilege of spending so many years with such a good organization and how the fans had been so good to him.

He reached out and tapped an open notebook on the table.

"I want to make sure this is in there," he said. "I want to thank the fans and my parents and, especially, Donzetta, you know, for putting up with me and this lifestyle for so long."

Often during our time together, a memory came back over and over again. The voices seemed together again: Earl Lawson, Pat Harmon, Bill Koch, Greg Noble, Enos Pennington—all of us gathered in the sports department—complaining about the baseball strike of 1981 and our charge to write about how people were spending their time and what they missed most during baseball's hiatus.

Late one afternoon, after finishing a story about pro softball, the phone rang. An older woman was calling. She was from Cheviot, a community on the west-side of Cincinnati, steeped in Irish and Germanic heritage, a part of town where—at the time—beer joints and bowling alleys were open all hours of the night and no one was ever late for work the next day.

She said she was just a baseball fan, but what she really missed was her friends. "I miss Marty and Joe," she said.

She talked about how life slows down when you are retired and fall into routine. She said that each night she and her husband would have dinner, put away the dishes, then go to the front porch and turn on the radio.

They sat, saying little, just listening to the game. Sometimes, she said, her husband fell asleep and sometimes she did, too.

They missed Marty and Joe, and they missed those nights on the porch. They had tried TV. They had tried cards and conversation.

"Not the same," she said. "Maybe we've been married too long...."

THERE ARE FANS WHO TURN THE TELEVISION sound off and listen to Marty and Joe on the radio. There are others who use Joe's voice as background while they putter in garages and shops. To them, Joe is not information, rather he is a *sound*, in which the words themselves are only faintly discernible. That sound is the evocation of a time in their lives when the future lay in front of them, as promising as their young and dreaming lives.

Paul Daugherty, a friend and colleague, admits to sitting on his deck in what he calls "the thick of a starry summer night" and listening to the radio.

"Nuxhall will be there," he writes, "his cadence somewhere between 33 rpm and molasses. It'll be slow and drowsy, and it will sound like baseball. It'll be just right."

Amen.

THE OLD FORM— WHEN JOE WAS ASKED IF HE COULD STILL

GET INTO HIS WINDUP, HE SAID, YES, HE COULD. BUT IT WOULD TAKE

A CRANE TO GET HIM OUT OF IT.

An historical footnote

While Joe Nuxhall is generally regarded as the youngest man
ever to appear in a major league game, he could be, actually, the
youngest to play in the 20th century. There is some evidence that
14-year-old Fred Chapman, from Little Cooley, Pennsylvania, pitched
in a game for Philadelphia of the American Association in 1887.
The American Association was a major league then and included the
Cincinnati ball club. While the details are somewhat ambiguous,
Chapman's career ended after five innings and four runs. He never
appeared in another game.

Resources

Bobby Alston, Hamilton, Ohio.
Dave "Yiddie" Armbruster, WLW Radio.
Ed Bailey, Cincinnati Reds,
    San Francisco Giants.
Sheldon "Chief" Bender,
    Cincinnati Reds.
Gene Bennett, Cincinnati Reds.
Rex Bowen, Dodger and Reds scout.
Marty Brennaman, Hall of Famer.
David Brewer, Friends of Rickwood
    Field.
Rob "Happy" Butcher, Cincinnati Reds
C.J. Cherre, St. Louis Cardinals.
Ned Colletti, San Francisco Giants.
Larry Conley, ESPN.
Bill Craig, Butler County Soldiers
    and Sailors Monument.
Bill "Seg Man" Dennison, WLW Radio.
Bobby DiBiasio, Cleveland Indians.
Conrad DuPuis, Navarre.
Sammy Ellis, Cincinnati Reds.
"Foots," ATL.
Jim Ferguson, National Association.
Bill Giles, Chairman Philadelphia Phillies.
Jim Greengrass, Cincinnati Reds.
Chuck Harmon, Cincinnati Reds.
Tommy Helms, Cincinnati Reds.
Larry Herms, Cincinnati Reds.
Jim Hickman, Cincinnati Reds.
Russ and Bert Hoard.
Jay "The Best" Horwitz, New York Mets
Larry Hall, Georgiana, Alabama.
Bob Howsam, former Reds President
    and General Manager.
Rick "The Commish" Hummel,
    St. Louis Post Dispatch.
Reuven Katz.
Clyde King, New York Yankees.
Ralph Kiner, New York Mets.
Dorothy Kurtz.

Vern Lundquist, CBS.
Danny Litwhiler, St. Louis Cardinals,
    Michigan State University.
Bobby Mattick, Toronto Blue Jays.
Rob Matwick, Houston Astros.
Hal McCoy, *Dayton Daily News*,
    Hall of Famer.
John Murdough, Cincinnati Reds,
Cincinnati Bengals.
Ron "Rufus" Millennor,
    Eddie Vedder fanatic.
Ed Mignery, former Hamilton High
    School football coach.
Willie McCovey, Hall of Famer.
Bob, Don and Gene Nuxhall.
Donzetta, Kim and Phil Nuxhall.
Naomi Nuxhall.
Jim O'Toole, Cincinnati Reds.
Ron Oester, Cincinnati Reds.
Darryl Parks, WLW Radio.
Sharon Pannozzo, Chicago Cubs.
Pete Rose, Cincinnati Reds.
Chris Sabo, Cincinnati Reds.
Murray Sapp, Birmingham, Alabama.
Jim Schultz, Atlanta Braves.
Larry Shenk, Philadelphia Phillies.
Howard Starkman, Toronto Blue Jays.
Steve Stewart, Cincinnati Reds.
Rick Stowe, Cincinnati Reds.
Bernie Stowe, Cincinnati Reds.
Sid Thrift.
Richard "Dick" Todd, Fox19 TV.
Billy Williams, Hall of Famer.
Charlie Wolf.

Texts

Allen, Lee, *The Cincinnati Reds*, Putnam & Sons, 1948.

Baseball Library.com

Burns, Ken and Geoffrey C. Ward, *Baseball: An Illustrated History*, Knopf, 1996.

Gilbert, Bill, *They Also Served: Baseball and the Home Front*, Crown Publishing Inc., 1992

Goldstein, Richard, *Spartan Seasons: How Baseball Survived the Second World War*, MacMillan Publishing, 1980.

The Fifties, David Halberstam, Ballantine Books, 1994.

James, Bill, *The Bill James Guide to Baseball Managers from 1870 to Today*, Scribner's, 1997

Lawson, Earl, *Cincinnati Seasons*, Diamond Communications, 1987.

Manchester, William, *The Glory and the Dream*, Little and Brown, 1974.

Raichler, Joseph L., *Baseball Encyclopedia*, MacMillan Publishing, 1979.

RetroSheet.org.

Stang, Mark, *Cardinals Collection: 100 Years of St. Louis Cardinals Images*, Orange Frazer Press, 2002.

Sulzberger, C.L. and Stephen Ambrose, *American Heritage New History of World War II*, Viking Press, 1997.

Wheeler, Lonnie and John Baskin, *The Cincinnati Game*, Orange Frazer Press, 1988.

Charlie Shelton's chronicle of Joe's playing career, on behalf of the Joe Nuxhall Foundation.

The photographs are from Joe Nuxhall's collection but for the photograph on page 253, courtesy Marty Brennaman.

Special thanks to Jim Borgman for permission to use his drawings.

Index

Adams, Bobby, 214
Alexander, Grover Cleveland, 98
Allen, John, 266
Allen, Lee, 36, 38–39, 82
Altman, George, 228
Amateur status, returning to, 172
Apgar, Dickie, 76
Armbruster, Dave "Yiddie," 250, 252, 254
Armstrong, Jack, 84
Arrigo, Gerry, 237
Atlanta, Georgia, 114
Autographs, 32

Bailey, Edgar Lonas, 199, 215, *222–223*, 229
Balata balls, 38
Baldwin-Lima Tool Works, 20
Bales, E. T., 113
Bambino, the Great, 30
Barber, Red, 244
Barger, Don, 77
Barons, the (see Birmingham Barons)
Bartels, Bob, *133*
Baseball, pitching, 101–103, 106–108
Baseball teams (see also Birmingham Barons;
        Cincinnati Reds)
    Class D, playing, 152–161
    Hamilton high school, 176–177
    Hamilton Moose Lodge amateur, *125*
    Lima Reds, 152–161
    Micks, 127
    minor leagues, 178–205
    Moose Lodge, 173
    Syracuse Chiefs, 148–149
    Washington Senators, 144
Basketball
    Dubois, Bud, 74–78
    grade school, 16
    high school, 173
    House of David, 186
    MVP award, *165*
    Shop league, 129, 173, 175–176
    Syracuse Nationals, 186
Bauer, Hank, 38
Beggs, Joe
    coaching and, 191
    game loss, 65
    with Joe and Bob Nuxhall, *178*
    twelve game wins, 98
Bell, Gus, *206*, 218, *222–223*

Bench, Johnny, 6, 233, *239*, 260
Bender, Sheldon "Chief," 189
Bergamo, Augie, 102
Berger, Wally, 46
Berra, Yogi, *216*
Bielemeier, Joe "Red," 166
Billingham, Jack, 260
Biltmore Hotel, 210
Birmingham, Alabama, 108–109, 110–123
Birmingham Barons, 110–123, *117*
Birmingham Black Barons, 120–121
Black Street bridge, 71–72
Blackwell, Ewell, 196, 204
Bloomington, Indiana, 142
Bottomley, Sunny Jim, 39, 98
Bowen, Rex, 41
Bragan, Jimmy, 240
Bramham, W. G., 161
Bray, Dick, 28, 82, 244
Breadon, Sam, 40
Brecheen, Harry, 230
Brennaman, Marty, 252–269
    about, 249–250, 255–261
    photographs with Joe, *257*, *267*
Bristol, Dave, 240
Broadcasting, 6–7, 238–271
    Marty Brennaman and, 12–13
    Miami University, 242
    retirement from, 266–271
    Ron Oester and, 32
Brosnan, Jim, 229
Browning, Jack, 176
Brucker, Earle, 210
Brunner, Bob, 127, 138, 157, 158, 167
Buck, Jack, 266
Burbank, Gary, 10, 269
Burger Beer, 244
Burgess, Smoky, 218
Burick, Si, 91–94
Burkhardt, Ken, *219*
Bush, Guy, *135*, 143, 146

Caciavely, Tommy, 159
Campanella, Roy, 204, 218
Caray, Harry, 244, 246, 248
Careers
    baseball, summary, 247
    broadcasting, 242–271
Carey, Max, 98

Carlton, Steve, 233
Carter, Arnold, 98, 108
Casey, Sean, 8
Celebrity, 72–79, 82–84
    St. Louis trip and, 68
Charlton, Norm, *11*
Cheney, Dick, 264
Child Labor Law Office, 113–114, *115*
Cincinnati Reds
    (see also Seasons)
    1945 spring training, 132, 134, 136–151
    1956 spring training, 220
    years playing with, 206–237
Circus, Nuxhall boys and, 24–26
Clay, Dain, 98
Clemente, Roberto, 274
Coaching, 190–191
Cobb, Ty, 116, 260
Coleman, Gordy, 228
Coleman, Ken, *267*
Colley, Frank M., 161
Collum, Jackie, *34*
Conduct, disorderly, 160–161
Conley, Gene, *104*, 218
Contracts
    broadcasting, 266
    Cincinnati Baseball club, 134, *139*, 139,
        149–150
    Cincinnati baseball club (1945), 134
    major league, 198
    professional leagues, 1945, *53*
    salary and, 192
    Syracuse Ball Club, 149–150
Cooper, Mort, 60, 102
Cooper, Walker, 96
Cox, Billy, 204
Crabtree, Estel, 94, 96, 100
"Cradle Snatching" cartoon, *188*
Craft, Harry, 98
Criscola, Tony, 98
Crosley Field, *23*, 28, 30–31
Crosley, Powel, 228
Crossley, Cap, 155, 166
Cuyler, Kiki, 46, 98

"D" Ball, 154
Dale, Frank, 241
Daley, Arthur, 220, 224
Daniels, Jake, 123
Daugherty, Paul, 276
Davidson, Teddy, 237, 238
Deacon, the (see McKechnie, Bill)
Dean, Dizzy, 43, 246
Depression, the great, 170–171
Derringer, Paul, 31, 47, 96, 98
Deviled eggs, 236
DeWitt, Bill, Sr., 228, 230, 234, 236
DiMaggio, Joe, 38
DiMaggio, Vince, 46
Dininger, Charley, 176
Ditches, digging, 26, 28
Dubois, Bud

about, 74–78
audition and, 44
basketball team and, 66
Dunn, Adam, 270
Duren, Ryne, 190

Eggs, deviled,, 236
Eisenhart, Jake, 103
Ellis, Sammy, 236, 240
Emswiler, H.W., 173
Erskine, Carl, 41, 218
Espy, Cecil, 250
Evans, Walter, *111*, 112, 117

Fallon, George, 102
Family life, 159, 167, 170–171, 270
"Fans in the Stands," 28, 82
Fausett, "Leaky" Buck, 100
Feller, Bob, 38
Ferrick, Tom, 220, *221*
Fieldhouse, Indiana University, 142
Fields
    burning in Muskingum County, 166
    Crosley, *23*, 28, 30–31
    Rickwood, (Birmingham), 115–117,
        120–121
    Sportsman's Park, 64
Florence, Paul
    Birmingham Barons, 109, 112
    child labor board, *115*
    with young Joe Nuxhall, *45*
Floridan Hotel, 199
Football, *75*, 168, 172–178
Ford's Field, 16
Fowler, Art, *34*, 215, 218
Foxx, Jimmie, 39
Freel, Ryan, 261
French Lick, 148
Frey, Lonnie, 98
Frick, Ford, 226
Frisch, Frankie, 98
Fry, John O., 136, 172, *177*
Furillo, Carl, 204, 218

Gabbard, Boomer, *151*
Gagliano, Phil, 248
Gailey, Dorothy
    about, 70–71
    baseball career and, 79
    Birmingham trip, 118
Gailey, "Papa" Joe
    about, 79, 158
    Birmingham trip, 118
    signing contract and, 82
    St. Louis trip, 70–71
Galehouse, Denny, 40
Garms, Deb, 102
Gashouse Gang, 246
Gerdeman, Norm, 236
Giles, Bill, 226
Giles, Warren, 82, 91, 127
    1945 spring training, 134

amateur status and, 172
Buck Fausett, 100
first impression, 43
letter to Joe, 84, *85*
Nuxhall contract and, 46
proposal to Orville Nuxhall, 47–48
Syracuse Ball Club, 150
Gillman, Sid, *177*
Goodman, Ival, 60, 98
Graham Hotel, 142
Grathwohl, Eldon "Red," 174, *177*
Gravlee, Denise, 115
Gray, Pete, 40, 123
Grayson, Frank "Pop," 140, 142, 143-144
Greenberg, Hank, 38
Greengrass, Jim, 191, 208, 214
Griffey, Ken Jr., 4
Grimes, Greg, 20

Hafey, Chick, 46, 98
Hamilton All Stars, 127–129
Hamilton Football team, *175*
Hamilton night, 213–214
Hamilton, Ohio, 22–28
Hamilton Sunday League, 24, *37*
Hamm, Dutch, 77
Harmon, Chuck, 214, 220
Harwell, Ernie, 244
Hatton, Grady, 196, 211
Heffner, Don, 232
Heinz, John P., 175
Helms, Tommy, 33–34, 240
Henry, Bill, 229
Herman, Babe, 39
Heusser, Ed, 96, 132
High school sports, eligibility, 170–174
Hitchhiking, 159
Hodges, Gil, 41, 204
Hornsby, Rogers, 210–213
Houston, Donzetta, 182, 184–185, *185*
    (see also Nuxhall, Donzetta)
Howell, Dixie, 205
Howlett, Grayle, 192
Howsam, Bob, 13, 38, 237, 240, 247–249
Hoyt, Dan, 161, 174
Hoyt, Waite
    evaluating pitches, 103
    with Joe, *231*
    Joe, letters to, 86–87
    retirement, 244
    return to Reds, 232
    signing, 43
Huey, Snip, 173
Hutchinson, Fred, 228, 236

Indiana University fieldhouse, 142
Iske, Hib, 26, 42, 127

Jackson, Shoeless Joe, 116
Jay, Joey, 229
Jobs, winter, 186
Joe Nuxhall Education and Character

Foundation, 275
Johnson, Deron, 236, *243*
Jones, Earl, 76
Jones, Tracy, 262
Just, Joe, 98

Kaiser, Al, 138, 157, 158, 167
Kansas City Monarchs, 120
Kansas, trade to, 228–229
Katz, Reuven, 266, 275
Kiner, Ralph, 237
King, Clyde, 38–39, 41
Kirkland, Willie, 227
Kluszewski, Ted
    All-star lineup, *222–223*
    with pals, *206*
    rising star, 196
    star, 214, 218
Konstanty, Jim, 98, 132
Kurowski, Whitey, 96

Laabs, Chet, 40
Labine, Clem, 218
LaMonda, N. B., 76
Larkin, Barry, 4
Lawrence, Brooks, *222–223*
Lawson, Earl, 198–200, 211–213
Lease, Joe, 116
Lima, 152-162
Lindner, Carl, 266
Linville, Shelby, 176
Lisenbee, Hod, 39, *135*, 143–144
Little Rock Travelers, 115–117
Litwhiler, Dan, 102, 106
Lobert, Hans, 64, 100
Lohrman, Bill, 96
Lombardi, Ernie, 31, 98
Long, Dale, 157, 166

Madison Elementary School, 16
Major league years, 202–241
Maloney, Jim, 229, *235*, *243*
Mantle, Mickey, 274
Maranville, Rabbit, 58, 98
Marion, Marty, 96
Marriage, 186–187
Marsh, Randy, 10
Marshall, Max, 98
Martin, Billy, 228
Mason, Paul B., 103
Mather, Chuck, 174, *177*
Matthews, "Wid," 41
Mattick, Bobby, 48, *111*, 112–113, 224
Mattick, Wally, 112
Mays, Willie, 220
McChesney, George, 176
McClendon, Lloyd, 262
McCool, Billy, 237
McCormick, Frank
    balata balls and, 38
    development of, 46
    enlistment and, 132

inspiration of, 72
star, 98
McCorry, Bill, 42–43, 82
McCovey, Willie Lee, 226–227, 232
McCullough, Jeni, 173
McDowell, H. L., 160–162
McGowan, Frank M., 115–116
McGuire, Bill, 127
McIntyre, Jim, 242, 246, 249
McKechnie, Bill, 13
    1925 season, 98
    about, 58
    celebrity and, 91
    inspiration of, 247
    Joe Nuxhall's tryouts and, 44–47
    Johnny Vander Meer and, 31
    scouting, Joe Nuxhall and, 43
    with young Joe Nuxhall, *45*
McKechnie, Bill Jr., *45*
McLeod, Ray, 143
McMannus, Larry, 64
McMillan, Roy, *206*, 208, 210, 214, ***222–223***
Meyer, Paul, 270
Miami Valley Championship game, 78
Michaels, Al, 249, 254
Miller, Eddie, 98
Miller, Leo, 181
Millville, 140
Minnich, Bud, 16
Minnich, Jack, 16
Moeller, Bill, 77, 82, 177
Moore, Louis (Mrs.), *115*
Morgan, Joe, 6, 32–33, 233
Motley, Ray, 242
Muncie Packers, 181–182
Murdough, John
    Bill McKechnie and, 59
    radio and, 246
    return to Reds, 230
    Rogers Hornsby, about, 210–211
    Roy McMillan and, 208, 210
    trade, Kansas City, 228–229
Musial, Stan
    final tour, 233–234
    hitting streak, 96
    home run, 1955, 218
    with Joe Nuxhall and Gene Conley, *104*
    pitching to, 60–61, 102, 138, 178
    Reds fans and, 226
MVP, shop league teams, 129

Negro leagues, 41, 120–121
Newcombe, Don, 218
Nolan, Gary, 240
Nuxhall, Bob
    with Don, measuring Joe's height, *73*
    eating at table with brothers, *19*
    family life, 16, 20–21
    with Joe and Joe Beggs, *178*
    school photograph, *27*
    shop league teams, 129
Nuxhall, Don

    with Bob, measuring Joe's height, *73*
    eating at table with brothers, *19*
    school photograph, *27*
Nuxhall, Donzetta, 213–214
    encouragement and, 192
    with family, *201*
    Hamilton night, *215*
    Joe's retirement and, 270
    marriage of, 186
Nuxhall, Evelyn, 79–81, 84, 86
Nuxhall, Gene, 16
    baseball and, 180
    eating at table with brothers, *19*
    family life, 20–21, 170
    school photograph, *27*
Nuxhall, Joe
    New York and, 208
    personality of, 113, 129–130, 160, 249
    physical description of, 92
    spirit of, 94
    statue of, 275
Nuxhall, Joe, photographs of
    (1941), *36*
    (1944), *50*
    (1945), major leagues, *63*
    (1946) football banquet, *177*
    (1949) with Bob Nuxhall and Joe Beggs, *178*
    (1954), sliding into base, *221*
    announcer's booth, *9*, *245*, *273*
    arguing with Ken Burkhardt, *219*
    baseball card, *194*
    with Bob and Don measuring height, *73*
    Bob Bartels and, *133*
    with Boomer Gabbard, *151*
    boys and, *197*
    with brothers, c. 1945, *69*
    child labor board, *115*
    with Cincinnati Reds team mates, *206*
    drinking gag, *145*
    eating at table with brothers, *19*
    eating, Cincinnati Reds, *209*
    with Evelyn, *83*
    Gabe Paul, salary and, *49*
    grade school, *14*
    Hamilton Moose Lodge amateur basebal
    Hamilton night, *215*
    interviewing Johnny Bench, *239*
    interviewing Maloney and Johnson, *243*
    interviewing Tom Seaver, *3*
    with Lisenbee and Bush, *135*
    Madison Elementary Team, *15*
    with Maloney and Walters, *235*
    with Marty Brennaman, *253*, *257*
    with Marty, Woodward, and Coleman, *267*
    with Milton Holly, *95*
    Muncie Packers, *183*
    Norm Charlton interview, *11*
    with Orville (1944), *89*
    with parents and record player, *51*
    with Phil, Donzetta, and Kim, *201*
    pitching, *2*, *5*

pitching, 1956, *34*
pitching, Cincinnati Reds, *203*, *259*
reaching to fans, *251*
school photograph, *27*
shop league basketball, *131*
signing autographs, *195*
sliding, against Phillies, *207*
sliding behind Del Rice, *225*
snowballs, *97*
spring break, *214*
in stadium (1944), *93*
Stan Musial and Gene Conley, *104*
Sunday league teams, *29*
with Waite Hoyt, *231*
with Wally Post, *187*
with Walter Evans and Bobby Mattick,
   111
in whirlpool, *153*
windup, *277*
Winton Place train stop, *56–57*
as youth, in baseball uniform, *29*
Nuxhall, Kim, *201*
Nuxhall, Naomi
   about, 70–72
   baseball career and, 66
   basketball games and, 77
   boys and school, 17
   Evelyn, 83
   Hamilton night, *215*
   High School Basketball team, *17*
   with Joe and Orville, *51*
Nuxhall, Orville
   baseball career and, 66
   family car and, *25*
   family life, 20–21
   Hamilton night, *215*
   with Joe (1944), *89*
   with Joe and Naomi, *51*
   Joe's celebrity and, 72
   legendary status of, 24
   proposal to, 47
   scouts and, 42
Nuxhall, Phil, 70, 200, *201*, 213–214
   Hamilton night, *215*

Oester, Ron, 32, 261
Ohio State League, 152
Ohio State University, The, 168
O'Neill, Buck, 120
O'Toole, Jim, 229, 240
Ott, Mel, 43

Pafko, Andy, 204, 274
Paige, Stachel, 120–121
Patterson, Pat, 42–43
Paul, Gabe
1950's salary proposal, *49*
   about, 194, 196
   expansion teams and, 228
   Nuxhall report and, 43
   recruitment and, 55, 65
   recruitment, Joe Nuxhall, 48–52

Rogers Hornsby and, 210–213
Pearl Harbor, attack on, 18
Pearl Jam, 8
Peddling, influence, 161
Peg Leg Sam, 119
Perez, Tony, 6, 233
Perkowski, Harry, 196, 212
Phillips, Harry, 175
Piegert, Earl, 76
Pinson, Vada, 112
Pitching
   1944, Birmingham, Barons, 113
   about, 5
   career end and, 240–241
   change-ups, 230
   Charlie Wolf and, 190–191
   Cincinnati Reds, *203*, 215, 218, *259*
   control of, 158
   curve balls, 147
   errors in, 128–129
   fastballs, 232
   first game, Cincinnati Reds, 96, 101–103,
      106
   high school, 180
   improvements in, 134
   to inside, 210
   Jim Greengrass on, 191
   Lima Reds, 160
   Lima Reds v. Newark, 159
   retirement and, *251*
   return to Reds, 232
   Roy McMillan and, 210
   Satchel Paige, 121
   Smokes game, 128–129
   summary, 247
   windup, *277*
Players, recruiting, 39–41
Podbielan, Bud, 212
Podres, Johnny, 218
Post, Wally, 184–186, *187*, 214, 218, 224
Presley, Elvis, 263–264
Press, scrutiny and, 198
Purkey, Bob, 229

Raffensberger, Ken, 196, 212
Ramsdell, Willie, 196
Recruitment, 50–66
   decision about, 66
   St. Louis trip, 54, 58–62, 64–65
Red Mountain, Birmingham, AL, 119
Reds, the (see Cincinnati Reds)
Reese, Pee Wee, 204, 218
Regal Room, 155
Reis, Eddie, 42–43
Rice, Del, *225*
Rice, Grantland, 98
Rickey, Branch, 40–41, 218, 241
Rickwood Field, Birmingham, 115–117,
      120–121
Riddle, Johnny
   1945 Cincinnati Reds spring training, 146
   Bloomington, IN, 142

music and, 147
    pitching control, 108, 117, 127
Roberts, Robin, 218
Robinson, Frank, 6, 112, *222–223*, 224
Robinson, Jackie, 41, 121, 204, 218, 220
Roosevelt, Franklin, 18–19, 148
Root, Fred, 16
Rose, Pete, 6, 233, 260, 261
    about Joe, 241
    Joe, broadcasting and, 249
Run averages (1944), 107
Ruth, Babe, 30, 116

Sabo, Chris, 261
Sapphire Room, The, 199
Salaries, 122
Sam, Peg Leg, 119
Sanders, Deion, 262
Sarringhaus, Paul, 168, *169*, 176
Savage, Randy, 264–265
Schmidt, Mike, 233
School, Reds Opening Day and, 90
Schott, Marge, 264–265
Schott, Stephen, 264–265
Scouting, 39–41
Scrutiny, press and, 198
Seasons
    1944 Cincinnati Reds, 91
    1949 Muncie Packers, 181–182, 191–192
    1952 Cincinnati Reds, 204–205, 210
    1954 Cincinnati Reds, 214, 220
    1956 Cincinnati Reds, 224
    1960 Cincinnati Reds, 227
    1961 Cincinnati Reds, 232–234
    1962 Cincinnati Reds, 233
    1964 Cincinnati Reds, 237
    1974 Cincinnati Reds, 254
    mid-70's, Cincinnati Reds, 262
Seaver, Tom, 262
Seeley, Bob, 127
Seghi, Phil, 196, 230
Segregation, 120–121, 220
Seoane, Isaac, 160–162
Seaver, Tom, *3*
Sewell, Luke, 210
Shannon, Mike, 266
Shephard, Bert, 39
Shoun, Clyde, 64, 98, 108
Signing agreement, 1945, 66
Simon, Randall, 7
Sipek, Dick, 112, 114, 123, 142-143
Smith, Lou, 140
Smokes Games, 126–128
Snider, Duke, 204, 218
Sollenberger, Harvey, *165*, 176
Sosa, Sammy, 4
Spahn, Warren, 38, 213, 218
Sportsman's Park, 64
Spring training
    1945 Cincinnati Reds, 143–149
    (1949), 188–189
    1956, Cincinnati Reds, 220

Cincinnati Reds, 1945, 132, 134, 136–151
St. Louis, recruitment trip, 54, 58–62, 64–65
Stengel, Casey, *216*
Stewart, Steve, 268
Stone, Naylor, 113
Stowe, Bernie, 209
Stowe, Rick, 269
Street, Gabby, 248
Sullivan, Claude, 242, 246, 249
Sunday League teams, 24, *37*
Sure-Fire Room, The 199
Suttles, George "Mule," 116
Swope, Tom, 132, 143
Symmes, John Cleves (Captain), 22, 24
Syracuse Ball Club, 149–150

Tebbetts, George Robert "Birdie," 214, *217*,
    220, *222–223*, 224
Temper, difficulties due to, 193, 196, *219*, 236
Temple, Johnny, 214, *222–223*
Texas League All-Star team, 193
Thompson, Junior, 98
Traynor, Pie, 46, 98
Treinen, Harold, 138
Tryout, Cincinnati Reds, 44–46
Tsuchiya, Thomas, 275
Tullis, Don, 77
Turner, Milkman Jim, 98

Van Cuyk, Chris, 204
Vander Meer, Johnny
    beginning career, 196
    inspiration of, 72
    interest in, 31
    loss to Cards, 65
    McKechnie, Bill, 46–47
    mentor to Joe, 6
Vargo, Ed, 228
Vedder, Eddie, 8, 10
Vincent, Al, 193
Vine Street, 16
Vulcan, statue of, 119–120

Wagner, Leon, 227
Wahl, Kermit, 146
Walker, Gee
    1944 season, 98
    entertainment and, 147
    friendship with, 189
    Jo Rene and, 189
    pitching, 93–94
Walters, Bucky
    caddie for, 147
    league wins leader, 132
    pitching, 96
    playing with, 6
    purchase of, 47
    shutout of Cards, 65
    twenty-game winner, 98
Walters, Ken, *235*
Waner, Paul, 39, 46
Warner, Roy, 247

Washington Senators, 144
Wehmeier, Herm, 143, 202, 227
Weight lifting, 132
Weintraub, Phil, 39
Werber, Bill, 98
Westercamp, Bernie, 143
"Whip," the, 204
Wiedemann (brewery), 244, 247
Williams, Billy, 226, 232
Williams, Ted, 38
Williams, Woody, 98
Willis, Dick, 20
Willis, Junior, 20
Wilson, Jimmie, 60, 100
Wilson Juniors (basketball team), *75*
Wilson Knights (basketball team), 77
Wolf, Charlie, 190–191
Woodward, Rick, 120
Woodward, Woody, *267*
World Championships, 262
World War II
    baseball and, 143
    life and, 36–49
    players and, 38
Wriggle, Joe, 76

Yellowhorse, Moses, 58

Zaharis, Babe, *216*
Zimbleman, Bill, 174

Greg Hoard came to Cincinnati in the winter of 1979 as a member of the *Cincinnati Post* sports department, where he was a feature reporter and columnist. He joined the *Cincinnati Enquirer* in 1984 as the Reds beat writer. He received numerous awards for his writing in Ohio and Indiana, but left journalism in 1990 for a career in television. Hoard worked for WLWT from 1990 through 1993, when he joined Fox19 as sports director. His career in television has always puzzled family members and close friends. His late uncle, Ted Sebastian, used to say: "Just proves folks will watch about anything on TV."